PREFACE BOOKS

General Editor: JOHN PURKIS

'A description of what the *Preface Books* were intended to be was included in the first volume and has appeared unchanged at the front of every succeeding title: "A series of scholarly and critical studies of major writers intended for those needing modern and authoritative guidance through the characteristic difficulties of their work to reach an intelligent understanding and enjoyment of it." This may seem modest enough but a moment's reflection will reveal what a considerable claim it actually is. It is much to the credit of Longman and to their [founding] editor Maurice Hussey and his authors that these words have come to seem no more than a plain statement of fact.'

(NATE NEWS)

Titles available in this series:

A Preface to Conrad *2nd edn*	CEDRIC WATTS
A Preface to Ezra Pound	PETER WILSON
A Preface to Greene	CEDRIC WATTS
A Preface to Hardy *2nd edn*	MERRYN WILLIAMS
A Preface to Hopkins *2nd edn*	GRAHAM STOREY
A Preface to James Joyce *2nd edn*	SYDNEY BOLT
A Preface to Jane Austen	C. GILLIE
A Preface to Keats	CEDRIC WATTS
A Preface to Oscar Wilde	ANNE VARTY
A Preface to Pope *2nd edn*	I.R.F. GORDON
A Preface to Samuel Johnson	THOMAS WOODMAN
A Preface to Shakespeare's Comedies	MICHAEL MANGAN
A Preface to Shakespeare's Tragedies	MICHAEL MANGAN
A Preface to Swift	KEITH CROOK
A Preface to Wilfred Owen	JOHN PURKIS
A Preface to Wordsworth	JOHN PURKIS
A Preface to Yeats *2nd edn*	EDWARD MALINS, JOHN PURKIS
A Preface to the Brontes	FELICIA GORDON
A Preface to Lawrence	GAMINI SALGADO
A Preface to Milton	L. POTTER

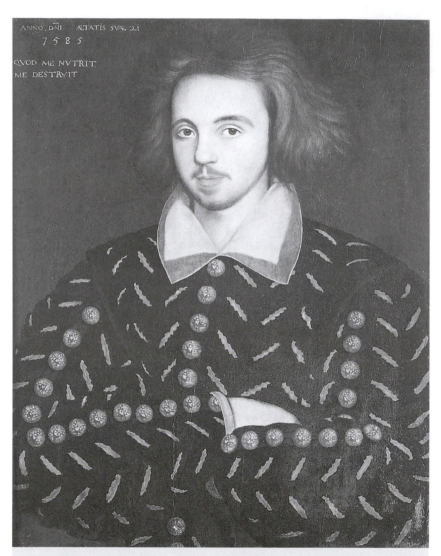

Portrait of a young man, believed to be Christopher Marlowe, from
Corpus Christi College, Cambridge. (By courtesy of the Master and Fellows of Corpus
Christi College, Cambridge. The College cannot vouch for the identity of the portrait.)

A PREFACE TO

MARLOWE

STEVIE SIMKIN

Longman

An imprint of **Pearson Education**

Harlow, England · London · New York · Reading, Massachusetts · San Francisco
Toronto · Don Mills, Ontario · Sydney · Tokyo · Singapore · Hong Kong · Seoul
Taipei · Cape Town · Madrid · Mexico City · Amsterdam · Munich · Paris · Milan

FOR AILEEN

Pearson Education Limited
Edinburgh Gate
Harlow
Essex CM20 2JE
England

and Associated Companies throughout the World.

Visit us on the World Wide Web at:
www.pearsoneduc.com

First published 2000

ISBN 0 582 31298 1 LIMP
      0 582 31299 X CASED

British Library Cataloguing-in-Publication Data
A catalogue record for this book can be obtained from the British Library

Library of Congress Cataloging-in-Publication Data
A catalog record for this book can be obtained from the Library of Congress

10 9 8 7 6 5 4 3 2 1
05 04 03 02 01 00

Typeset by 35 in 11/13pt Bembo
Production by Pearson Education Asia Pte Ltd.
Printed in Singapore

CONTENTS

LIST OF ILLUSTRATIONS

ACKNOWLEDGEMENTS

Some of the material that appears in the *Jew of Malta* chapter has previously been published in *Studies in Theatre Production* and *On-Stage Studies*. My thanks to the editors and publishers of these journals for permission to use this material.

I would like to acknowledge four works that have been essential to my research: Millar MacLure's *Christopher Marlowe: The Critical Heritage*; William Tydeman and Vivien Thomas's *Christopher Marlowe: The Plays and their Sources*; and Charles Nicholl's *The Reckoning*, whose fascinating detective story provided a vivid and illuminating glimpse through the shadows that surround Marlowe's life and death. James Shapiro's *Shakespeare and the Jews* was an invaluable source for the research on *The Jew of Malta*.

Colleagues in the School of Community and Performing Arts at King Alfred's have been generous in their support of research time that facilitated work on this book and related research, and I owe them all a debt of gratitude. In particular, I would like to thank Rob Conkie for stepping into the breach and relieving me of some teaching duties as the book neared completion.

Tim Prentki, Stephen Hawes and Paul Chamberlain provided wise guidance and advice on the research and rehearsal for the King Alfred's Performing Arts Company production of *The Jew of Malta* that I directed in the winter of 1997. Special thanks are due to the actors and crew members who worked so hard to make the project a success, in particular Tom Rennie (Barabas) and Natalie McGrath (assistant director). Thanks also to the panellists who took part in the heated debate at the colloquium that followed one performance of the play.

For invaluable feedback on draft chapters, thanks to Peter J. Smith, Mick Mangan, Roger Richardson, Geoff Ridden, Tim Prentki and Stephen Hawes. Thanks also to the series editor, John Purkis, for guiding the book through to completion, to Magda Robson, Jane Powell and Liz Mann at Longman, and to Katy Coutts for copy-editing so swiftly and thoroughly. Any flaws that remain are, of course, entirely my own.

Finally, I owe the greatest debt of gratitude to my wife, Aileen, and our children, Jamie and Matthew, for love, support and just putting up with it all.

Stevie Simkin, Winchester, 29 April 1999

A NOTE ON TEXTUAL REFERENCES

For discussion of Marlowe's poetry, I have used Stephen Orgel's 1971 edition of *The Complete Poems and Translations* (Penguin). All references to Marlowe's plays are based on the Revels Plays editions, as follows:

Bawcutt, N.W. (ed.) 1997. Christopher Marlowe, *The Jew of Malta*. Revels Plays edition. First published 1978. Manchester University Press

Bevington, David & Rasmussen, Eric (eds) 1993. *Doctor Faustus*. Revels Plays edition, Manchester University Press

Cunningham, J.E. (ed.) 1999. *Tamburlaine the Great*. Revels Plays edition. First published 1981. Manchester University Press

Forker, Charles R. (ed.) 1994. Christopher Marlowe, *Edward II*. Revels Plays edition, Manchester University Press

Oliver, H.J. (ed.) 1968. *Dido Queen of Carthage* and *The Massacre at Paris*. Revels Plays edition, Methuen.

References to Shakespeare's works are to the one-volume *Norton Shakespeare*, edited by Stephen Greenblatt, Walter Cohen, Jena E. Howard and Katharine Eisaman Maus (W.W. Norton & Company, 1997).

Note that spelling has been modernized in almost all quotations. Original spellings remain where such details are relevant to the discussion.

INTRODUCTION

The Preface Books series approaches the work of the author from a particular perspective: by introducing the writer via a biographical sketch and a survey of his or her cultural and social context, it encourages readers to root their understanding of the texts in the period in which they were produced. The titles given to the two opening chapters — 'Marlowe in his time' and 'The time of Marlowe' — aim to reflect the commitment to a contextual approach. At the same time, both chapters urge a degree of caution, warning against the impulse to draw straightforward conclusions about Marlowe's work from a knowledge of his life and times. In Elizabethan London his plays attracted large audiences, provoked respect, parody and vituperative jealousy among rival playwrights, and drew the sharp eye of the state censor. Marlowe himself was a remarkable and provocative figure, and it is tempting to correlate the controversial issues that the plays address with what we know (or think we know) about him, his personality and his beliefs.

Marlowe remains, for many critics, intricately bound up with his subject matter: if we choose to read *Edward II* as the story of a king brought down by his all-consuming love for another man, it is difficult not to make a connection with Marlowe's reported declaration 'That all they that love not tobacco and boys were fools'. *Doctor Faustus* and *The Jew of Malta*, in their different ways, can be seen to cast a sceptical eye on religion, and we learn that Marlowe was arrested on account of supposed heretical and atheistic beliefs — 'monstrous opinions', as his one-time friend and fellow playwright Thomas Kyd referred to them. Even Marlowe's poetry caused controversy: an edition of his translations of Ovid was one of a number of books that the Archbishop of Canterbury ordered to be burned six years after his death. *Tamburlaine the Great* and *The Massacre at Paris* revel in their garish violence and *Edward II* includes one of the most shocking executions in stage history. But Marlowe himself remains perhaps more famous than his plays: his violent death at the age of 29, stabbed through the eye in a fight (we are told) over a bill for food and drink, intrigues us. For many, Marlowe is the Icarus of his age, soaring beyond acceptable boundaries and paying the price. However, as we shall see, the multiple stories that we can gather of Marlowe's life and, in particular, of his death are like pieces from different jigsaw puzzles, each one startling and intriguing in its own right, but stubbornly refusing to fit with any of the other pieces. Any attempt to squeeze specific interpretations of his work into the same jumble of 'evidence' needs to be treated with a degree of circumspection.

There is a familiar image that adorns the cover of a number of works by and about Marlowe – a striking portrait of a handsome Elizabethan man that has been used so often that we tend to forget that there is no direct evidence at all to prove that it is actually Marlowe's likeness. At the fringes of Marlovian studies lurk the scholars who would hitch his wagon to a bigger star. Members of the Marlowe Society have launched a hopeful vessel into the troubled waters of the Shakespeare authorship controversies. An annual competition, the Calvin and Rose G. Hoffman prize, was established to encourage scholarship in the field with the ultimate aim of finding someone who will furnish 'irrefutable and incontrovertible proof and evidence . . . that all the plays and poems now commonly attributed to William Shakespeare were in fact written by Christopher Marlowe'. In his own time, Marlowe eclipsed Shakespeare; today, he is compared (almost invariably unfavourably) with him, except by those who wish to prove the two writers were one and the same person. Once again, Marlowe's identity shifts in and out of focus. On the south side of the River Thames, a painstakingly researched replica of the Globe theatre, first built in 1599, has been erected, providing a site for the revival of Shakespeare's plays in 'Shakespeare's theatre'. Not far away, in the basement of an office block, the foundations of the Rose ('Marlowe's theatre') lie in a foot of soil and water. Since April 1999, a sound and light show designed to give visitors some idea of the original construction and history of the theatre has been on offer.

Although a degree of awareness of the context in which Marlowe lived and wrote is crucial to an understanding of his work, dramatic texts matter because they persist, they have an after-life, and they will mean something different in each new context in which they are revived. This book places a particular emphasis on the plays in performance, devoting attention both to what we can determine about their production and consumption in Elizabethan times, and examining how modern interpreters have approached them. Marlowe's plays have sharp edges: they are disconcerting texts in many varied ways, and 400 years have, in most instances, failed to wear those awkward edges down. Marlowe's *Jew of*

Malta deploys anti-Semitic stereotypes in the cause of a brutal black comedy, and his *Tamburlaine* depicts, with a degree of irony that is hard to determine, the mighty acts of a fourteenth-century tyrant who slashes and burns his way through central Asia. Tamburlaine has the virgins of Damascus impaled on spears by his cavalry and casually hands over the women of another conquered city to be raped by his soldiers. At the time of writing this introduction to complete the book, rereading those passages cannot help but bring to mind the savage ethnic conflict in the Balkans, and the horrifying stories that are emerging from a shattered Kosovo.

The book ends with a concluding chapter entitled 'Marlowe in our time', which provides an assessment of some of the ways in which Marlowe's work has penetrated our contemporary culture, and investigates how theatre practitioners and other artists, working in various media, have explored his plays or else appropriated them for specific agendas. In the critical survey section, studies of individual plays consider recent productions; the discussion of *The Jew of Malta* explores, in a postscript, a particular attempt to read the play systematically 'against the grain' in order to make it speak *about* (rather than simply speak out) ethnic oppression.

Marlowe's brief life and slim volume of work retain their fascination because of the position they occupy at the intersection of a number of different discourses: religious, political and cultural. But any answers to the puzzles of his plays lie not in what we know (or what various dubious acquaintances of Marlowe's would have us know) about their author's life. Instead, the interplay of past and present constantly generates new meanings for these texts. It is the aim of this book to enable the reader to approach Marlowe's work on those terms, recognizing the texts as documents determined by their original contexts, while being open to the new ways in which they may continue to resonate, 400 years later.

PART ONE

THE WRITER AND HIS SETTING

Chronological table

Year	Marlowe's Life	Literary/Theatrical Events	Historical Events
1558			Death of Mary I and accession of Elizabeth I
1559			Act of Supremacy and Allegiance: restoration of Protestant church in England
1560		Geneva translation of the Bible	
1562		Norton and Sackville's *Gorboduc*	
1563		John Foxe's *Acts & Monuments*, first edition	
1564	6 Feb?: born at Canterbury	23 April?: William Shakespeare born at Stratford	
1565–7		Golding's version of Ovid's *Metamorphoses* published	
1565			Great Siege of Malta
1566		Edward Alleyn born	
1568			Mary Queen of Scots imprisoned
1570			Elizabeth I excommunicated
1571			Battle of Lepanto: Turks defeated by Christian forces
1572			Aug: St Bartholomew's Day Massacre
1576		The Theatre opens; first Blackfriars opens (mostly used by boy companies)	
1577		The Curtain theatre opens; Holinshed's *Chronicles* published	
1578–9	Educated at King's School, Canterbury, on a scholarship		

Year	Marlowe's Life	Literary/Theatrical Events	Historical Events
1580	Dec: at Corpus Christi College, Cambridge, as a Parker scholar		
1581	17 Mar: matriculates		
1581–6?	Long periods of absence from Cambridge, apparently working for the Government's secret service		
1582		Sidney writes *Astrophil and Stella* (not published until 1591)	
1584	Receives his BA degree		
1585–9			Civil wars in France
1586	Writes *Dido Queen of Carthage*, possibly in collaboration with Thomas Nashe	Death of Sidney	Babington Plot uncovered
1587	Receives his MA degree; probably writes *Tamburlaine* in this year; it is staged in 1587 or 1588	Kyd's *The Spanish Tragedy* Rose theatre built	Mary Queen of Scots executed
1588	May have written *Doctor Faustus* about this time		Defeat of Spanish Armada
1589	18 Sept: Marlowe and Thomas Watson imprisoned over death of William Bradley in street brawl; Marlowe on bail in Oct, discharged Dec		Henri III of France assassinated; succeeded by Henri of Navarre (Henri IV)
1590	*Tamburlaine* first published	Early parts of Spenser's *Faerie Queene* published	
1590/1	Writes and sees *The Jew of Malta* performed about this time		
1591	Sharing work room with Thomas Kyd	Shakespeare's *Henry VI* parts 1–3 first performed Sidney's *Astrophil and Stella* published	
1591/2		Shakespeare's *Taming of the Shrew, Comedy of Errors, Richard III*	
1592	In the Netherlands, counterfeiting money		Plague; theatres closed for long periods

Year	Marlowe's Life	Literary/Theatrical Events	Historical Events
1592	*Edward II* probably written and staged in this year, possibly also *The Massacre at Paris*		
1593	Writes *Hero and Leander* 12 May: Kyd arrested, and heretical papers discovered in the rooms he shares with Marlowe 18 May: warrant issued for Marlowe's arrest 30 May: killed by Ingram Frizer in Deptford 1 June: buried 2 June: Baines accuses Marlowe of heresy 28 June: Frizer pardoned 29 June: Richard Cholmeley accuses Marlowe of atheism		Plague; theatres closed for much of the year July: Henri IV of France converts to Catholicism
1594	*Dido* and *Edward II*, and possibly *Massacre*, published	Nashe's *The Unfortunate Traveller*	7 June: Roderigo Lopez executed
1595		Death of Kyd The Swan theatre opens	
1596		Shakespeare's *The Merchant of Venice*	
1597 –1600		Edward Alleyn retires from the stage	
1598	*Hero and Leander* published		
1599	Marlowe's translation of Ovid's *Amores* banned and burned	Globe theatre opens	
1600–5		Alleyn returns to the stage, then retires to theatre management; dies 1626	
1603			Death of Elizabeth I; accession of James I
1604	*Doctor Faustus* 'A-text' published		
1616	*Doctor Faustus* 'B-text' published		
1633	*The Jew of Malta* published		

CHAPTER 1

MARLOWE IN HIS TIME

'A dead man in Deptford': the Marlowe myth

On Wednesday 30 May 1593, four men spent the day together in a house owned by a woman called Eleanor Bull in Deptford, a town set on the Thames, south-east of London. Ingram Frizer was an up and coming businessman beginning to make his fortune via financial investments in property and commodities. Robert Poley was an agent in Queen Elizabeth's secret service who had worked in various shady capacities across the European continent. Nicholas Skeres was another dubious character who had connections with various moneylenders in London, as well as associates in the Elizabethan criminal network. The fourth man in the group was Christopher Marlowe, a young, successful, university-educated writer who had scored a number of notable successes with plays performed at the Theatre and the Rose, two of the early purpose-built playhouses in London. Having spent the day in each other's company at Widow Bull's, they took supper together and Frizer, Skeres and Poley settled down to a game of backgammon. Marlowe lay down on the bed in the sparsely furnished backroom. Suddenly, a violent dispute erupted between Frizer and Marlowe, possibly provoked by a disagreement over the bill for the day's food and drink. A fight broke out in which Marlowe beat Frizer around the head with Frizer's dagger, and in the struggle Frizer regained control of his weapon and stabbed Marlowe in the face, the point of the dagger probably entering the top of his eye socket. Death was instantaneous.

It may seem odd to begin an account of Marlowe's life at the point of his death. But one of the reasons why Marlowe continues to fascinate, 400 years or more after he died, is because it seems that we know more about his death than we do about his life: the coroner's report on his death, meticulously detailed, is at the head of a family tree of documentation about the incident. Stories about his death quickly proliferated in a process akin to Chinese whispers: the narrative is embellished with increasingly gruesome detail, becoming more and more outlandish as it is handed from one teller to the next. The coroner's report clearly identifies Marlowe as the aggressor: 'it so befell that the said Christopher Morley, on a sudden & of his malice towards the said Ingram aforethought, then and there maliciously drew the dagger of the said Ingram' and 'gave the aforesaid Ingram two wounds on his head of the length of two inches & of the depth of a quarter of an inch' (cited in Wraight & Stern, 1993, p. 293). The report continues:

> and so it befell in that affray that the said Ingram, in defence of his life, with the dagger . . . gave the said Christopher then & there a mortal wound over his right eye of the depth of two inches and of the width of one inch; of which mortal wound the aforesaid Christopher Morley then & there instantly died . . .

The report makes it very clear how it perceives the killing – that Frizer acted 'in the defence and saving of his own life'. We will return to this shortly, but it is worth tracing first some of the transformations this story underwent in the years following Marlowe's death.

Thomas Beard was a Puritan who had been at Cambridge with Marlowe and would later be Oliver Cromwell's schoolmaster. According to Beard, writing in his book *Theatre of God's Judgements* (1597), Marlowe was 'by practice a playmaker, and a poet of scurrility' and a blasphemer who had 'denied God and his son Christ . . . affirming our Saviour to be but a deceiver . . . and the holy Bible but vain and idle stories, and all religion but a device of policy' (cited in MacLure, 1995, pp. 41–2). Incidentally, Beard actually uses the name 'Marlin' for Marlowe – as we shall see, Marlowe's name is as slippery as the stories of his life and death. Beard, rabid in his condemnation of theatre and fanatical in his religious beliefs, must have been overjoyed to find a man justly punished by God who was not only a playwright but someone rumoured to have been an atheist. Though it is impossible in medical terms, in the light of the report of Marlowe's wound, Beard maintains that Marlowe 'even cursed and blasphemed to his last gasp'. So terrible was the manner of Marlowe's death, according to Beard, that it was 'not only a manifest sign of God's judgment, but also an horrible and fearful terror to all that beheld him' (cited in ibid., pp. 41–2). Pressing the point home, as it were, with all the grim satisfaction of the zealot, Beard concludes:

But herein did the justice of God most notably appear, in
that he compelled his own hand which had written those
blasphemies to be the instrument to punish him, and
that in his brain, which had devised the same.

[cited in ibid., p. 42]

Francis Meres, writing in 1598, refers to Beard's account in his collection of jottings, quotations and literary gossip *Palladis Tamia*. Here, we
learn that Marlowe was, apparently, 'stabbed to death by a bawdy serving man, a rival of his in his lewd love' (cited in ibid., p. 46). The
nature of this 'lewd love' is left unspecified, but one possible interpretation is that it is hinting at Marlowe's reputed homosexuality (Nicholl,
1992, p. 68). Certainly the familiar glib phrase, 'all they who love
not tobacco and boys are fools', had already passed into the folklore
gathering around his posthumous reputation, along with his supposed
opinion that Christ and St John were lovers. It would be ill-advised to
use these scraps of 'evidence' to draw a straightforward conclusion that
Marlowe himself was a homosexual, however: to impose modern understandings of sexual orientation onto the early modern period ignores
the immense cultural shift that separates us from the Elizabethans. As
we shall see when we come to study Marlowe's historical tragedy *Edward
II*, there were significant differences in attitudes to and conceptions of
sexual relationships 400 years ago.

We now have Marlowe cast as both lewd and heretical. William
Vaughan, writing some years later (*The Golden Grove*, 1600), adds some
gruesome detail: 'he stabbed this Marlow into the eye, in such sort,
that his brains coming out at the dagger's point, he shortly after died'.
He also reinforces the idea that Marlowe's death was an act of God:
'Thus did God, the true executioner of divine justice, work the end of
impious Atheists' (cited in Wraight & Stern, 1993, p. 307). Another
furious religious tirade, blessed with the catchy title *The Thunderbolt of
God's Wrath against Hard-Hearted and Stiff-Necked Sinners* (1618), the work
of one Edmund Rudierd, also drew on Beard, but managed to turn
the story into a warning against playwrights and actors in general:

But hearken ye brain-sick and profane poets, and players,
that bewitch idle ears with foolish vanities: what fell upon
this profane wretch, having a quarrel against one whom
he met in a street in London, and would have stabbed
him: But the party perceiving his villainy prevented him

with catching his hand, and turning his own dagger into
his brains, and so blaspheming and cursing, he yielded up
his stinking breath: mark this ye players, that live by
making fools laugh at sin and wickedness.

[cited in Wraight & Stern, 1993, p. 307]

Marlowe's death, then, is interpreted in a number of different ways:
first as a warning against atheism; then, connected with some kind of
immoral sexual practice; and now taken as proof of God's disapproval
of the theatre. When we begin to look in more detail at Elizabethan
society, we will explore further the opposition to the theatre that existed
among certain influential sectors of the population. What is important
to notice at this point is the fact that Marlowe's unusual and untimely
end is appropriated for different purposes by different writers. The 'facts'
of the case mutate as they filter through different accounts. This gives
us some kind of insight into how history works – less a collation of
facts than a process of telling stories about the past. It is a notion we
shall return to when we come to look at the story Marlowe told about
the reign of Edward II. But to return to Vaughan's account: for the
Puritans, it seems, the story of Marlowe's death is underpinned by a
notion of God's hand in human affairs, meting out suitable punishment
for the heinous sins of blasphemy and atheism. How Marlowe acquired
this reputation is another thread that we will trace shortly. But there is
another tale to be told about Marlowe, and in order to unravel it, we
need to return to his origins and trace his life from its humble begin-
nings in Canterbury in 1564.

Early years

Some rudimentary details of Marlowe's early years can be traced. He
was born the son of John Marlowe, a shoemaker in the ancient city
of Canterbury, and Katherine, formerly Katherine Arthur. Of their nine
children, Marlowe was the second, and the oldest that survived. He
was also the only one of the boys to live beyond infancy; four of his
sisters also lived to adulthood. We know that Christopher was born in
February 1564, but it is after this bare fact that we stumble over the first
gap in his biography, and we pick up the story again when Marlowe
acquires a scholarship to attend the King's School, Canterbury, at the

13

age of fifteen (although it may be that he started at King's before this date). Here Christopher would have received a thorough grounding in Latin and Greek grammar, and some ancient literature. He would have learnt about Roman history, as well as the familiar Greek and Roman legends. Canterbury, situated along the route from Dover to London, was a busy city, and Marlowe would have grown up in a lively atmosphere that was lent by virtue of its position something of a cosmopolitan air. One event it is safe to assume Marlowe witnessed, as a child of nine, was the procession that moved down the High Street in September 1573, as Elizabeth I made her royal visit to Canterbury Cathedral; it is likely that the spectacular pageantry would have made a strong impression upon him (Wraight & Stern, 1993, p. 23). Spectacles of another kind were provided by travelling bands of players – records survive of visits by a number of companies during Marlowe's time in Canterbury, among them Lord Strange's Men, a group that would become closely associated with Marlowe's own work. We know, too, that plays were regularly staged at the King's School, and although there is no direct proof that Marlowe himself performed, it seems fairly likely that he did. He may well have taken part in performances by students at Cambridge, too: records survive of performances at Corpus Christi College during Marlowe's time there.

In the winter of 1580, Marlowe arrived in Cambridge as the Archbishop Parker scholar at Corpus Christi College, one of the oldest colleges in the university which itself dates back to the twelfth century. Matthew Parker had been Archbishop of Canterbury from 1558 until his death in 1575. The Cambridge connection came via Parker's period as Master of Corpus Christi College from 1544 to 1553. Three scholarships were established by the terms of his will (Parker had already set up a number of others), and Marlowe qualified for the first of these, which was set aside for a native of Canterbury educated at the King's School. University life then was a very different experience from what it is now, as we might expect, but the immensity of that difference may still astound us: the student's regime actually sounds more like a monastic lifestyle than anything else. Rising at four for prayers at five and breakfast at six, the students would attend a morning of classes lasting until dinner at noon: the first half of the afternoon would be taken up by more classes, leaving the rest of the day for private study. The afternoon classes might often involve attendance at debates: university examinations were conducted orally at this time, with a student required either to attack or defend a particular proposition in a kind of verbal combat with his peers. To receive his BA, the student would have been required to offer four such demonstrations of his skill in debate, two offensive and two defensive. The curriculum was again classically based, with a thorough programme of classical philosophy at its centre. Generally, students resided in college for eleven months of the year, although there were many instances of this rule being broken. Indeed, it appears that some questions were raised over Marlowe's progress from the BA to the MA element of this degree because of his erratic attendance record. Marlowe lodged in a converted storehouse with three other scholars. Many of the students at Corpus Christi would have been younger than Marlowe, since the usual age for entry was fourteen. Although he arrived at Cambridge in December 1580, Marlowe was seventeen when he formally matriculated in March 1581. A total of six years' study led to an MA, which Marlowe achieved in 1587. As a Parker scholar, he would have been expected to embark on a career in the church. However, it seems clear that Marlowe had very different ideas about where his future lay. He wrote *Dido Queen of Carthage* while at Cambridge, as well as some poetry (including translations of the erotic poetry of the Latin writer Ovid) and very probably most of the first part of *Tamburlaine the Great.*

At Cambridge we can locate a number of these fragments of biographical data that make the puzzle of Marlowe's life so alluring. In 1953, a portrait was discovered amidst a pile of rubble left by builders repairing the Master's Lodge at Corpus Christi (see the Frontispiece). Charles Nicholl provides some fascinating speculative background to the portrait in his investigation of Marlowe's death, *The Reckoning* (1992), and the discussion here of the mystery surrounding it is indebted to that book. Although badly damaged, the painting was sent to the National Portrait Gallery, where it was authenticated as Elizabethan – an inscription bears the date 1585 – and, after restoration, it was hung in the dining hall of the college. Although the painting gives no clue as to who the sitter for the portrait was, it does tell us that the subject was 21 years of age at the time: Marlowe's age in 1585. As we have already noted, Marlowe entered university unusually late, and it is unlikely that there were many – if any – other students of this age at that time. In 1585, he had received his BA and was embarking on his MA. This makes it more likely that the portrait is indeed of Marlowe. One of the mysteries surrounding the painting is its own history: it does not appear in a list of paintings belonging to the college compiled in 1884. The implication is that it was at some stage taken down and stored away, and then forgotten. Some scholars, assuming it *is* a portrait of Marlowe, have speculated that it might have been removed in the aftermath of Marlowe's death and the scandal surrounding the event. Again, speculation piles upon speculation, but there are undoubtedly some good reasons for believing that it might be his portrait. Some of the reasons are soundly and logically based, whilst others are founded on a degree of romanticism that can be hard to resist, particularly when we read the Latin inscription beneath: '*Quod me nutrit me destruit*': 'that which nourishes me destroys me'. It is, as we shall see, a haunting and a provocative line, and one that fits conveniently into the Marlowe myth that we are now beginning to piece together; this has made it all the more tempting to assume that it is his portrait.

Trying to reconstruct Marlowe's time at Cambridge is another game of deduction and speculation, but the most mundane of sources have the potential to offer up rich, intriguing clues, solutions and possibilities. These sources include the college accounts (complete apart from the 1585–6 academic year records, which are missing), which show the payments he received as a Parker scholar, and the Buttery book, which details expenses on food and drink for individual students. Scholars such as Frederick Boas (1940), Wraight & Stern (1993, first published 1965) and Charles Nicholl (1992) have studied the patterns of these records (there are photographs of some of the relevant pages in Wraight & Stern's appendices), and made some fairly safe deductions from them. Their conclusions lead us back into the shadows that enveloped Marlowe at Eleanor Bull's house in Deptford in May 1593. The records of attendance are not extraordinary for the first three years of his university career: a couple of periods of absence lasting six weeks each technically exceeded the college regulations, but were not unheard of. However, the 1584–5 session sees a sudden drop in Marlowe's total scholarship payments: with the scholarship working on the basis of a shilling a week for every week the student was in attendance, the amounts paid to Marlowe during this academic year total only 19*s*. 6*d*. The Buttery book fills in some of the detail for us, suggesting that Marlowe was absent for eight weeks between April and June and nine weeks between July and September, returning for the end of the Trinity term. For the next year, the Buttery book is all we have to go on, and it indicates another April–June truancy; and in 1587, college accounts show a further absence of a couple of months by the time the Lent term wound up on 25 March.

Marlowe's absences had, of course, not gone unnoticed, and he was initially refused permission to proceed from his BA to his MA degree. The decision was overturned by a letter sent to the Cambridge authorities from Elizabeth's Privy Council:

Whereas it was reported that Christopher Morley was determined to have gone beyond the seas to Reames [Rheims] and there to remain, their Lordships thought good to certify that he had no such intent, but that in all his actions he had behaved himself orderly and discretely whereby he had done her Majesty good service, and deserved to be rewarded for his faithful dealing: their Lordships request was that the rumour thereof should be allayed by all possible means, and that he should be furthered in the degree he was to take this next Commencement, because it was not her Majesty's pleasure that any one employed, as he had been in matters touching the benefit of his country should be defamed by those that are ignorant in th' affairs he went about.

[cited in Nicholl, 1992, p. 92]

Scholars have proved fairly conclusively that this Christopher Morley was our Marlowe; I have already noted in the discussion of Thomas Beard's account that Marlin was one alternative form for Marlowe's name, particularly in his days at Cambridge; Morley was another. 'Reames' is the French city of Rheims where the English College had been established, one of only a handful of Catholic seminaries established in Europe for Englishmen. The rumour that Marlowe had visited Rheims would have implied that he had defected not only in religious terms, from England's Protestantism to France's Catholicism, but in political terms too. What the Privy Council's letter implies is that Marlowe, far from being a political and religious traitor, was in fact a loyal patriot. What we seem to have is a classic example of the undercover agent, working behind enemy lines.

Marlowe and Sir Francis Walsingham

The mystery of Marlowe's life and death deepens, and we must pause as we take what may seem a fairly modern concept – the secret agent – and locate it in its Elizabethan context. A fuller account of the politics of Elizabethan England can be found in chapter 2, which also discusses the ways in which politics and religion were profoundly intertwined. For now, it is enough to bear in mind that England under Elizabeth was a Protestant nation, but one that was forced to meet the Catholic challenge on a number of fronts, both internationally (particularly in relation to the imposing empires of France and Spain) and internally. The Protestant Elizabeth had been preceded by her Catholic sister Mary Tudor, who had reigned from 1553 to 1558; Mary Queen of Scots (also Catholic) laid claim to the English throne (she was technically speaking Elizabeth's heir) and consequently remained a thorn in Elizabeth's side until her execution in 1587. One of the chief weapons in Elizabeth's struggle against the Catholic threat was her secret service, and the key player in that organization was Sir Francis Walsingham. Walsingham, who was the father-in-law of the poet Philip Sidney, had spent a good deal of the 1550s abroad, becoming fluent in French and Italian and establishing contacts in those countries that would prove invaluable in the future. In 1568 and 1569, he was able via his Italian contacts to feed information to Sir William Cecil, Elizabeth's right-hand man for most of her reign, about potential threats to the English queen, and between 1570 and 1573 he served mostly in France, working to establish some kind of settlement between France and England. But the so-called St Bartholomew's Day Massacre on 24 August 1572, when thousands of Huguenots – French Protestants – were massacred at the instigation of Charles IX and his mother Catherine de Medici, brought these efforts to an end. (Marlowe's *The Massacre at Paris* is a dramatization of that slaughter and its aftermath.) Walsingham left Paris soon after, returning to take up the post of Secretary of State, which he retained until his death in 1590. Walsingham was a Puritan and, particularly in the wake of the Huguenot massacre, obsessively devoted to the cause of stamping out the Catholic threat. He poured considerable amounts of his own wealth into financing the secret service, and his spies were everywhere. Although some government funds were at Walsingham's disposal, the Elizabethan secret service remained outside the formal organization of the government. It is worth bearing in mind that there were no standing armed forces at this time either, armies being raised as and when necessary. With the secret service more akin to a network of paid spies and informers than to a formal and hierarchical marshalling of agents, loyalties were notoriously fickle and the accuracy of information, gained by word of mouth and by intercepting correspondence, was wildly unpredictable.

Although we cannot know for sure that Marlowe travelled to Rheims – it may only be part of the kind of malicious gossip that dogged him for much of his short life – it is quite possible that he did. This was a particularly volatile time: the Spanish Armada would sail against

England the year after Marlowe's mysterious first disappearance from the university records. Marlowe's work for Walsingham may have included a part in the foiling of the Babington Plot, a conspiracy to assassinate Elizabeth and install Mary Queen of Scots on the throne, authorized by Mary herself. The Rheims seminary was a significant piece in the jigsaw of this particular plot, since the double agent Gilbert Gifford was firmly established at the seminary, and, deeply trusted by Mary and her associates, was able to feed crucial information to Walsingham in the months leading up to the arrests. It was the discovery of the Babington Plot that gave Walsingham the excuse he needed to execute Mary, and so remove this particular Catholic threat altogether. Whether or not Marlowe was involved, Robert Poley certainly was: playing the part of a Catholic loyal to Mary's cause, it was his manipulation of Babington that secured an account of the plot that also implicated Mary herself. This is the same Robert Poley who was one of the party present at Eleanor Bull's on the day that Marlowe died.

Walsingham had spies in foreign courts; places such as the English College at Rheims were also obvious target areas for his operatives, since the Jesuit seminary was not only a training school for Catholic missionaries but a haven and rallying point for those who dissented from Elizabeth's Protestantism. It seems entirely possible that Marlowe spent some time at Rheims during his absence from Cambridge: the rumours of his travel to that place coupled with the Privy Council's assertion that 'he had been in matters touching the benefit of his country' point to that conclusion. Scholars have also noticed that in times following his periods of absence, Marlowe seems to have been particularly extravagant, and this would suggest that he had been generously rewarded for the service he had done his queen, although any such payment seems to have been unofficial, since he does not appear in the accounts of the Queen's Chamber where other agents' fees are listed. If Marlowe did indeed travel to Rheims about this time, it would appear he operated as a spy, using the cover of being a convert to Rome. In this role, he would have been able to ascertain details of real converts and feed back this information to Walsingham. Intriguingly, it seems that another Walsingham, Thomas, second cousin to Francis, worked for the secret service: Thomas Walsingham, a year Marlowe's senior, would become the playwright's friend and patron. Again, pieces of the jigsaw suddenly snap together, since Ingram Frizer, whose dagger pierced Marlowe's eye socket, worked for Thomas Walsingham at the time of Marlowe's death. But while the pieces seem to fit, these new connections simply throw up further questions about Marlowe's death. Once again, 'facts' mutate into alternative histories. Was the brawl a quarrel over the bill? Was it God's justice on a sinner? Or might it have been a political assassination?

Marlowe's theatrical career

After the difficult but finally triumphant tussle for his Master's degree, Marlowe sets off for London and promptly disappears from our sight for a short period: his exact whereabouts over the next couple of years are uncertain. We do know that by September 1589 he was lodging with Thomas Watson in Norton Fulgate, close to the Curtain theatre, in one of the so-called 'Liberties' – districts lying on the outskirts of the city that were outside the jurisdiction of the City authorities. Those who existed in the margins of the law chose to inhabit the Liberties – prostitutes, criminals, vagrants, lepers. Interestingly enough, the first public, purpose-built theatres, known as playhouses, were erected in the Liberties, north-east of Norton Fulgate, followed by the famous play-houses such as the Globe which appeared on the south side of the Thames, again outside the jurisdiction of the City Fathers (the reasons why the Elizabethans chose to build their theatres there, and the consequences of that decision, are explored fully in chapter 2). Norton Fulgate, known as a good residential district despite some of the more dubious elements of its population, was situated to the north-east of the centre of London and to the south of Finsbury, in an area of marshy land called Moorfields. Marlowe's way into the city would have been through Bishopsgate, which would frequently have been decorated with the heads of executed criminals. Bedlam, the London madhouse, was located on Bishopsgate Street in Moorfields, and Finsbury Fields was a popular site for duels.

As a Parker scholar, Marlowe would have been expected to proceed from university into the ministry. We cannot know whether or not Marlowe himself ever seriously considered this as an option. It is doubtful whether anyone would have thought it likely by the time he graduated from Cambridge. It seems that he had harboured literary ambitions from his early days as an undergraduate: his first play, *Dido Queen of Carthage*, was probably written in 1586 and was preceded by some poetry. The title-page of the first printed edition of *Dido* (1594) tells us that it was first performed by the Children of Her Majesty's Chapel. We do not know exactly when the play was performed but since the rather faddish boys' companies were in decline by the time Marlowe left Cambridge, it is likely to have been before 1587. It is generally accepted that, by 1585, Marlowe had also translated the sequence of poems *Amores* written by the Roman poet Ovid. We cannot know for sure exactly when Marlowe wrote this work, since earliest publication dates are notoriously unhelpful in determining dates of composition. We do know that a number of surreptitious editions of Marlowe's elegies appeared towards the end of the century. In keeping with Marlowe's tendency to attract controversy and outrage, in June 1599 one of these posthumous editions was banned by the church, and those copies that could be found were seized and burned. Marlowe also translated some of Lucan's *Bello Civili* ('Civil War', also known as *Pharsalia*, after one of the battles Lucan records). This history of Julius Caesar's career operates as a warning of the horrors of civil war. While Ovid's *Amores* are shocking for their frank sexual content, Lucan's work is striking in the Elizabethan context for its contemporary relevance: as we have already noted, the threat posed by Mary Queen of Scots as contender for the English throne was not removed until 1587.

It is likely that Marlowe wrote at least part of his first major play, *Tamburlaine the Great*, towards the end of his time at Cambridge. It was probably first staged by the Lord Admiral's Men at James Burbage's venue in Finsbury, the Theatre, the first purpose-built public playhouse. Edward Alleyn, one of the greatest of the Elizabethan actors, and the man who would go on to play the roles of Barabas in *The Jew of Malta* and Doctor Faustus, would have taken the title role here, too. *Tamburlaine* probably premièred in 1587. Some critics have argued that the two parts of the play were conceived and written as a whole – a coherent, ten-act piece. It seems more likely that Part Two was written in haste to capitalize on the success of the first. The playwrights, theatre managers and companies then were as concerned with profits as, say, Hollywood film producers are now, and it is probable that the form in which we have received *Tamburlaine* was shaped as much by commerce as by artistry. In any case, it is clear that the plays were a tremendous success, remaining a familiar fixture in the repertoire of the Lord Admiral's Men. Philip Henslowe (d. 1616), owner of the Rose playhouse where most of Marlowe's plays were performed in his lifetime, kept detailed records of his receipts (recorded in what has come to be called his 'Diary'), and he lists numerous performances of *Tamburlaine* in 1594–5. The thundering rhetoric of the verse, the spectacular visual effects (there are a number of notable references to the striking colours in Tamburlaine's changing costumes, tents and banners), the graphic violence, all contributed to the play's popularity. Marlowe was also breaking new ground

with *Tamburlaine*. The Prologue is a bold proclamation, an advertise-
ment for Marlowe as theatrical pioneer:

> From jigging veins of rhyming mother-wits,
> And such conceits as clownage keeps in pay,
> We'll lead you to the stately tent of War . . .

[I.Prologue.1–3]

There are signs here of what we may come to recognize as particular
Marlovian traits as we become better acquainted with his work: a good
deal of scorn for the current standard of the drama, impatience with
its unadventurous style and an implied criticism of the way it panders
to lazy audience expectations. As we shall see in the full discussion of
Tamburlaine, the play may not have been as revolutionary as its Prologue
would like to claim, but it remains a defining moment in the development of English drama.

By 1587, then, Marlowe had already made a name for himself among
the London dramatists. This was the heyday of the so-called 'University
Wits', a group of writers for the stage who had either passed from or
passed over the professional careers they would have been expected to
follow, and chosen instead to make their fortune writing for the various companies of players located in and around London. The epithet
'Wit', incidentally, does not imply wit in the sense we are most familiar with; it denoted intellect rather than a sharp sense of humour. Other
members of the group included George Peele (1558?–1597?), John Lyly
(1554?–1606) and Robert Greene (1560?–1592), the latter a bitter, probably envious rival of Marlowe's. The emergence of the term 'University
Wit' marks a significant shift in the production of English drama, moving from the guild-based Mystery cycles, through the maturing growth
of the touring troupes of players, to the establishment of something very
close to the profession of playwriting, an occupation to which well-
educated gentlemen might devote themselves. The University Wits would
have been familiar with Greek and Roman drama, and often would
have been involved in performances within their colleges. There was a
firmly established tradition at Cambridge, and shortly afterwards at Oxford,
of staging both classical plays and works written by undergraduates.
Although it is more likely that most of a typical graduate's knowledge
of Greek would have come via translation, his fluency in Latin would
have been taken for granted. The students read widely in Latin poetry,
history and philosophy, and even their knowledge of Christian doctrine

would have come chiefly via Latin versions both of the Bible and of the writings of the Church Fathers. There is in Marlowe a good deal of confidence in the scope of his classical allusions, and not a little self-indulgence. Marlowe's classicism also locates him in the vicinity of the humanist tradition: the revival of classical learning that was at the root of humanism took place in part as a reaction against the rigidly Christian scholastic tradition that had dominated the Middle Ages. It should not surprise us to find a writer with a reputation as an atheist choosing to place himself within the more anthropocentric school of humanism, and steeping his writing in the classics. It is clear, too, that a fair number of audience members must also have enjoyed these allusions.

This said, there were certainly significant dramatists outside the circle of the University Wits: Thomas Kyd (1558?–1594?), author of the remarkable and highly influential *The Spanish Tragedy* (1592), was one of those who did not receive a university education. Shakespeare was not university-educated either; he was in London at the same time as Marlowe, but, whilst Alleyn was strutting the stage as Tamburlaine, Shakespeare may still have been a few years away from seeing his first plays staged. When he did make his debut, it was probably with the *Henry VI* trilogy, which owed something of a debt to *Tamburlaine the Great*, just as his *Merchant of Venice* would draw upon Marlowe's *The Jew of Malta*. Marlowe reappears in extant records in the autumn of 1589. By then he had almost certainly written *Doctor Faustus*: as we shall see later, the text of this play is unstable, coming down to us in two radically different versions, and any record of its early stage history is lost. However, it was repeatedly revived, and was evidently another great success in the theatre.

While the première of *Faustus* is not recorded, the next stage in Marlowe's troublesome personal career is: this time he was involved in a brawl, or a duel, which ended in the death of one William Bradley. As in the case of Marlowe's own death, the details of the victim's injuries are precise: a wound in the right side of the chest six inches deep and an inch wide. The root of the quarrel seems to have been a debt owed by Bradley to a friend of Thomas Watson – Watson was a friend of Marlowe's, and it is possible that he and Marlowe shared lodgings together. On the afternoon of 18 September 1589, Bradley accosted Marlowe in Hog Lane in Norton Fulgate (possibly this is where Marlowe was lodging at the time). They drew upon one another, and a duel began. Shortly afterwards, Watson intervened and Marlowe withdrew, since the true quarrel lay between the two of them, and the conclusion of the fight was Bradley's death at Watson's sword-point, who was himself also wounded. Marlowe and Watson apparently did not make any attempt to escape arrest – to flee would effectively have been to admit guilt – and they were locked up in Newgate Gaol (on the site now occupied by the Old Bailey) on suspicion of murder. Their trial the following day acquitted them, the jury accepting the plea of self-defence. Marlowe was bound over to keep the peace and fined £20, and released within two weeks of his arrest. It was clear to the jury that Marlowe had withdrawn from the fight, and there were no more charges for him to answer. Watson was less fortunate: although he was acquitted when the full case was finally heard in December 1589, he had to wait, in gaol, until February of the following year before he finally received his royal pardon.

It was around this time that Marlowe wrote *The Jew of Malta*, which seems to have been another tremendous box office success. Henslowe's diary records ten performances between February and June 1592, each with substantial receipts. It is assumed, too, that these performances were revivals, since the diary entry does not note the 26 February 1592 performance as a première (Henslowe customarily wrote the letters 'ne' against certain plays in his records, and although we cannot be certain, it seems likely that this denoted a new play, although it could also refer to a new version of a play, or a new production). During the period July 1592 to December 1593, the Privy Council ordered the closing of the playhouses due to the threat of plague: a short month of playing was permitted during this period, and a performance of *The Jew of Malta* was accordingly slotted in. Further performances are noted in 1594, 1596 and 1601. For better or worse, the play's harsh stereotyping of Jewishness and its savage black humour touched a nerve with Elizabethan audiences, and it helped to consolidate Marlowe as the great London playwright of the time. It may be that the 1594 performance was arranged in the wake of the execution of a famous Jew, Dr Roderigo Lopez, a royal physician who had been accused and convicted of treason. Certainly it would have been in keeping with the practice of the theatre managers to cash in on contemporary events.

By 1592, Marlowe was in trouble again. It seems that government business had taken him abroad once more, this time to Flushing in the Netherlands, where he was arrested for counterfeiting currency (a full account of the incident can be found in chapter 25 of Nicholl's *The Reckoning*). Flushing, a Dutch town owned by the English, with an English governor and army, was notorious for this kind of activity. From the evidence that exists, it seems that Marlowe and his fellow agent Richard Baines had a falling out, each accusing the other of taking their 'performances' as counterfeiters too far and trying to make their own personal profits out of government work: Baines first accused Marlowe of persuading a goldsmith to forge some coins, only one of which, a Dutch shilling, was actually used. Baines also claimed that Marlowe was intending to defect to the Roman Catholic church. Marlowe retorted that he was only testing the goldsmith's skill, and said Baines was equally implicated in the arrangement with the goldsmith. According to Marlowe's account, he was merely acting as an *agent provocateur*, as we believe he may have done in Rheims. In the upshot, Baines's word was taken over Marlowe's. The two of them were sent back to England, with Marlowe and two others as prisoners and Baines accompanying them. Sir Robert Sidney (the poet and national hero Philip Sidney's younger brother), Flushing's governor, sent a letter with them detailing the facts of the case for Lord Burghley. We do not know what happened to Marlowe in the fallout from the business at Flushing. He may have been imprisoned for a couple of months. Whatever the case, he certainly escaped with a light sentence, since the official punishment for forging false currency was to be boiled to death in oil. We do know that he must have been out of prison by May 1593 since by then he was involved in another street brawl, this time with a couple of constables. He was fined and bound over to keep the peace. Within a few weeks, he would be dead.

It was probably in the year 1592 that Marlowe's final two dramatic works, *Edward II* and *The Massacre at Paris*, were written, although, as with *Faustus*, hard evidence that would help us date the first production of *Edward II* is impossible to trace. Henslowe's diary lists *The Massacre at Paris* as having been staged at the Rose by Lord Strange's Men in January 1593, and it does bear the 'ne' mark that implies this was a première. Both plays are historical dramas, and on this account they seem to go together. Critical consensus dictates that *Edward II* is stylistically the most mature of Marlowe's work. *The Massacre at Paris* has come down to us in a badly mangled form; it is generally accepted that the printers used a text that was reconstructed from memory, possibly by one or some of the actors, possibly by a prompter or someone else involved in the production. For this reason, it is almost impossible to make judgements that date the play by examining its style, but it does share some features with *Edward II*; the conjecture that these plays do mark the abrupt end of his career as a dramatist seems the most sensible one. In the space of twelve months from December 1592, it is believed that between 10,000 and 11,000 people died of the plague in London – about 5 per cent of the city's population. The theatres were closed for long periods in 1593, and this meant financial ruin for some: neither the Queen's Men nor Lord Pembroke's Men survived. It also meant that playwrights were forced to find other ways of making ends meet. Shakespeare's two narrative poems *Venus and Adonis* and *The Rape of Lucrece* might have been the result of this particular force of circumstance, and it is likely that Marlowe wrote *Hero and Leander* at the same time. The text, which Marlowe never completed, was finally published in 1598, five years after his death.

'Monstrous opinions': Marlowe and transgression

It is now 1593, and we are approaching Marlowe's final turbulent weeks. The brawl in Deptford does not take place in a vacuum, for at the time of his death Marlowe was awaiting a hearing before the Privy Council on a charge of atheism. It is clear that Marlowe had made a good number of enemies for himself by this time, and before we look closely at the run-up to the issue of a warrant for his arrest, it is important to understand the extent to which Marlowe had already offended many sensibilities with his 'monstrous opinions'. As far back as 1588, Marlowe had been ruffling feathers in the London theatrical world. Robert Greene, one of the University Wits, was by all accounts a talented and prolific writer who led a debauched lifestyle and died in extreme poverty and misery, his final gesture being a deathbed pamphlet entitled *A Groatsworth of Wit* (1592). The pamphlet was written as a warning against Greene's fellow playwrights in general and, it would seem, against Marlowe in particular. Before this, Greene had already made what many read as an envy-fuelled attack on *Tamburlaine* in his *Perimedes the Blacksmith* (1588). Some of what he writes remains obscure, the contemporary resonance long since gone, but it is clear that he has Marlowe in his sights (it is possible that the other 'Gentleman Poet' is Shakespeare) when he declares:

> I keep my old course, to palter up something in
> prose, using mine old poesy still . . . although lately two
> Gentlemen Poets, made my two mad men of Rome beat
> it out of their paper bucklers: and had it in derision, for
> that I could not make my verses jet upon the stage in
> tragical buskins, every word filling the mouth like the
> fuburden of Bo-Bell, daring God out of heaven with that
> atheist Tamburlan, or blaspheming with the mad priest of
> the sun: but let me rather openly pocket up the Ass at

Diogenes hand: then wantonly set out such impious
instances of intolerable poetry, such mad and scoffing poets,
that have prophetical spirits as bold as Merlin's race . . .

[cited in MacLure, 1995, pp. 29–30]

What is rather clever about Greene's attack is the way in which he
manages to associate closely, even to identify, Marlowe's opinions with
those of his character Tamburlaine: Marlowe and Tamburlaine, he suggests, are both blasphemers. The reference to Merlin is also obliquely
aimed at Marlowe via a pun on Marlin – another familiar spelling of
Marlowe's (or Marley's, or Morley's) name. Such complications over
nomenclature were common in a society which still worked mostly within
an oral tradition, and where the spelling of the language remained volatile.
Merlin would have been pronounced as Marlin by the Elizabethans,
and Marlin was a form of his name that was particularly familiar in
Cambridge, where the two men had previously been acquainted. Greene
is even more explicit in *A Groatsworth of Wit*:

Wonder not, (for with thee will I first begin), thou
famous gracer of Tragedians, that *Greene*, who hath said
with thee (like the fool in his heart), There is no God,
should now give glory unto his greatness: . . . Why
should thy excellent wit, his gift, be so blinded, that
thou shouldst give no glory to the giver? Is it pestilent
Machiavellian policy that thou has studied? O peevish
folly! What are his rules but mere confused mockeries,
able to extirpate in small time the generation of mankind.
. . . The broacher of this diabolical atheism is dead, and in
his life had never the felicity he aimed at: but as he began
in craft, lived in fear, and ended in despair.

[cited in MacLure, 1995, p. 30]

This time, Greene is not only associating Marlowe with atheism but
also accusing him of being in thrall to the philosophy of Machiavelli,
who makes an appearance in the Prologue to *The Jew of Malta*, and who
would have been familiar to the Elizabethans as a figure of evil and
duplicity. In itself, *A Groatsworth of Wit* counted for little. It was probably largely ignored. But it is significant in that it sowed the seeds for
the accusations of heresy and atheism that were to follow.

27

In the spring of 1593, the atmosphere in London was volatile. Distrust and discontent aimed at the immigrants in the city – chiefly Flemings and French Huguenots – was beginning to reach boiling point, and the threat of rioting was becoming more real each day. Notices, the Elizabethan equivalent of graffiti, were being pinned up around the city, and it was one of these, set upon the boundary wall of a Dutch church, that sparked off the controversy that would envelope Marlowe. His associate Kyd had been working, with other writers, on a dramatization of the life of Sir Thomas More who had served as Sheriff of London during a period of similar unrest in the city. These men had a sharp eye on the profit principle: lean times came in the wake of the temporary closures of the theatres, and they no doubt had high hopes of a box office hit to replenish the coffers as soon as the plague went into some kind of remission. Unfortunately, the censor's eye for potential trouble was as keen as the dramatists' was for a money-spinner. The Master of the Revels refused to pass the play for performance and demanded that a scene depicting an insurrection be cut. For Kyd and his associates, it was back to the drawing board.

The Council of the Star Chamber had by now decided on a thorough and invasive form of action that advocated the search of properties and the arrest of anyone thought to be involved in seditious activities. It is not clear why Kyd's lodgings were targeted: it might have been the business with the Thomas More play. The notice on the Dutch courtyard wall had been signed with the pseudonym 'Tamburlaine'. The tone of the attack is grimly familiar in an age that is accustomed to the brutal threats and crude illogic of racist discourse:

> You strangers that do inhabit this land,
> Note this same writing, do it understand.
> Conceive it well, for safeguard of your lives,
> Your goods, your children, and your dearest wives . . .
> Cut-throat-like in selling, you undo
> Us all, and with out store continually you feast.
> Our poor artificers do starve and die.

> [cited in Nicholl, 1992, pp. 284–5]

Charles Nicholl shows how the text of the libel seems to echo some of the preoccupations of Marlowe's work, and he finds in particular traces of *The Jew of Malta* and *The Massacre at Paris* (p. 286). Kyd, as a known associate of Marlowe's, may have been suspected of writing the notice.

Whoever the author of the so-called Dutch Church libel may have been – and it is impossible to know (although Nicholl's speculations are intriguing and worth reading) – it was Kyd who found himself under arrest when his rooms were searched and an heretical manuscript found among his papers; the script was labelled by the authorities 'vile heretical conceits denying the deity of Jesus Christ our Saviour found amongst the papers of Thomas Kyd prisoner which he affirmeth he had from Marlowe' (cited in Wraight & Stern, 1993, p. 239). Heresy and atheism are almost interchangeable terms at this time, but however the formal accusation is framed, it is clear that these are profound, punishable offences. Interrogation and, most likely, torture on the rack followed for Kyd. In addition to physical pain, there was the torment of the prospect of being burned at the stake for heresy. The outcome was two detailed statements by Kyd that pointed the finger of blame directly at Marlowe. Reading the two letters he addressed to the Lord Keeper, Sir John Puckering (almost certainly written in June, shortly after Marlowe's death), it is hard not to feel pity for Kyd: the abject terror beneath the formal and reverential service is plain. It seems Kyd never recovered from his spell in prison, and he died within a year. This extract captures the tone of the letters:

> When I was first suspected for that libel that concern'd the state, amongst those waste and idle papers (which I cared not for) and which unasked I did deliver up, were found some fragments of a disputation touching that opinion affirmed by Marlowe to be his, and shuffled with some of mine (unknown to me) by some occasion of our writing in one chamber two years since . . .
>
> [cited in MacLure, 1995, p. 32]

In the second letter the accusations against Marlowe are made more explicit:

> Pleaseth it your honourable lordship touching Marlowe's monstrous opinions, as I cannot but with an aggrieved conscience think on him or them, so can I but particularise few in the respect of them that kept him greater company. Howbeit in discharge of duty both towards God, your lordships and the world thus much have I thought good briefly to discover in all humbleness:

first, it was his custom when I knew him first and as I
hear say he continued it in table talk or otherwise to jest
at the divine scriptures, gibe at prayers, and strive in
argument to frustrate and confute what hath been spoke
or writ by prophets and such holy men.

[cited in ibid., p. 35]

Kyd goes on to claim that Marlowe had said St John had been Christ's
homosexual lover – 'that Christ did love him with an extraordinary love';
that he esteemed St Paul 'a juggler', and that 'things esteemed to be done
by divine power might as well have been done by observation of men'
(cited in ibid., p. 35). At what point these accusations emerged during
the interrogation we cannot know, but the Privy Council seemed confident that it had enough information to reel Marlowe in: a warrant
was issued for his arrest on 18 May 1593, with orders to seek him at
the home of Sir Thomas Walsingham in Kent. He was apprehended
there and returned to London, appearing before the Council. Oddly
enough, he was not imprisoned at this point, but released on bail and
ordered to report back daily to the Council. If we recall again the dispute over his graduation, it seems likely that whatever influence he had
then had come back to prise him out of a tight corner once more.

Richard Baines comes back into the frame at this point: with the
Flushing business no doubt still in his mind, he would presumably have
been very satisfied to find himself appointed to investigate Marlowe's
alleged atheism. Part of that report was submitted to the council
around the time of Marlowe's death, and the list of supposed heresies
is exhaustive: this time, it is Moses who is the 'juggler'. The sexual slant
of Marlowe's blasphemies is heavily accentuated ('That the woman of
Samaria and her sister were whores and that Christ knew them dis-
honestly'; 'That St. John the Evangelist was bedfellow to Christ . . . that
he used him as the sinners of Sodoma'; 'That the Angel Gabriel was
bawd to the Holy Ghost, because he brought the salutation to Mary').
There are accusations that recall Marlowe's graduation controversy ('that
all Protestants are hypocritical asses') and the Flushing incident ('That
he has as good right to coin as the Queen of England'), and accuse
him of proselytizing for his atheist cause ('almost into every company
he cometh he persuades men to atheism willing them not to be afeared
of bugbears and hobgoblins, and utterly scorning both God and his ministers') (cited in MacLure, 1995, pp. 37–8). It is in Baines's report that
we find the infamous quip he attributes to Marlowe, 'That all they that

love not tobacco and boys were fools' (cited in ibid., p. 37). From here, it is just a short step to the fanatical tirades of Thomas Beard and his successors.

We are brought full circle to the mystery of Marlowe's death. Charles Nicholl's attempt to reconstruct the events leading up to the fight in Deptford in his book *The Reckoning* (1992) is intriguing and ingenious, and its proposed solution to the mystery, emphasizing the political intrigue, is bold and fascinating, but Nicholl wisely remains circumspect as he draws his conclusions. The depth of his research traces connections between disparate figures associated with Marlowe which are often astonishing, but he concedes that 'the final truth about Marlowe's death lies hidden under these layers of reconstruction . . . Only fragments remain: scraps of paper, pieces of a jigsaw, the nagging sense of unfinished business' (Nicholl, 1992, pp. 328–9). In the next chapter we will look at the broad context in which Marlowe wrote his plays and poems: the historical, social, political and religious conditions that impacted on his work, and in which his work intervened. In the documentation of Marlowe's life from which we have attempted to construct some kind of coherent narrative (but only one out of a range of possibilities), there are elements that we recognize as 'human', immediate, vivid. There are other elements that we may find very alien if we try to fit them within the kind of perspective we use to make sense of our own lives and the world around us. As we move from the story of Marlowe's life to his context, and to his work, it will be vital to preserve this sense of 'otherness': in order to comprehend Elizabethan culture, in order to achieve some sense of the way in which Marlowe's plays worked in the theatres of his time, we need to remind ourselves constantly that we are in a world that is very different from our own, and that piecing that world together will inevitably be a varied experience: some areas of the picture will suddenly snap together and become very clear and vivid. At other times we will find that we can only speculate or make informed guesses as to how the world seemed through the eyes of an Elizabethan. It is this open, diverse and volatile response to Marlowe's work that will release its full potential.

CHAPTER 2

THE TIME OF MARLOWE

'But that was in another country': cultural difference

One of the biggest challenges to anyone approaching Marlowe's plays either on stage or on the page is the gap of 400 years that separates our era from his. The study of the literature of the past has traditionally been founded on the notion that human beings have remained fundamentally the same throughout history; great writers were understood to tap into those essential aspects of humanity, and it was in this that their greatness was said to inhere. But since the 1970s these notions – essential humanity and the idea of great literature – have been subject to some close scrutiny, and have been challenged by many; more often, the debates have been constructed around the figure of Shakespeare, the epitome of the so-called universal genius. Marlowe, a more marginal figure in terms of his canonical status, puts an interesting spin on these debates for two reasons: firstly, he does not share Shakespeare's sense of personal anonymity (what we know about Marlowe, though scant, is undoubtedly colourful), and secondly, a play like *The Jew of Malta* raises difficult questions about texts transcending their contexts. The chief aim of this section is to give an overview of the Elizabethan culture in which Marlowe lived his short life, paying close attention to politics, religion, literature and the theatre, those areas that impinged most directly upon him. The impression the chapter is designed to leave is one of otherness rather than familiarity: that 400-year gap is hugely significant, and is not to be dismissed unthinkingly, with an appeal to a vague conception of 'universality'. The past is another country.

It is difficult, in such a limited space, to create a very full picture of the profoundly different culture that was Elizabethan England. Perhaps some of the most seemingly trivial aspects of human life are as good a place to start as any, since their apparent insignificance is actually an indication of how we tend to take such things for granted. In terms of simple daily routine, then, the seasons regulated social activity to a much greater extent than they do today, and activities would be structured around sunrise and sunset. On dark winter nights the day would end much earlier, with supper, prayers and bed following fairly quickly after work finished, since poorer households could scarcely afford the cost of candles or other means of artificial light. The summer allowed time (and the appropriate climate) after work for music, dancing, and other recreations, and the cycle of the moon would sometimes allow for some limited after-dark activities. Competing for the attention of those seeking entertainment in London were the public playhouses, gambling houses and brothels, as well as bear-baiting pits. Public executions, when scheduled, would in themselves constitute an outing.

Sanitation in the sixteenth century was primitive by any modern standard. In the city streets, duels could be provoked by pedestrians in confrontation over who would be permitted to 'take the wall' (that is to say, to walk closest to the walls of the houses in order to avoid stepping in the streets, which were routinely clogged with animal and human excrement and other waste). The sight and smell of faeces, urine and sweat that we tend to be shielded from in the developed world today would have been very much more familiar to the Elizabethan. Not only would this impact on daily life, in everything from disposing of slops and cleaning chamber pots, to the hazards of walking past open second-floor windows, but it had important implications for health, too. In a world that had very few ways of fighting infection, death, disease and disfigurement were much more familiar parts of everyday life. Syphilis, carried back from the Americas, was believed to be spread by women (a belief that tells us much about the misogyny endemic in the culture). It often killed, but when it did not, it would usually disfigure. The high visibility of syphilis meant that its victims were often publicly vilified, particularly since it was thought to be a punishment from God for sexual licence. Medical knowledge was a dangerous amalgam of science and superstition, with an array of physiological and psychological disorders attributed to the supernatural. The skin of a recently hanged man, for instance, was understood to be a treatment for certain skin diseases, which were rampant among the lower classes, again chiefly as a result of poor hygiene and sanitation: often unable to afford a change of clothes, they would wear the same garments week after week. Congenital abnormalities were taken as signifiers of the supernatural: Anne Boleyn, one of Henry VIII's wives, had an incipient sixth finger on one hand – a convenient signifier of involvement in witchcraft. When Henry had had enough of her, he accused her, among other things, of sorcery; the fact that the second child she bore was deformed and stillborn added to the weight of 'evidence' against her.

The difference between life expectancy in 1990s Britain (78 for women, 72 for men) and early modern England (between 32 and 40) is startling. Mortality rates also varied wildly over time, dependent as they were on such factors as epidemics and bad harvests which might lead to widespread starvation among the poorer classes. Epidemics caused widespread panic: typhus and bubonic plague were the worst, with the latter visiting the teeming capital almost every year. Once the death toll reached 30 in London, the theatres would be shut down, since it was believed that the disease spread quickly in crowded places. In the worst outbreak, in 1603, it is estimated that approximately 23 per cent of the population of London was wiped out. Malaria and tuberculosis were also common. The perils of childbirth were significant both for mother and baby, and the dangers are well known and well documented. Child mortality was also high, chiefly due to disease but also to the frequency of accidents in the home. Burns were more often inflicted and less easily treated than they are today, and frequently led to infections that were impossible to cure. Of the young fatalities, little boys, apparently left to wander from the home, more frequently drowned, while girls, helping or playing in the house, suffered more domestic accidents (Laurence, 1996, p. 85). It is not unreasonable to assume that attitudes to death differed from those that are current today, both as a result of the greater prevalence of Christian belief and due to the fact that, with cures scarce and haphazard, prayer was often the only option. Death was understood not as a simple physical occurrence, but as one stage in a supernatural process. Abbott's *Life Cycles in England, 1560–1720* discusses the diary of Ralph Josselin, a parson living in the first half of the seventeenth century. The entry for 23 February 1648 reads:

> Whereas I have given my mind to unseasonable playing at chess . . . Whereas I have walked with much vanity in my thoughts . . . have served divers lusts too much in thoughts and actions, whereas both body and soul should be the Lord's who hath called me to holiness, God hath taken away a son.

> [Abbott, 1996, p. 29]

In a world where death hovered close by, and where the majority believed their lives to be in the hands of a higher power, the sense of control over one's life and the lives of loved ones was precarious. A number of social historians have noted how weekly church attendance brought with it the awareness of the proximity of death, with the tombs and gravestones indoors and out, the wooden crosses in the graveyard, and the engraved skulls and skeletons lining the walls. Catechisms and numerous reminders and admonitions concerning the imminence of death were familiar subjects of the ballads and chapbooks that were prevalent in the popular culture of the time. The connection between death, sickness or misfortune and the judgment of God in these texts is a familiar one. Beginning at birth, human earthly existence was seen as a journey towards death, at which point the soul passed from the body into eternity. The appearance of the body after death was perceived as an important sign of the subject's spiritual state. Even more important was the ability to die well: with few cures and few means of effective anaesthesia, the dying often had plenty of time to contemplate their end.

The human soul, heaven and hell, salvation and damnation: these are concepts that would have seemed immediate and concrete to an average Elizabethan in a way that we may find hard to imagine. Although this was undoubtedly a time of immense religious and cultural upheaval, belief in the supernatural remained dominant, though by no means unchallenged. The drama of the medieval era (from which *Doctor Faustus* is quite clearly descended, as we shall see) was populated by abstractions – the qualities, say of Mercy or Mischief, were personified, and even the human figure was an allegorical Everyman rather than an identifiable individual. This makes medieval drama relatively inaccessible to many modern minds, but to a mind that was conditioned to think of the human in terms of a split between the spirit and the body, the one eternal, the other transient, the earthly world was only a poor shadow of the spiritual dimension, and in that sense the abstractions were more 'real' than we can possibly imagine. There is a danger of homogenizing here, and this has been a failing in earlier scholarship in both historical and literary studies. Elizabethan society encompassed a very broad range of beliefs, even if by today's standards that range would seem extremely limited. Atheism today is understood to constitute the rejection of the idea of God and, usually, any form of the supernatural; for the Elizabethans, any deviation from orthodoxy could be termed atheism (Marlowe was himself accused of it), which should give some indication of how much more heterodox belief was 400 years ago. Superstitions clustered around all aspects and routines of human life, particularly the key moments of birth, baptism, marriage and death. Astrology, lent authority by its classical roots, was also deeply embedded in the beliefs of the people:

from it came the idea that the human body was composed of the four elements of fire, earth, air and water, and that planets influenced the body via the effect their movements had on these four components. Medical practice was founded on the idea of the four humours, each of them equivalent to one of the four elements. Belief in witchcraft was widespread. According to Anne Laurence's fascinating social history of *Women in England, 1500–1760*, between 1542 and 1746 approximately 1,000 people were executed for witchcraft in England. Comparatively speaking, the English were much less ferocious prosecutors of supposed witches than other Europeans. Scotland, which at that time had a population a third the size of England's, had twice as many executions for witchcraft. It is worth noting that between 80 and 90 per cent of those accused of the 'crime' during this period were women (Laurence, 1996, p. 219).

Elizabethan justice and punishment was a swift, public and brutal process, though no worse (and often much more lenient) than other European countries. Still, poisoners would usually be sentenced to be boiled to death in water or lead – this is the end that Barabas meets in Marlowe's *The Jew of Malta*. Heretics were usually burned at the stake; the monarch preceding Elizabeth, Mary I, executed a large number of Protestants who were regarded as martyrs – over 270 were executed between 1553 and 1558 (Routh, 1990, p. 156). Witches were drowned or burned; thieves would be hanged or have their hands chopped off; offenders who refused to plead at their trials would be pressed under heavy weights until they either agreed to plead, or else were crushed to death. The refusal to plead was an option for some, since it meant that one would not die a convicted felon, and so property could pass to one's family instead of being confiscated by the Crown. Offences against the state were met with 'the greatest and most grievous punishment used in England', as reported by William Harrison in his *The Description of England*:

> . . . drawing from the prison to the place of execution
> upon an hurdle or sled, where they are hanged till they be
> half dead, and then taken down, and quartered alive; after
> that, their members and bowels are cut from their bodies,
> and thrown into a fire, provided near hand and within
> their own sight . . .

> [cited in Evans, 1988, p. 286]

Francis Barker has done some painstaking research studying the records that survive of executions during the reigns of Elizabeth and James I.

His conclusion was that, in each of the years during that time, 'on average at least 371.5 were put to death by hanging, 7.94 were killed by the *peine forte et dure* [pressed to death], and a further 176 probably died in jail' (Barker, 1993, p. 178). By scaling that up to take account of the difference between populations then and now, it seems that the equivalent figures in modern Britain would be a staggering 4,599 executed, 98 pressed to death, and 2,179 dead in gaol each year (p. 179). Barker also submits that these are likely to be drastic underestimates, though they seem to be the most accurate figures available on the surviving evidence. Execution was a common and very visible part of Elizabethan life. The heads of traitors were routinely mounted on the archway of London Bridge, and would have been seen by many as they went about their business, since the bridge was the only means to cross the Thames except by boat. The very public and often protracted performance of harsh justice was highly theatrical, a spectacular display of the extent to which the state held sway over its subjects. The extremity of the violence perpetrated, the ingenuity with which the body could be dismembered in the process of hanging, drawing and quartering, were powerful demonstrations of state power. It is tempting to link the event of a public execution, complete with stage, players (the priest, the executioner, the condemned man) and audience, with the frequent occurrences of executions and tortures in early modern dramatic texts. And, as we shall see, Marlowe's plays include their own fair share of violent deaths, each with different sets of implications.

As we begin an inevitably cursory glance at personal relationships in this society, it is worth reminding ourselves again of the significance of the historical gap that separates us from the Elizabethans. Lawrence Stone, commenting on the writing of women's history in particular, has a useful rule that we would do well to bear in mind: 'Thou shalt not assume the ubiquity in the past of modern emotional patterns – neither pre-marital love, nor conjugal affection, nor maternal devotion to children' (Stone, 1985, p. 21). Stone has argued that familial affection is a comparatively recent phenomenon, and that the way mother, father and children related to one another at least up until Tudor times was profoundly different from in the modern family. His thesis has been widely challenged: there is certainly enough evidence from documents of the period to suggest that the kind of emotional bonds that exist today between partners, and between parents and children, were present then. But we need to remain cautious when we attempt to interpret these relationships through a modern perspective, for amidst the familiarity, there was much that is odd by our own standards. In the first place, the Elizabethan household featured roles and relations between husband and wife that were clearly defined, and based on scripture. According to Genesis 12.16, God said to Eve that 'In sorrow thou shalt bring forth children and thy desire shall be to thy husband, and he shall rule over thee'. It was assumed to be part of the natural order that men were superior to women, and it seems likely that domestic violence was consequently fairly widespread, and to a certain degree expected and tolerated. The story of Adam and Eve was also taken as a warning about women's seductive and deceitful nature, and the consensus was that they were to be kept under close surveillance. The plots of many plays that fit into the popular 'revenge tragedy' genre of the Jacobean period revolve around sexual intrigue, husbands' anxiety of their wives' adultery and the need to police supposedly highly volatile female sexuality: women were thought to have greater sexual appetites than men.

For the women's part, the pain and peril of childbirth were understood as part of God's judgment on Eve. Infant mortality rates were, unsurprisingly, high, and as a consequence childbirth had its own particular superstitions and rituals associated with it – untying knots and unlocking doors were thought to ease delivery. In this society, the role of the woman was clearly defined: she was expected to keep the house in order and to raise children. Although privileged women might have had some assistance from servants, the vast majority would not have done. It has traditionally been assumed that children, particularly girls, married very young, but recent research has yielded a more complex picture, and it seems that ages varied according to region, social status and other circumstances. Canon law did not recognize a marriage until the male was fourteen years of age and the female twelve. Among the property-owning classes, marriages would often be made politically (and so often arranged at a younger age), although the notion of marriage for companionship, the norm today in Western society, is thought to have begun to emerge during the Tudor period. Amy Louise Erickson usefully summarizes the attitude that seemed prevalent at this time when she writes that 'It was commonly expected that love should be not the precursor to marriage, but its outcome' (Morrill, 1996, p. 97). Education for women was chiefly aimed at fitting them for their roles as wives, training them as efficient householders and obedient partners. Women were not perceived as full members of society in the way that men were; having no representation in Parliament, and no say in law-making, it was more often their husbands who would be held responsible for regulating their behaviour. The legal status of the woman in Elizabethan England is a signifier of her position in other spheres, too: exchanged as property between males in marriage arrangements, positioned below the male in the spiritual order of things, she was always subservient to him, and deprived of any sense of self-determination or autonomy. The satirical literature that grew up around the notion of the disobedient wife – the husband-battering 'shrew' – is a strong indicator of how firmly the relative status of man and woman was embedded in the culture, and how any aberration was seen as something monstrous, ludicrous, or both.

Old and new historicism

Approaches to literature which attempt to 'historicize' the texts under discussion are not new. From the time that literary studies became institutionalized as a profession, around the 1930s, a strong historical strand has been present in the scholarship. The literary critic who is perhaps the most well-known Elizabethan scholar of the mid-twentieth century is E.M.W. Tillyard. Tillyard's historical approach was in part a response to the tendency among the most influential figures in the field of literature, such as F.R. Leavis, to divorce texts from their contexts and to insist on the primacy of 'close reading' and detailed textual study. Tillyard's historicism was a straightforward kind of analysis that sought to assess the significance of the wider social context of a work of art to an understanding and full appreciation of that work. Tillyard's *The Elizabethan World Picture* (1944) has generally been taken as the epitome of this kind of approach, partly because it has in the past been such a popular and widely read introduction to early modern culture in England, recommended by teachers and lecturers to generations of students. Tillyard's book is grounded in the idea that it is possible to identify and recover a 'mindset' which represents a coherent body of beliefs of a particular age that were 'taken for granted', 'a part of the collective mind of the people', as he puts it (Tillyard, 1970, p. 18). From this starting point, Tillyard postulates Elizabethan society as one that understood itself as being centred on a divine order, with a so-called 'great chain of being' defining that order: a chain within whose length every thing, animate and inanimate, had its place. The picture was of a unified, hierarchical system imposed from above that operated in this fashion spiritually, intellectually and socially. Tillyard saw this system reflected in the drama of the period, with comedies inevitably resolving conflict into harmony, and the tragedies representing the breakdown of order.

Tillyard's book would prove to be influential from the time of its publication, although it certainly did not go unchallenged in the decades that followed. The pre-eminence of *The Elizabethan World Picture* from the time of its publication until the 1970s has perhaps become something of a myth in itself. As Graham Bradshaw has shown (1993, pp. 1–8), a number of critics including Wilbur Sanders (1968) and Norman Rabkin (1967) published key works that took issue with Tillyard's monolithic view of Elizabethan culture. However it is probably fair to say that, while dissent was evident in scholarly circles, Tillyard's book rapidly took on seminal status in schools and undergraduate programmes. It was not until the 1970s that a generation of critics emerged who challenged Tillyard on more fundamental grounds, arguing that historical periods are not unified entities, but tend instead to be discontinuous, overlapping and contradictory. Instead of a mindset, a 'world picture', we find that within any particular era there will be several competing explanations of the way the world works. Influenced by Marxist philosophers and cultural critics, literary scholars began to study literature in the light of emerging debates about ideology.

Ideology is one of those elusive terms that can be used to mean many different things, but for the purposes of this present discussion, it is understood to signify a set of socially shared meanings: in a way, it is roughly equivalent to the notion of a mindset, or a world picture. Ideology produces systems that explain who we are, how society is structured and how the world works. The difference between Tillyard's notion of a mindset and the way ideology is understood to work is that the latter is not univocal. Tillyard's assumption seems to have been that a set of beliefs existed to which everyone subscribed unquestioningly. Ideologies, by contrast, are understood to exist in parallel, often in competition with each other. Ideology is also more complex in that it is often understood to operate at an unconscious level. It may be that there were those who believed in the rigidly hierarchical system Tillyard proposes; but other individuals and groups may have resisted or contested the established social order that was erected on that belief in a great chain of being. Those near the top of the human section of that chain would obviously have had a vested interest in endorsing, maintaining and propagating the belief that God had ordained a position in the hierarchy to each living thing. But the early modern period was one of massive social upheaval, particularly in economic terms, with the birth pangs of new kinds of capitalism sending shock waves across Europe that would have been impossible to ignore, though some were certainly provoked to advocate the status quo even more forcefully. This introduces another connotation of the term 'ideology': the ways in which certain ideas about how society works are propagated for political purposes have been explored by several key cultural theorists, most acutely by Louis Althusser. For Althusser, ideology was necessarily a distortion of reality: in his own terms, it is 'a "representation" of the imaginary relationship of individuals to their real conditions of existence' (Althusser, 1971, p. 152). This is important for our purposes, because that distortion of reality is understood to function by a variety of means (education, the political system, the judicial system, and so on) which includes literature, drama and other cultural forms.

All this is crucial to a study of Marlowe, since both his life and his work have been understood to be subversive in the sense that they challenged the dominant ideology of the time. Drama is one of the means by which ideology operates, and by placing play-texts alongside other documents from the period – texts written, perhaps, by lawyers, theologians, popular writers, politicians, pamphleteers, and even monarchs (James I was particularly prolific) – we can see how tightly woven the theatre was into the social fabric. Drama constructs meaning: it is one 'signifying practice' among many, to use Anthony Easthope's useful term (Easthope, 1991, p. 5). Such signifying practices can never be politically neutral, for they are means by which we interact with one another in society. The critic Alan Sinfield talks about how literary writing makes an appeal for recognition – in effect, a play says 'The world is like *this*, isn't it?' – and this has to be political, whether it is on the micro scale of personal politics or the grander scale of state or international politics (Sinfield, 1994, p. viii). Dramatic texts of the period have been identified as very lively sites of contestation, or combat, between conflicting ideologies (whether religious, political or social), and their potential in this respect was recognized by those who had much to lose and gain in that society. The monarch's Master of the Revels, who saw all scripts of new plays and licensed them for production, would censor any material considered seditious. Nevertheless, the potential of drama in ideological terms is heightened by the context of public performance: circulating a pamphlet questioning the divine right of the monarch, for existence, is certainly subversive, but its potential impact is hard to judge. Staging the deposition of a king in front of several hundred citizens is something else again.

A number of new historicist critics, notably Greenblatt (1994, first published 1980) and Tennenhouse (1986), have used a broader understanding of the notion of performance to interrogate the ways in which both Elizabeth I and James I 'staged' their authority. Both of them seemed to understand the potential of performance, and found plenty of opportunities to put their power on display. Elizabeth's famous appearance amongst her troops at Tilbury in 1588, riding in armour through their ranks, prompted one who was there to talk of her having 'passed like some Amazonian empress through all her army' (Neale, 1934, p. 297). Roger Sales cites a description of her procession through London on the day before she was crowned in 1558. The author describes the city as a 'stage wherein was shown the wonderful spectacle of a noble hearted princess toward her most loving people', and the quotation that Sales includes has a strong sense of the histrionic about it:

> And on the other side her grace by holding up her hands, and merry countenance to such as stood far off, and most tender and gentle language to those that stood nigh to her grace, did declare herself no less thankfully to receive her peoples good will, than they lovingly offered it unto her.
>
> [cited in Sales, 1991, p. 27]

A familiar example of ideology at work in the sixteenth century, and of the way it interacts with drama, literature and culture in a wider sense, is this iconic figure of Queen Elizabeth I, perhaps still one of the most instantly recognizable of all English monarchs along with her father, Henry VIII. The designation of certain paintings of her as, for example, the 'sieve', 'pelican' and 'ermine' portraits, identify the symbols that those portraits feature. Each symbol represents particular qualities, such as chastity (the sieve) and charity (the pelican) (see Morrill, 1996, pp. 232–3, 352). One of Elizabeth's cleverest and most successful strategies during her long reign (45 years) was to remain unmarried, while, for much of that time, always appearing to be on the brink of one political marriage or another. The last time she came close to a union was with the Duke of Alençon in 1579. Since she was 45 years old by this time, when the marriage did not happen (primarily due to the predictable problem of the Frenchman's Catholicism) it was then clear that she would not be providing an heir to her throne.

The arts were instrumental in the development of the cult of the Virgin Queen, which in some ways worked as a substitute for the cult of the Virgin Mary that was simultaneously being dismantled in the wake of a Protestant monarch (Elizabeth) replacing a Catholic one (Mary I). Julia Briggs, in *This Stage-Play World* (1997), identifies an interesting passage in the prologue to a play by Thomas Dekker, *Old Fortunatus* (1599): the conversation scripted for the old men may be a little mischievous, but it gives a good sense of the way in which Elizabeth had become a semi-mythical figure:

1. Are you then travelling to the temple of Eliza?
2. Even to her temple are my feeble limbs travelling. Some call her Pandora; some Gloriana; some Cynthia; some Belphoebe; some Astraea; all by several names to express several love. Yet all these names make but one celestial body, as all those loves meet to create one soul.
3. I am of her country, and we adore her by the name of Eliza.

[cited in Briggs, 1997, p. 223]

These classical references are all chosen to express one or other of the Queen's attributes: Pandora ('all gifts'), Gloriana (Spenser's name for his Faerie Queene), Cynthia (another name for Diana, goddess of the moon, associated with hunting and with chastity), Belphoebe (the huntress-goddess of Spenser's poem), and Astraea (goddess of justice and innocence). Edmund Spenser's *Faerie Queene* (1590–6) is undoubtedly the most elaborate celebration of the Elizabeth cult. Spenser is fairly explicit about his intentions in a letter to Walter Ralegh, which was used as a preface to the 1590 edition of the first three Books:

In that Faery Queen I mean glory in my general intention, but in my particular I conceive the most excellent and glorious person of our sovereign the Queen, and her kingdom in Fairy Land.

[Spenser, 1979, p. 40]

There is a reciprocal process here of production and consumption: while Spenser endorses and develops the cult of Elizabeth in the *Faerie Queene*, at the same time the cult creates a space, or a demand, for the celebratory literature, masques and portraiture – the two feed off each other. Spenser's poem helps to establish the legitimacy of this 'version' of Elizabeth, and in so doing has a part to play in the propagation of the ruling class's ideological position.

As we grapple with fragments of different perspectives on Elizabethan society by its contemporaries, whether in historical accounts, religious and political pamphlets, or in the literature of the time, we see that the coherent 'world picture' pieced together in Tillyard's account is only one possible configuration, and one that is coloured by those with a vested interest in a hierarchical social order. In this sense, the representation can never be a neutral and unbiased one. However, the other significant factor we have not taken into consideration is Tillyard's own agenda. When Tillyard created his neatly framed depiction of an Elizabethan golden age, he was writing in the early 1940s. *The Elizabethan World Picture* was published in the middle of the Second World War, and the book needs to be understood in that context. The idea of a golden age, of a people living in harmony, with each member of the society assigned to his or her own place within that divine order, is clearly bound up in the politics of nationalism that were unsurprisingly regarded as crucial to the war effort. Other works of the period have come to be viewed in a similar light, notably G.M. Trevelyan's *English Social History* (1942). In another medium entirely, the standard analysis of Laurence Olivier's film version of *Henry V*, released in 1944, now takes as a given its complicity with the same patriotic initiative. The issue of representation will recur throughout this study of Marlowe's work, as well as his life: his biography is itself a collection of fragments that refract an array of different perspectives. In the study of the plays, the track record of analysis and stage history reveals a number of different reconfigurations of the texts' meanings. When Derek Jarman, for instance, makes a film based on *Edward II*, it is important to recognize that he is writing with an agenda of promoting gay rights in an era of censorship; a performance of *The Jew of Malta* in Nazi Germany is going to have a particular set of intended and received meanings, also, that would be different from those generated by a performance in Britain in the 1990s; and so on. Although there are always limits on the bounds of interpretation – there will be a point, finally, where the words refuse to be forced to mean something that they patently do not mean – it is important to bear in mind that one can sometimes travel a long way before those boundaries are reached, even before the text itself is edited, censored or rewritten.

Politics and religion in Elizabethan England

Politics and religion in Elizabethan society were inseparable in a way that might be hard for us to understand today. Though there are societies in the modern world where the two are still deeply implicated in one another – the conflict in the north of Ireland and the wars in the former Yugoslavia at the end of the twentieth century are two grimly familiar scenarios – the tendency is, at least in largely secularized societies such as Europe and North America, to conceptualize them as distinct. It is vital, if we are to gain any great insight into the social context within which Marlowe's plays were produced, to understand something of the ways in which politics and religion interacted in Elizabethan England, for Marlowe's texts are scarred with the traces of religious and political conflict. Furthermore, as we have already seen, his own life (and possibly his death, too) seem to have flared up and burned out at the point where the two collided. In order to understand the Elizabethan context, moreover, we have to review something of the history of the English throne leading up to the reign of Elizabeth, the last of the Tudor dynasty. Although at the turn of the millennium the British monarchy matters chiefly only in terms of symbol and heritage, in early modern times political power rested with the monarch, who governed through his or her Privy Council, which determined policy.

The centrality of the monarchy in religious affairs is starkly symbolized by the establishment of the king as Supreme Head of the church via the Act of Appeals and Supremacy in 1533 during the reign of Henry VIII (1509–1547). The act cemented Henry's new authority, establishing the king as 'institute and furnished by the goodness and sufferance of Almighty God with plenary, whole and entire power, preeminence, authority, prerogative and jurisdiction' (cited in Morrill, 1996, p. 226). The substitution of king for pope as supreme authority was one landmark of the religious revolution known as the Reformation that took place during the sixteenth century, bringing to an end the supremacy of the pope in western Christendom and the establishment of the Protestant faith. Though the movement itself is largely associated with Martin Luther and Jean Calvin, the two great religious figures of the Reformation, the gradual displacement of the pope as the central authority in European affairs had been under way throughout the preceding centuries, manifest in all aspects of these diverse cultures and societies. The English reformation differed from the revolution on the continent for a number of reasons, most significantly in the fact that it was more of a 'top down' reform in England than anywhere else. In Switzerland and the Netherlands, for instance, the rebellion against Rome had started among the people, and resulted in such conflagrations as the Peasants War, which raged across Germany in 1524–5 (ironically, a revolt that was condemned by Luther, despite the fact that the movement's appeal for agrarian reform was to a large extent fired by his doctrines, appealing to divine law over earthly authority). In England, the break with Rome was from the top down in the sense that it came about in the first place as a result of Henry VIII's desire to rid himself of the first of his six wives, the staunchly Catholic Catherine of Aragon. By 1527, Catherine had produced only one child that had survived (a daughter, Mary), and Henry decided to divorce her. When the pope refused to annul the marriage, Henry secretly married Anne Boleyn (who produced one child, the girl who would grow to be Elizabeth I and reign from 1558 to 1603). Henry had the archbishop of Canterbury pronounce his divorce from Catherine, was excommunicated by the pope, and proceeded to install himself as supreme head of the church. In the meantime, a raft of new legislation stopped all taxes due to Rome and confiscated all monastic land, which amounted to at least 20 per cent of the country.

Anne Boleyn did not last more than a few years. Her first child had been a daughter, the second a boy, deformed and stillborn. Henry was ready to move on. His third wife, Jane Seymour, died in childbirth but did produce a son, Edward, in 1537. However, the boy's constitution was delicate and, probably due more to pressure from his advisors than his own inclinations, Henry was persuaded to marry again, and three more marriages followed, to Anne of Cleves (1539), Catherine Howard (1540–2) and, finally, to Catherine Parr. None of these unions bore any children, however, and it was the sickly Edward VI who succeeded to the throne at the age of nine. He reigned until 1553, dying at the age of sixteen. During his short life Edward carried the standard of Protestantism, showing a profound interest in theology and church doctrine. He was succeeded (for less than two weeks) by Lady Jane Grey, before Mary I ascended the throne in 1553.

Mary I, daughter of Henry and Catherine of Aragon, was as anxious to establish a successor as her father had been. As a female monarch, her own authority was always unstable; there were many who would never have accepted her legitimacy on the throne simply because she was a woman. Her marriage to Philip, the Spanish heir, was a risky decision, provoking a xenophobic English populace. As it turned out, it was an unsuccessful match, and Philip only twice set foot on English soil, each time for the briefest of visits. For the powerful players in the Council, Mary's phantom pregnancy in 1555 effectively signalled her end as a significant figure in terms of succession, and they began to look towards Elizabeth's prospects. In the meantime, Mary attempted to undo the work of the Reformation in England, reconciling the nation to the pope, and persecuting so-called heretics: between 1555 and 1558 nearly 300 Protestants were burned at the stake. The policy backfired, however, with the martyrdom of these Protestants only serving to strengthen the anti-Papist cause. Other dissenters fled to the continent, where encounters with unadulterated Calvinism also served to reaffirm Protestant resolve.

We come now to Elizabeth I, who became queen in 1558 at the age of 25, six years before Marlowe was born. Elizabeth's Protestantism had meant that her position while Mary reigned was always a precarious one. Once on the throne, she moved quickly to establish a national church in the Protestant mould: as far as the establishment was concerned, the religious revolution was over and a new order had been set in place. In the wake of this, religious conflict began to flare up around those who supported the national church and those who saw the reformist mission as having been only half completed in England: these Puritans used the House of Commons to pursue their aims, despite Elizabeth's attempts to limit discussions of religion there. The Puritan influence remained a significant factor in affairs of state as well as locally, as we shall see later when we investigate the place of the public theatres in London life. After the abiding obsession with establishing heirs – and specifically male heirs – to the English throne, which had lasted some 40 or 50 years, Elizabeth's position was startling and, for many in the Council, profoundly disturbing. From the beginning she announced her intention to reign as a virgin queen, though a number of proposed marriages were mooted. But Elizabeth's virginity left the matter of succession wide open: until her death in 1568, Lady Catherine Grey, sister of the unfortunate Jane, might have been able to claim under the terms of Henry VIII's will. More importantly, the Catholic Mary Queen of Scots loomed as a larger threat, being next in line in hereditary terms. When Elizabeth succeeded Mary I, Mary Queen of Scots, who was married to the French king Francis II, denounced her on the grounds of illegitimacy (since Elizabeth was the child of Henry VIII's second marriage) and began styling herself Queen of France and of England. Francis died in 1560, and Mary, a virtual outcast at the French court, returned to Scotland the following year to take up the Scottish throne. Elizabeth was now faced with the next heir to the throne hovering on the other side of the border; furthermore, this was an heir that was openly challenging the legitimacy of Elizabeth's own claim to the monarchy. As things fell apart in Scotland for Mary, due to a series of poor judgements in her marriages and affairs, she was forced to abdicate in the face of opposition from Scottish lords, and finally sought Elizabeth's protection in England. She would spend the last nineteen years of her life in imprisonment. After a series of Catholic plots against Elizabeth were linked, justly or not, to Mary and her confederates, Elizabeth was finally persuaded to sign a warrant for her execution. She was beheaded on 8 February 1587.

Without going much further into historical detail, it should be clear how deeply implicated politics and religion were with each other at this time. The discussion of dates, famous names and laws and statutes can leave an impression that the Reformation was achieved solely by political process, when in fact it was part of a much deeper cultural shift, the development of which is far more complex and difficult to assess than a record of acts of Parliament. The conflicts erupted not only between monarchs and popes, but also between common lawyers and the ecclesiastical courts, and between individual churchmen and members of the laity. At ground level, there is strong evidence to suggest that anticlericalism was a significant part of the social fabric long before reforms were established at the level of church and state. Historians cite such diverse sources as court records of assaults on clergymen, diaries, and literary artfacts. Chaucer's *Canterbury Tales* include a number of satirical portraits of churchmen – the original depictions are a sign of how deeply rooted the anticlericalism was, since the *Tales* first appeared at the end of the fourteenth century. The fact that they were reprinted five times between 1478 and 1526 suggests that they became increasingly popular during this period of immense change (Dickens, 1993, p. 318). Some time later, we can make a tentative connection between the popular and the political when we examine the kind of satire Marlowe unleashes on Catholicism in his play *The Jew of Malta*: this is a form of political propaganda that would presumably have gone down well with the majority of a London theatre audience as well as Queen Elizabeth and her court. In this sense, not only were religion and politics enmeshed in one another, but theatre and society were, too. For this reason, it is important to understand something of the context of a play like *The Jew of Malta*, since the way it resonated in its own culture, at the time it was composed, will be very different from the way it resonated in Britain in 1987 when staged by the Royal Shakespeare Company. The differences would be starker if it had been performed in, say, Berlin in 1939 or Israel in 1947.

The issue of cultural difference is again paramount when we come to investigate Marlowe's religious beliefs. There are passages in the major plays that might strike us as being unorthodox for an Elizabethan, and we shall consider these in more detail in the following chapters. *Doctor Faustus* is obviously remarkable for its portrayal of a man brave or foolish enough to dismiss hell as a 'fable' while conducting a conversation with a devil, but there are numerous other examples in *Faustus* and elsewhere of what an orthodox Elizabethan would perceive as heresy. There is a constant temptation, not easily resisted, to make a connection between the tale and the teller in Marlowe's case because there are a number of documents accusing him directly of holding heretical opinions. But whenever we find Marlowe accused of atheism (the charges were levelled at him by a number of his contemporaries), we need to remind ourselves of the context: in a nation still deeply riven in terms of its state religion, any deviation from the current norm was likely to be slapped down with the labels 'atheism' and 'heresy'. The most shocking forms of heresy for an orthodox Elizabethan would have been those that questioned the sanctity of scripture as the word of God, and forms of dissident belief that questioned the doctrine of the Trinity, whether in the form of Arianism (denying the Son's equal status) or Unitarianism (maintaining that God exists in one person only). Frequently, unorthodox belief would be linked with social and political deviancy, a connection Robert Greene made when he accused Marlowe of Machiavellianism and atheism in 1592 in his *Groatsworth of Wit*:

> Is it pestilent Machiavellian policy that thou hast studied?
> . . . The broacher of this Diabolical Atheism is dead, and
> his life had never had the felicity he aimed at: but as he
> began in craft, lived in fear, and ended in despair . . .

> [cited in MacLure, 1995, p. 30]

Chapter 1 details the list of charges that were drawn up against Marlowe by various witnesses just before his death (see pp. 29–31). A warrant for Marlowe's arrest was issued on 15 May 1593 in connection with an initiative by the authorities to hunt down anyone propagating 'unsafe' opinions: again, religious dissent is identified as something so subversive that it necessitates detention and interrogation. Thomas Kyd is arrested and tortured for information about Marlowe. Baines writes a denouncement of Marlowe which includes charges of atheism, homosexuality and proselytizing. The emphasis on the sexual slant of Marlowe's supposed heresies is not accidental: as we shall see in our study of *Edward II*, the relation between sodomy and political and religious unorthodoxies was one that was frequently invoked at this time. It is hard to gauge the extent to which scepticism and atheism might have spread during this time of religious turmoil. Certainly, in the atmosphere of conflict and dissent that characterized the age, it is likely that the beliefs of many may have been shaken, since the bedrock of orthodoxy was unstable. At the same time, as Marlowe's own case goes to prove, it was unsafe to be too outspoken with any views that could be construed as radical.

Theatres and theatre-going

In the late 1570s and early 1580s, the travelling companies of players that had routinely toured the country, performing in makeshift venues such as the courtyards of great houses and in public halls, began to establish themselves in London. The first purpose-built theatre in England was erected in London in 1576 and called, simply, the Theatre. The Curtain opened nearby the following year. In 1587, the Rose was erected on the south side of the Thames, and it was here that Edward Alleyn (1566–1626) installed his company, the Lord Admiral's Men, who would perform Marlowe's chief works: the roles of Faustus, Barabas and Tamburlaine were made famous by Alleyn, one of the great tragedians of the era. Marlowe's untimely death put a stop to a fruitful partnership between writer and star actor. The first Globe, perhaps the most famous of the Elizabethan theatres, was first built in 1599 from recycled timber from the Theatre. Although some of the history may well be apocryphal, it is said that when the ground rent for the Theatre's site was put up, Burbage decided to move the entire playhouse to a cheaper site. The story goes that the Theatre was dismantled under cover of night and the beams were slid across the frozen surface of the River Thames. The establishment of permanent bases for performance gave the players some legitimacy and began the process of professionalizing their work. The economic structure of the companies reflects the emergent spirit of capitalism: theatre companies tended to consist of 'sharers' – leading actors who split profits from the box office between them – and hirelings, who were paid a weekly wage. Shakespeare had a share in the company known as the Lord Chamberlain's Men, later renamed the King's Men. The elements of risk, capital outlay, shareholders and so on that characterized the expanding theatre business are indicators of an economic shift that was underway in society more generally.

The Act for the Punishment of Vagabonds (1572) had classed players alongside rogues and vagrants. But Elizabeth and James I were both strong supporters of the theatre, and helped to legitimize the profession by acting as patrons to the theatre companies: the Queen's Men were established in 1583. A Master of the Revels had the task of organizing the entertainments at court; he also operated, in effect, as a state censor, ensuring that nothing controversial would be performed. All new scripts had to be submitted to the Revels office to be checked for offensive material. A good example is Shakespeare's *Richard II* (1595?), the first printed edition of which was published in 1598 without act 4 scene 1, which depicted Richard's deposition. The second and third quartos also omitted it. By the time of the fourth quarto, in 1608, in a less volatile political climate, the scene was finally restored. We cannot know for sure whether the scene was performed or not during this decade of the play's stage history, but scholars speculate that it may well not have been.

Despite the royal interest in theatre, which was at least on the face of it a benign one, the theatre entrepreneurs still had some powerful enemies. The City Fathers, who were in effect the local government of the City of London, had a strong Puritan streak. Although the survival of one or two virulently anti-theatrical tracts can result in an overstatement of the case, it is clear that the Puritans in general did disapprove of theatres and theatre-going. Although critical opinion remains divided on the issue, many maintain that it was largely due to a strong Puritan presence in Parliament that the theatres were shut down in 1642 for a period of eighteen years. In the late sixteenth century, as the profession was beginning to secure a foothold in London, the Fathers made vociferous complaints to the Privy Council, and for this reason the theatres were built outside the Mayor's jurisdiction, in the so-called Liberties – areas such as Shoreditch and Southwark. According to the Puritans, the theatres attracted thieves and prostitutes, and this was difficult to deny. They also argued that they were unhygienic places, and would breed disease and, in particular, the plague. The latter was a real danger, as we have already seen, though the part played by fleas and rats in the spreading of the plague had yet to be discovered. Puritan objections, however, did not rest solely on these peripheral issues, but involved the performances themselves. One of the defining features of Protestantism, and of Puritanism in particular, was its shunning of all ceremony, spectacle, and church iconography. Although Elizabethan staging was in some respects primitive by modern standards, it was at least visually spectacular, with richly covered tapestries at the back of the stage and expensive, elaborate costumes. According to the Puritans, much of the drama of the time was immoral and bred immorality in its performers and audiences. The tales of murder and sexual intrigue that were so popular, as well as the bawdy content of some of the comedies, horrified them. Needless to say, in an era (and in a particular movement) so intent on a natural order of things, there were also strong objections to the practice of men dressing as women to play the parts of the females (although, since standards of decency forbade women to perform, they could hardly have expected anything else). This excerpt from Philip Stubbes's *The Anatomy of Abuses* (second edition published 1583) is characteristic: responding to the notion that the plays provide good examples to learn from, Stubbes's reply drips sarcasm:

> truly so there are; if you will learn falsehood; if you will learn cozenage; if you will learn to deceive; if you will learn to play the hypocrite, to cog, to lie and falsify; if you will learn to jest, laugh and fleer, to grin, to nod and mow; if you will learn to play the Vice, to swear, tear and blaspheme both heaven and earth; if you will learn to become a bawd, unclean, and to devirginate maids, to deflower honest wives; if you will learn to murder, flay, kill, pick, steal, rob and rove; if you will learn to rebel against princes, to commit treasons, to consume treasures, to practise idleness, to sing and talk of bawdy love and venery . . . and finally, if you will learn to contemn God and all His laws, to care neither for Heaven nor Hell, and to commit all kind of sin and mischief, you need to go to no other school, for all these good examples may you see painted before your eyes in interludes and plays.

[cited in Evans, 1988, pp. 11–12]

There are some revealing phrases here: although Stubbes's scatter-gun approach is obviously aimed at hitting every conceivable target, the mention of treason is significant. The theatre laid itself wide open as a potential space for ideological contestation: this is why it created so much disquiet. The playwrights and the companies were not simply providing entertainment: in some ways, they functioned as something roughly equivalent to our news programmes, or topical debates and documentaries. The most frequently cited example of a play intervening in political events of the time is the aforementioned *Richard II*. Robert Devereux, the earl of Essex, led his followers into London in 1601 in an attempt to seize the throne from Elizabeth. The day before the march, the Lord Chamberlain's Men, Shakespeare's company, were paid by Essex's supporters to stage a performance of *Richard II*. As a result, one of the shareholders of the company, Augustine Phillips, was called before the Privy Council to provide an explanation, though he was later released. Franco Moretti, discussing the debasement of a monarch that Shakespeare so graphically stages in *King Lear*, notes that 'Having deconsecrated the king, tragedy made it possible to decapitate him' (Moretti, 1992, p. 46). It is a bold move to make this kind of connection between Lear and King Charles I, executed in 1649, and it certainly has a sense of poetic hyperbole about it. At the same time, it serves as a striking caption for the potential interplay between early modern politics and theatrical performance.

'Conjuring books': the playwright and the text

One of the reasons why Marlowe's work is so fascinating is that it is located at a critical turning point in the development of English drama. In contemporary Western theatre we tend to have a clear notion of the playwright as a more or less independent agent working alone on a script in a way that is not very different from the practice of another creative artist, such as a novelist or a poet. Playwrights are assumed to have full ownership of and authority over the texts they have created, and this manifests itself in the identification of a piece as 'David Hare's new play', in the legal apparatus of copyright ('Harold Pinter is hereby identified as the author of this work in accordance with Section 77 of the Copyright, Design and Patents Act 1988'), and in the traditional call of the audience at a successful première: 'Author! Author!' The situation is complicated, of course, when a play comes to be staged. Once a text is opened up in rehearsal to the creative engagement of a director, actors, and others associated with the production, the status of that play in terms of 'authorship' becomes more complex. However, in terms of the published text, when we pick up a volume of Caryl Churchill's plays, we would tend to take it for granted that that book contains the words that Churchill wrote, revised and finalized by Churchill herself. For the most part, while accepting that this is a generalization, our confidence will be justified.

However, when we come to a collection of Shakespeare's Complete Works, or Marlowe's, things are not as clear-cut as they might appear by contemporary standards. That collection of plays one lifts off the shelf in a bookshop or a library is not, strictly speaking, a volume of 'Christopher Marlowe's plays', in either a legal or a philosophical sense. In the Elizabethan theatre, once a playwright finished his work, he would effectively sell it to the company he worked for (in Marlowe's case, the Lord Admiral's Men), and it would then become the property of the company. In this respect it differs from the legal claim mentioned above that Pinter has over his work. Again, the cover of the book deceives us when it says we have in our hands 'Plays by Christopher Marlowe': since none of Marlowe's original manuscripts survive (with the possible exception of one single page of *The Massacre at Paris*), we have no concrete proof that the versions of the play we have inherited are accurate versions of what he wrote. An assumption that the text we are accepting is a play 'by Christopher Marlowe' ignores a number of crucial processes that will have shaped it on its journey from Marlowe's first manuscript to the neatly bound book on the shelf.

Details of the publication histories of each of Marlowe's plays can be found in the appropriate chapters, but a brief description of one or two of them will help clarify the problems about authorship under discussion here. The oldest surviving text of *The Jew of Malta* is 1633; we estimate that the play was first performed in 1589 or 1590, and it is impossible to know how the play may have evolved over that time from its 'original' version. The text we have inherited of *The Massacre at Paris* is widely acknowledged to be a very poor one, its frequent oddities and occasional gibberish implying that it has been constructed from memory by members of the company. This was fairly common practice, a way of 'pirating' playtexts, particularly popular ones. The best guess for its date is 1602 (Oliver, 1968, p. xlix), for a play that probably dates from around 1592. *Doctor Faustus* is in some ways even more problematic, having survived in two distinct early versions – the 'A-text' appeared in 1604, and the 'B-text' made its first appearance in 1616 (it is possible that *Faustus* was premièred as early as 1588 or 1589). There are numerous, often highly significant differences between the two: in effect, we have two distinct plays. The notion of recovering 'Marlowe's play' – that is to say, what Marlowe originally wrote – is a vain hope. Even in the case of the earliest text of 1604, it is generally agreed that the play was probably the result of a joint effort on the part of two or more writers.

The collaborative nature of performance in the Elizabethan theatre is another important reason why it is wise to be wary of assuming a text we have inherited can be taken straightforwardly as 'Marlowe's play'. It is quite possible that Marlowe collaborated on the 'original' script of *Doctor Faustus*, for instance, before it was handed on to the company. I have already noted that, once a script was handed over to the company, the playwright ceased to have any legal ownership of it. This is not the only sense in which the author relinquished his work. In an age where printing was still a lengthy and expensive process, only one or two full transcripts of the play would generally have been available to the company who owned it. From the one copy marked up as a performance text, the 'book-keeper' would copy out the actors' parts in the form of scripts, or 'sides' that contained only their lines and cues, plus entrances and exits. In the process of taking the script from the playwright's study to the playhouse, when it would be copied at least twice, sometimes three times, before reaching the actor, there were plenty of opportunities for errors to slip in, or even deliberate alterations. Furthermore, it seems likely that a new play would have remained in a state of flux during the brief rehearsal period, with room for improvisation, cuts and other alterations by the players as they rushed to get it ready for performance. There is clear evidence that certain kinds of player in particular were accustomed to improvising and extemporizing. In a famous passage of *Hamlet* the hero, briefing a company of actors before their performance, warns the leader of the troupe: 'And let those that play your clowns speak no more than is set down for them' (3.2.34–5). Critics have tended to identify the clown Will Kemp as the target of this barbed comment; Kemp was an actor with the Lord Chamberlain's Men, Shakespeare's company, from 1594 to 1599. Ironically, it is quite possible that the scene between the two gravediggers in *Hamlet* (5.1) could have been subjected to just this kind of improvisation.

All of this has implications for the way in which we view the plays, and in particular the relation between them and their author. The play read privately from a page enacts a similar interpretive process as reading a novel: the words of the novelist, or playwright, are interpreted by the individual who is reading the book. When a play like *Doctor Faustus* is staged, however, its interpretation involves a number of people – the director, the company of actors, possibly a dramaturg who might advise on cuts or produce an edited script – and in this sense Marlowe's script (if it is Marlowe's) becomes only one element in the creation of the performance event. This is all in advance of the performance itself, which is then 'read' by an audience both individually and collectively. Other elements of the performance (elements which are not a part of the process of reading a text, dramatic or otherwise) will inevitably impinge on the consciousness of members of the audience: costume, decor, music, the physical presence of the actors and their positions on stage. When we learn that the script a company begins with today may already be far removed from Marlowe's 'original', and that parts of the play may well have been composed by another writer altogether, it is clear that we need to understand the phrase 'Marlowe's *Faustus*' as a signifier that stands for a much more complex relationship between the text and its creators.

Theatre conditions and conventions

The design of the outdoor theatres reflected their roots in the impro-
vised performance spaces of earlier decades. They were constructed around
the shape of the courtyard, with the stage, round or octagonal, coming midway into the space. The audience sat on three sides around it,
either at ground level, or in galleries round at the levels of one or two
upper floors. The central area was open to the sky, and the groundlings
would mill around the stage, paying a penny for the privilege (whilst those
sitting would pay an extra penny for access to the galleries). To give
some sense of perspective, the weekly wage of an unskilled labourer
would have been five or six pence a day, and a loaf of bread and a pint
of ale would also have cost a penny each (McDonald, 1996, p. 236).
Performances would take place in the afternoons, so no artificial lighting was required. The main stage would be permanently open to the
scrutiny of the audience – no curtain to bring a scene to a sudden, climactic end, or to mask a change of set. At the back of the stage there
was the 'tiring-house' which was used both as a dressing-room and as
wings, storing props and set, and providing several entrances through
gaps in the curtains. Above the tiring-house was a balcony which provided a third level – it might be used as battlements, for example, for
the balcony scene in *Romeo and Juliet*, or for the appearance of the Good
and Bad Angels in *Doctor Faustus*. There was also a level beneath the
stage – a trapdoor was set in the floor of the stage and from this opening devils or ghosts might emerge: in *Hamlet*, the ghost of Hamlet's father
is heard knocking beneath the stage. Faustus was almost certainly
dragged through it by devils at the end of that play. As far as we can
tell, the Elizabethans used very little scenery. This is explained in part
by their preoccupation with the classical theatre – following the ancient
Greek model, the back of the stage consisted of a permanent, elabor-
ately decorated scene – and partly by necessity (act 4 of Shakespeare's
Anthony and Cleopatra, for example, has thirteen scenes, some as short
as four or six lines long). However, they did use numerous props, such
as crowns, swords, scrolls, and so on, as well as pieces of furniture. Lists
of props from the period even include a bay tree (to symbolize a gar-
den, presumably) and a hell-mouth that may well have been used in
the scene where Faustus is dragged away by the devils to his eternal
damnation.

This brief description of the Elizabethan stage, though sketchy,
should give a fairly clear impression of how it differed from modern
theatres, which are more often based around the so-called proscenium

arch model. The emergence of the proscenium arch is to some extent bound up in notions of the 'real': the arch works almost like a picture frame, or even a cinema or TV screen. Inside that frame, people move about, creating an illusion of another world of other lives. The arch also conceals the lighting rig, and perhaps items of the set – painted flats, etc. – which can be raised and lowered to indicate a change of setting. An illusion of reality is reinforced by the *hiding away* of the lighting rig and unnecessary pieces of the set. The proscenium model encourages the audience to believe that what is going on on stage is '*really happening*'. In *Doctor Faustus*, on the other hand, one throne will indicate a royal chamber, and – the extreme example – some kind of painted wooden construction will signify the entrance into Hell. This is how the Elizabethan dramatists worked: the audience's imagination was engaged by a cross and a table, for instance, and this set off a chain of associations: the props – an altar – the inside of a church. These visual cues are often supplemented by characters' speeches, with characters giving detailed descriptions of the supposed setting.

There is also a significant difference in the relationship between actor and audience in the two models. The proscenium tends to emphasize a division between actor and audience. This, of course, helps to sustain that illusion that the stage world is another world, complete in itself, and that the figures on the stage are real people leading real lives – we are uninvited voyeurs, observing through the space where the fourth wall should be. In Elizabethan drama, by contrast, the division between actor and audience is much more fluid than it is in naturalism. The most obvious illustration of this flexible boundary is the soliloquy, where an actor addresses the audience directly to reveal inner feelings, or to confide a plan, or merely to provide necessary plot details (as we shall see, Marlowe exploits this device very profitably in *The Jew of Malta*). By contrast, maintaining distance between actor and audience is essential to a naturalistic play in order to preserve the illusion of reality being conjured up on stage.

This discussion of differences in stage practice leads us on to a more complex and more interesting debate around the evolution of acting styles. A couple of terms commonly used by theatre practitoners are 'characterization' and 'motivation': actors talk about finding their motivation for a speech or action; they might complain that something a director asks them to do seems to them to be 'out of character'. There is a strong emphasis here on *internalizing* the acting process: the actress will want to trace the path of her thoughts and emotions, trying to understand exactly why her character says what she says, or does what she does, at any particular moment of the play. She is seeking out the *motivation* for each speech and action. This tendency to internalize, to develop a sense of the psychology of the character, often inventing a past history that informs the character's behaviour in the play, is rooted in the acting system developed by the Russian actor and director Konstantin Stanislavsky (1863–1938). Although the detailed picture of the history of acting styles is more complex, it is fair to say that Stanislavsky's System and its descendant, the Method, inform common sense notions about what acting is, at least in Britain, America and much of Europe (although parts of continental Europe are more under the control of approaches derived from Brecht's theory and practice). Although Stanislavsky's System stressed the importance of a balance between inner experience and outer expression, in its current form it remains heavily internalized.

From what we can tell, the Elizabethan actor worked within a very different tradition, with very different assumptions and techniques. For one thing, Elizabethan actors relied more heavily on gesture: certain poses, movements of the hand and so on would have been recognized as signalling certain emotions. The style would probably have been cruder, more bombastic. This is probably still familiar to us, since the style persisted, in various shades and hues, even into the twentieth century. Today, we would generally refer to this practice as 'ham acting': we would probably associate it most readily with melodrama and silent movies. It is worth noting that this more external acting style was necessitated in part by the nature of the theatres themselves – performing in the vast open space of a place like the Globe theatre, without any clever technology to boost the acoustics, the actors would have been forced to belt out their lines to be heard at all at the back of the gallery. A replica Globe theatre, which opened in the mid-1990s, was built close to the original site near the River Thames, and experiments here have shown that it tends to coerce actors into a more 'telegraphic' style of acting, with facial expressions and gestures exaggerated, and the voice making similar compensations. However, there are other equally significant factors. A company of Elizabethan actors might have had 40 plays in its repertoire in any one year. Today, a rehearsal period for a major production at a mainstream theatre such as the National Theatre in London can last anything between eight and twelve weeks; by contrast, the Elizabethans might have had a total of about 24 hours to get a new play on its feet. In addition, actors were given only their own lines to learn. They would never have had the luxury that modern actors enjoy of a complete script: one guesses that they would not have seen the point of it. The astounding fact that a leading actor of the time such as Edward Alleyn would have played about 70 roles in the space of three years gives some idea of the scale of their task: in the face of this, it is unlikely that any actors would have had time or inclination to indulge in the kind of 'research' and psychological profiling that is standard practice amongst actors today.

This is not to say that neither playwright nor actor brought any kind of so-called 'character' into their work. It is clear that there were major developments within the period itself: as far as we can tell, during Shakespeare's heyday a new term was coined for the art of acting. Up to this point, the accepted term had been 'playing' – so, Richard Burbage 'played' the part of Richard III. However, at some time around the turn of the century the term 'personation' was introduced. It is thought by some critics that the more subtle, more complex style of acting demanded by Shakespeare's work in particular led to the new term. The two different styles are actually quite neatly embodied in two of the most famous actors of the period, Richard Burbage (the star of the company to which Shakespeare belonged) and Edward Alleyn (Marlowe's lead actor). From contemporary reports we can deduce that Alleyn's style belonged to the old school, while Burbage was more progressive. As more plays were performed in the indoor 'private' theatres such as the second Blackfriars (1600) and the Phoenix (1616), the greater intimacy of the acting space could be interpreted as having allowed scope for a greater naturalism in acting technique – actors were no longer bellowing to be heard at the back of the galleries, and more audience members were closer to the stage. But this takes us beyond the span of Marlowe's career.

There is another, more profound difference between the modern and the early modern when we talk in terms of 'realism' and 'reality' in relation to theatrical representation. We would probably find a character like Miss Julie in Strindberg's play of that name far more real than, say, the 'character', or, rather, the allegorical figure, of Mischief in the play *Mankind*. But what about Faustus? In what sense is he more real than Mischief? Does he have more of an identity that we would recognize? Does he have what we could identify as a *subjectivity*, a sense of himself as an autonomous being or unified self? To reiterate, it is difficult for us, spanning a gulf of 400 years or more, to begin to think like an Elizabethan – even if we decide to posit such a thing as a 'typical' Elizabethan, a move which critiques of Tillyard have problematized. But, while maintaining some such reservations, we can perhaps begin to acknowledge that Marlowe, and the figures that populate the plays he wrote, inhabited a physical and mental world that was profoundly different from our own. Consequently, we need to be wary of assuming that our own experiences automatically parallel theirs. At every level, there is a profound 'otherness': most fundamentally of all, perhaps, the sense of oneself as an individual was something that emerged only gradually with the break-up of the medieval social, economic and religious order and the momentous changes in the societal and psychological landscapes. Under the older social order, one's significance was founded on one's place within a rigid social hierarchy; with the emergence of capitalism, a man or woman's personal existence became much more significant: people came to be seen in terms of what they owned, what they could buy, and what they could sell (even if it was only their labour). It is this kind of contrast, or the conflict of competing world-views, that was touched on earlier in the discussion of Tillyard's notion of the Elizabethan world picture. As we have seen, the change was not only political and economic, but spiritual also: with the rise of Protestantism, there was a shift towards the importance of oneself as an individual in relation to God, and the idea of working out one's own personal salvation, as opposed to the more rigid and long-established law of the Roman church. As we shall see, *Doctor Faustus* dramatizes with great force one of those ideological crises – the conflicting understandings of the relation between God's prescience (or predetermination) and human free will.

The process of putting a play of this period into performance brings the stark differences between Marlowe's time and our own under intense scrutiny. The actor who approaches the role of Faustus, Barabas, Edward or Isabella with a twentieth-century mindset will be repeatedly derailed by the stubborn refusal of these *personae* to conform to modern notions of character, of psychological consistency and 'motivation'. Their otherness is rooted both in the difference between early modern and modern subjectivities – the notion of the self – and in differing priorities for the playwrights, for whom psychological realism seems not to have been of paramount importance. In this respect, quibbling over Marlowe's characterization is a little like complaining that a portrait painted by Picasso does not resemble a face. Marlowe's work in this sense could be seen as something far removed from our own understanding both of what an effective piece of drama is, and of what it means to be human. However, as we shall see, the plays can be powerful theatrical events, often shocking and provocative, though their power may not necessarily reside in their supposed 'relevance' to our own society, or their insights into the way we lead our own lives. In Faustus's being torn apart by the conflict of heavenly and infernal impulses, in Tamburlaine's rampant, mercilessly destructive political egotism, Barabas's single-minded self-interest, and Edward's retreat from the responsibilities of power into the cocoon of his forbidden love affair, there is plenty in Marlowe's fairly slim collection of writings that might offer this kind of connection, illuminating our own lives and societies at the end of the twentieth century. But in reading and watching the plays, what is more striking is the extent to which they uncover the particularity and peculiarities of their own time, and it is in this that their riches are most fully revealed.

PART TWO

CRITICAL SURVEY

CHAPTER 3

SCOURGE OF GOD:
Tamburlaine the Great

'Revenge, war, death and cruelty'

Tamburlaine certainly made a considerable impact on London cultural life when it exploded onto the stage in 1587. In its own fashion, it could be seen as the first 'blockbuster' of its time, or, more accurately, the first blockbuster and its sequel: *Tamburlaine* actually consists of two distinct plays, first written and performed some months apart. It is clear that the plays quickly earned a degree of cultural status which positioned them as milestones in the evolution of Elizabethan drama. It is possible that Marlowe's death revived and maintained some interest in his work, because we know that both parts were still in the repertory of the Admiral's Men in 1594–5. During that season, the two parts were played at Henslowe's Rose several times, a couple of nights apart, where they proved very profitable. However, the plays inspired almost as much vituperation as admiration, and surprisingly quickly became targets for parody and satire. Within a few decades of Marlowe's death, they would vanish from the public stage for hundreds of years. And yet, when the main performance space in London's National Theatre was opened in 1976, it was the two parts of *Tamburlaine* that were chosen to mark the event. Like so many aspects of Marlowe's life and work, contradictions seem to lie at the heart of this play and its impact on its audiences.

Tamburlaine would have been a familiar figure to the London audiences that flocked to see Marlowe's plays. The name Tamburlaine is a corruption of the original Timur (or Temur) the Lame, thought to derive from a hostile characterization of his physical appearance. Timur, it appears, was crippled on his right side, with bones in both his leg and his arm fused, probably from battle wounds (Geckle, 1988, p. 32). He was probably born in the 1330s, his heritage the great Mongol empire. He was himself a descendant of Chinggis (or Genghis) Khan (*c.*1167–1227), who founded the empire, although by the time Timur arrived on the scene, this vast area had begun to fragment into a multitude of separate kingdoms.

It was here that Timur's conquests began. When Marlowe depicts Tamburlaine appealing to his followers for his right to rule, he strikes an accurate note: Beatrice Forbes Manz notes how Timur 'rose to power within a confederation of unruly tribes, whose loyalty he could keep only by means of a career of conquest' (Manz, 1989, p. 12). He was recognized as a brilliant military tactician. It seems Marlowe's sources are accurate too in the way they represent Timur's perceived relation to good fortune, or divine intervention, although historical records seem to depict him as skilful manipulator, using religion carefully and diplomatically in the cause of his quest for power, and not as the god-baiter of Marlowe's plays. From his base in Samarkand, in Uzbekistan, Timur set out to conquer Persia, Azerbaijan, Armenia and Georgia, sacked Delhi, invaded Syria and Anatolia, and captured the Ottoman sultan in Ankara in 1402; his final campaign was an attempt to invade China. By this time, mortally ill, he had to be carried in a litter. He died in Utrar in 1405 and although he named a grandson as his successor (not a son, as Marlowe has it), fifteen years of war ensued as his descendants struggled for power.

In the same way that Marlowe would later shape his sources to create a compelling drama out of the stories of the life of Edward II, he drew on a wide range of texts to construct a narrative out of the various accounts of Tamburlaine's exploits. In the first scene of Part One we are introduced to the weak and ineffectual Mycetes, King of Persia, who dispatches one of his lords, Theridamas, to deal with the Scythian Tamburlaine, up to now more an irritant than a substantial threat. When Mycetes leaves the stage, his brother Cosroe, contemptuous of Mycetes's inadequacies as monarch, is crowned king by three other Persian lords. The second scene depicts Tamburlaine wooing his captive Zenocrate, daughter of the Soldan of Egypt and due to marry Alcidamus, King of Arabia. Theridamas meets Tamburlaine, is suitably impressed, and becomes his ally against his former king, Mycetes. In the following scene (I.2.1), Cosroe resolves to enlist Tamburlaine in his cause against the Persian king. An intervening scene (I.2.2) finds Mycetes and Meander preparing their army for battle, and in I.2.3 Cosroe finally meets Tamburlaine and becomes allied to him. Mycetes enters (I.2.4), desperately looking for a place to hide his crown, and he is followed by Tamburlaine. After an amusing argument over the crown, both return to battle, and in the following scene (I.2.5) Tamburlaine enters victorious. Cosroe makes Tamburlaine regent of Persia. Meander also switches sides. But no sooner has Cosroe left the stage than Tamburlaine, musing on the idea of being a king, suddenly and perversely resolves to challenge Cosroe for the crown he has just handed over to him. Cosroe is outraged by Tamburlaine's challenge (I.2.6); in battle he is defeated and mortally wounded (I.2.7). Tamburlaine claims the Persian throne.

Act 3 depicts the siege of Constantinople and introduces Tamburlaine's next opponent, Bajazeth, the Turkish emperor, who sets himself up as a formidable adversary. The second scene (I.3.2), an interlude of sorts, stages a conversation between Zenocrate and her attendant lord Agydas. It appears that Zenocrate has fallen in love with Tamburlaine. Agydas is incredulous. Tamburlaine overhears Agydas, and his thinly veiled threat – Techelles is sent with a naked dagger to 'salute' him – frightens Agydas into killing himself rather than face death at Tamburlaine's hand. Meanwhile Tamburlaine (I.3.3) dismisses Bajazeth's basso (ambassador), sent to warn him to back down in the face of overwhelming numbers; Tamburlaine declares his faith in his 'smiling stars'. Bajazeth enters, and a direct challenge follows. They prepare to do battle, handing over their crowns to their women (Zenocrate and Zabina) for the duration of the combat; the women exchange insults. Tamburlaine is victorious in the battle, Bajazeth's 'contributory kings' are all killed and their crowns claimed by Tamburlaine's allies, and Zabina's crown is given to Zenocrate. Tamburlaine asserts that he will not ransom Bajazeth: it is power not wealth that motivates him. Act 4 opens with the Soldan of Egypt raging over the loss of his daughter Zenocrate. A messenger arrives with news of Tamburlaine's approaching army, and the Soldan declares his determination to 'scatter and consume them in his rage' (I.4.1.34). The messenger reports that Tamburlaine uses three colours for his tents and banners, with white symbolizing mercy, before they turn red (only non-combatants will be spared) and finally black (everyone will die). Back in Tamburlaine's camp, Bajazeth is brought forward caged (I.4.2). Tamburlaine humiliates him still further by using him as a footstool to mount his throne. He awaits the surrender of the people of Damascus, vowing he will show no mercy if they do not, despite Zenocrate's pleas on behalf of her homeland. Meanwhile the Soldan marshalls his forces with his allies the King of Arabia and the Egyptian Capolin (I.4.3). Tamburlaine's colours are now red (I.4.4), and although Zenocrate begs Tamburlaine to raise the siege of her father's city, he refuses. As act 5 begins, the governor of Damascus sends four virgins to plead with the black-clad Tamburlaine, who condemns them to be slaughtered by his cavalry (I.5.1). Zenocrate grieves as Damascus falls. Tamburlaine marches to confront the Soldan's army, leaving Bajazeth and Zabina to curse their fate. Bajazeth finally kills himself by dashing his brains out against the cage, and when Zabina finds him dead, she goes insane and also kills herself. Zenocrate grieves for Damascus but also fears for the fate of Tamburlaine and begs Jove and Mahomet to forgive him, but Tamburlaine is victorious: the King of Arabia enters, mortally wounded, and dies in Zenocrate's arms. Tamburlaine has Zenocrate's father the Soldan as his prisoner, but restores Egypt to him, and Zenocrate, finally to become Tamburlaine's wife, is crowned as his queen.

Part Two opens with a reluctant truce being planned by Orcanes King of Natolia and Gazellus the Viceroy of Byron with Sigismond King of Hungary (II.1.1). They unite in a common cause against Tamburlaine. Sigismund swears by Christ and Orcanes by Mahomet as they make their pact. In scene 2 we are back in Tamburlaine's camp. Bajazeth's son Callapine, Tamburlaine's prisoner, persuades Alemeda his keeper to help him escape. Callapine swears revenge on Tamburlaine as he leaves (II.1.2). Finally, Tamburlaine himself makes his first appearance in the second part, along with Zenocrate and his sons: it is evident that some twenty years have passed since the end of Part One. Tamburlaine doubts his sons' manliness, and two of them (Celebinus and Amyras) compete in their professions of bloodthirstiness, while the third (Calyphas), notably less enthusiastic, is branded a 'bastardly boy' by his furious father (II.1.3.69). Tamburlaine's kings offer him tribute and report on their military expeditions and conquests. The second act opens with Frederick of Buda and Baldwin of Bohemia trying to persuade Sigismund to break the truce and surprise Orcanes, who, having sent most of his troops to deal with Tamburlaine, has left himself dangerously exposed. Sigismund is reluctant to break a holy promise but is finally persuaded by the idea that he can play the role of 'scourge' against the infidel (II.2.2). Orcanes is preparing to march against Tamburlaine when a messenger arrives with news of Sigismund's treachery. In the following scene, Sigismund is killed and his army defeated (II.2.3). Orcanes, the Moslem, attributes his victory to Christ's fury at the Christian king breaking his promise. Act 2 ends back in Tamburlaine's camp and finds Zenocrate seriously ill, attended by her husband, sons, their kings and a troop of physicians (II.2.4). Tamburlaine delivers a great rhetorical speech expressing his love for the 'divine Zenocrate' before she dies.

Callapine is crowned emperor of Turkey by Orcanes and his allies (II.3.1), and forces are marshalled to defeat Tamburlaine. Act 3 scene 2 depicts Tamburlaine in the throes of his wild grief, burning to the ground the town of Larissa where Zenocrate has died. He tutors his sons in the arts of war, cutting his own arm to display his bravery. Meanwhile, at the walls of an enemy fortress, Theridamas and Techelles challenge the captain to surrender; he refuses (II.3.3). Inevitably, the following scene depicts victory for the Persians and the defeated captain dies (II.3.4). His wife, Olympia, prepares to commit suicide, also killing her son, but is captured by Techelles and Theridamas before she can carry it through. Callapine, Orcanes and their allies are gearing up to defeat Tamburlaine and, in a face-off, the two sides indulge in a long exchange of threats (II.3.5). Act 4 opens with another scene depicting the differences between Tamburlaine's sons. Calyphas's lack of enthusiasm for battle enrages Tamburlaine and he kills his own son in front of an appalled Orcanes. The subplot involving Theridamas and his love for the captured Olympia reaches its conclusion (II.4.2) as Olympia tricks him into killing her, and then we are back to Tamburlaine, victorious again, making his entrance in a chariot drawn by the defeated Turkish kings (II.4.3). He exults over them and prepares for his next challenge – the city of Babylon. The citizens of Babylon plead with their governor to surrender but he refuses (II.5.1). After the inevitable defeat, Tamburlaine has the governor strung up on the city walls and shot to death. He orders all the citizens of the city to be drowned, and he burns the Moslem holy books. Just as the scene concludes, Tamburlaine is suddenly stricken with a sickness, but he remains defiant. Callapine and the King of Amasia, calling on Mahomet for revenge, prepare to attack Tamburlaine while he is still recovering from besieging Babylon (II.5.2). The play ends with Tamburlaine's kings grieving over their ailing leader. A map is spread out and Tamburlaine reviews the extent of his empire, lamenting what is left unconquered (II.5.2). He hands his crown on to his son Amyras and dies.

Tamburlaine in the theatre

There are numerous references to the two parts of *Tamburlaine* in contemporary documents, both in the immediate wake of its first performances, and for some time afterwards. Some of the many references to the play that occur in contemporary documents are 'neutral', helping us to date the play, and giving some enlightening insights into stage practice. A letter written by Philip Gawdy to his father and dated 16 November 1587 refers to an accident that happened when the Lord Admiral's Men (the company for which Marlowe wrote) performed a play Gawdy does not specifically name:

> . . . having a device in their play to tie one of their fellows
> to a post and so to shoot him to death . . . one of the

player's hands swerved, his piece being charged with a
bullet, missed the fellow he aimed at and killed a child,
and a woman great with child forthwith, and hurt an
other man in the head very sore.

[cited in Chambers, 1945, II, p. 135]

Although we cannot be certain, the episode being referred to is probably the shooting of the governor of Babylon in act 5 scene 1 of the
second part of *Tamburlaine*. Other references are more intriguing for the
degree to which they are edged with admiration or envy. As we have
already seen, Robert Greene (1560?–1592) was to launch a venomous
attack on Marlowe's supposed atheism in his *A Groatsworth of Wit* (1592).
Greene was evidently preoccupied with the young poet, very probably
jealous of his phenomenal success, and he makes a reference to Part
Two of *Tamburlaine* in his prefatory epistle to *Perimedes the Blacksmith*,
published in 1588, the year after the play premiered. He mentions 'two
Gentlemen Poets' who have mocked him for his failure to 'make my
verses jet upon the stage in tragical buskins', and writes of one of them
whose work he notes as 'daring God out of heaven with that Atheist
Tamurlan . . .' (MacLure, 1995, p. 29). Greene makes a clear association
between Marlowe the writer's opinions on the one hand, and those of
his character Tamburlaine on the other, prefiguring the accusations of
atheism he would elaborate in *A Groatsworth of Wit*. Just as critics have
continued to romanticize the writer and his work by associating him
with his creation Doctor Faustus, so Marlowe has been compared, too,
with aspects of Tamburlaine, crystallized in Tamburlaine's blasphemous
burning of the Koran (II.5.1). The play and its hero crop up in another
fascinating context: in 1593, Marlowe's fellow playwright Thomas Kyd
had been arrested under suspicion of having authored a xenophobic piece
of propaganda displayed on the wall of a Dutch church in London (and
which has become known as the Dutch Church libel). The libel launched
an attack upon foreign communities in the city, threatening a massacre,
and was signed 'Tamberlaine' (see chapter 1, 'Marlowe in his time',
pp. 28–9, for a fuller discussion of the incident). It was another document to be catalogued in the case against Marlowe the subversive, whether
or not he had been directly involved in its composition or its display.

   With regard to the very first performances, we can be reasonably
confident that the second part was composed in response to the box
office success of the first, the sequel to a blockbuster. The end of Part
One gives no indication that there may be a sequel, and the prologue

to the second part declares that 'The general welcomes Tamburlaine received / When he arrived last upon our stage / Hath made our poet pen his second part' (II.Prologue.1–3). Commercial pressure, and the inclination to capitalize on a successful formula, is something we associate readily with contemporary Hollywood cinema, and it may come as something of a surprise to find that we can look at the business of Elizabethan theatrical entrepreneurs in an analogous way. There is certainly a sense in Part Two of a writer going through the motions, and the paucity of source material is evident. In the past, critics have devoted much scholarship to investigating the artistic integrity of the two parts as one whole, and some, such as Helen Gardner (1942) and G.I. Duthie (1948), have disputed the common perception that has tended to denigrate Part Two, coming up with accounts of varying plausibility to argue for its relative strengths. There is some valuable speculation in Gardner's account: she points out how the play structures its episodes around events linked to the main plot conceptually, showing that although 'Man's desires and aspirations may be limitless, . . . their fulfilment is limited by forces outside the control of the will' (Gardner, 1942, p. 19). However, it is obvious that Marlowe had plundered his historical sources fairly comprehensively by the time the first part was finished, and was left to cast around for inspiration for the second. The fact that recent stagings have tended to cut the second half far more heavily than the first is an indication of the relative paucity of real drama in the sequel.

For various reasons, and with varying degrees of approval or opprobrium, the *Tamburlaine* plays passed into common currency in the theatrical community. They were widely (and badly) imitated. Shakespeare makes a glancing reference to what was evidently one of the most famous moments and most memorable speeches: as Tamburlaine enters in a carriage drawn by the kings he has conquered, he cries 'Holla, ye pampered jades of Asia!' (II.4.3.1); ten years later, Shakespeare tips his hat to Marlowe when he has Pistol, in *2 Henry IV*, talk of 'packhorses, / And hollow pamper'd jades of Asia' (2.4.140–1). Other writers, or teams of writers, who recalled the moment in subsequent plays include Jonson, Chapman and Marston, Dekker and Ford, and Beaumont and Fletcher (Levin, 1984, p. 59). This scene depicting Tamburlaine in his carriage, along with the staging of Bajazeth braining himself against his cage (I.5.1), are the two moments that reverberate most commonly through the drama and other documents of the time. The other aspect of the first performances that seems to have made a particular impression is Edward Alleyn's acting (the plate on p. 72 is thought to depict Alleyn as Tamburlaine). There is a plethora of references to stalking,

Engraving of Tamburlaine in Richard Knolles, *The Generall Historie of the Turkes* (London, 1603), p. 236. Believed to be a portrait of Edward Alleyn. (Reproduced by courtesy of the Director and University Librarian, the John Rylands University Library of Manchester.)

stamping, roaring and strutting in relation to Tamburlaine, almost all of them mocking a style of acting seen as outmoded by the time it is recorded (Levin, 1984, pp. 62–3). Ben Jonson's remark in his *Timber, or Discoveries* (1640) is symptomatic: Jonson contrasts what he calls 'the true Artificer' with the writer whose language 'fl[ies] from all humanity, with the *Tamerlanes*, and Tamer-Chams of the late Age, which had nothing in them but the *scenical* strutting, and furious vociferation, to warrant them to the ignorant gapers' (MacLure, 1995, p. 50). Here and elsewhere, the perception is of a close correlation between the style of the actor and his playwright. A tract dating from 1597 describes a man pacing a room with 'bent . . . brows' and 'furious [g]esture . . . as if he had been play-ing Tamberlane on a stage' (cited in Gurr, 1963, p. 98), and Andrew Gurr makes reference to a number of other descriptions of performances of the role so closely identified with Alleyn, noting how it quickly became 'proverbial' (ibid., p. 99). Alleyn's style was certainly identified as 'barn-storming', and since we know that his Marlovian lead roles were crucial in determining his status in the early modern theatre, it is reasonable to assume that the style in which they were written at least in part deter-mined the mode in which they were played. Even in a late twentieth-century interpretation of the role such as Anthony Sher's (RSC 1992), it seems it is difficult to escape the tendency towards the histrionic: Sher rolled his eyes, prowled the stage constantly, and savoured Marlowe's sonorous lines in a virtuoso performance that, though sometimes bor-dering on self-parody, appeared to be precisely what the text required.

It seems that the bold theatricality of the first productions of *Tamburlaine* extended beyond the rhetoric of the texts and the acting style of its star player. Philip Henslowe's diary includes various items in his lists of stage props and costumes that were used for this particular play, including 'Tamberlaine['s] bridle' (used to yoke the captive kings to his chariot), 'Imperial crowns' (crucial to the symbolic play of power), 'Tamberlaine's coat with copper lace' and 'Tamberlaine's breeches of crimson velvet' (Foakes & Rickert, 1961, pp. 320–2). We know that spectacle was a significant element of Elizabethan stage practice, and it is particularly important in these plays. It may be that Marlowe was responding to the reception of the first play when he wrote more visu-ally striking set pieces into Part Two. The second part is punctuated with coronations, and features Tamburlaine's burning of a city and of the Koran, sieges, the scaling of the walls of Babylon, and the savage execution of its governor. The greater demands on staging that Part Two entails suggests that the second half was destined for a theatre like the Rose rather than for the more informal spaces that may have been used for Part One.

The impact that the plays had on English theatre was massive, but the attention they received in their time made them easy targets for their critics as the forms of the drama and styles of performance evolved rapidly in a hothouse atmosphere of innovation and experimentation. In retrospect, then, the Prologue unwittingly contains something of an ironic joke at its own expense when it boldly asserts that *Tamburlaine* represents a radical departure:

> From jigging veins of rhyming mother-wits,
> And such conceits as clownage keeps in pay,
> We'll lead you to the stately tent of War,
> Where you shall hear the Scythian Tamburlaine
> Threat'ning the world with high astounding terms . . .

[I.Prologue.1–5]

From the start, Marlowe is scornful of the competition, although it is unclear whether his remark is a sideswipe at the kind of entertainment that conventionally preceded and concluded the performance of a play, or a pot-shot at a rival company. The disparaging term 'jigging' may refer to doggerel verse, or the jigs traditionally performed by clowns like Will Kemp, Robert Wilson and Richard Tarlton during the course of an afternoon's entertainment at one of the playhouses. The phrase 'high astounding terms' is an apt description of Tamburlaine's characteristically inflated style, but before too long, as we have seen, the towering verse Marlowe wrote for his hero would become the butt of critics' jokes, even while the plays themselves, it seems, remained very popular.

Nevertheless, we must be careful not to underestimate the significance of the plays in terms of the development of dramatic verse. Marlowe was one of the first playwrights to take blank verse from epic poetry to the English stage: the use of five-stress lines that were unrhymed had a hugely liberating effect, freeing writers from the tyranny of rhyming couplets ('jigging veins of rhyming mother-wits', perhaps), while also pinpointing the pattern (five stresses) that seems to replicate most closely the natural rhythms of English speech. That said, the *Tamburlaine* plays remain fairly conservative in terms of metrical experimentation, sometimes sticking uncomfortably rigidly to iambic pentameters (where an unstressed syllable is followed by a stressed syllable). This dying speech of Cosroe's is characteristic:

> The strangest men that ever Nature made!
> I know not how to take their tyrannies.
> My bloodless body waxeth chill and cold,
> And with my blood my life slides through my wound.

> My soul begins to take her flight to hell,
> And summons all my senses to depart:

[I.2.7.40–5]

The same speech illustrates Marlowe's tendency to reel off end-stopped lines, where the sense and the metre coincide with a pause at the end of a line. Although Marlowe does make use of three-stress and four-stress lines too, there is a fairly consistent pattern where the final stress of a line falls heavily on its final syllable, and this can have a monotonous effect:

> Come, happy father of Zenocrate,
> A title higher than thy Soldan's name,
> Though my right hand have thus enthrallèd thee,
> Thy princely daughter here shall set thee free –

[I.5.1.434–7]

Often, Marlowe's tendency to revel in the exotic names of his *dramatis personae* contributes to the sense of metrical precision: as well as the name of Tamburlaine himself, we have for example Zenocrate, Theridamas, Techelles, Olympia and Bajazeth, the latter often powerfully deployed as a three-stress word. The daring use of these names is often astounding, creating an impression of splendid exoticism. Although the verse in the *Tamburlaine* plays is certainly more controlled and less adventurous than his later work, it is also fair to say that its martial, stately tone befits the subject matter. Ben Jonson's over-familiar description of Marlowe's 'mighty line', though now a commonplace, is a neat epithet that has yet to be improved upon.

The first part of *Tamburlaine* was most likely written while Marlowe was still at Cambridge, possibly in 1586 or 1587. The *Tamburlaine* plays were the only ones that Marlowe would have seen in print: they appeared in 1590. The fact that someone took the trouble to print them is further testimony to their popularity. The Stationers' Register actually lists them as 'The two commical discourses of Tomberein the Scythian shepherd', and the printer, Richard Jones, notes that he has left out some comic scenes, 'some fond and frivolous gestures', as he calls them, which he considered to be unsuitable in the context of 'so honourable and stately a history' (cited in Chambers, 1945, IV, p. 422). The notion of *Tamburlaine* being in any way comic might surprise us – Jones printed on the title-page a more appropriate description ('Tragicall Discourses') – but, as we shall see, there are touches of real humour remaining in the plays as they have come down to us, even if that humour is often dark, sour and sardonic. It is likely, though by no means certain, that the comic business that was included in performance, and which was excised by Jones, would have been added by the company rather than by Marlowe. Furthermore, the preface addresses itself to 'the Gentlemen Readers and others that take pleasure in reading Histories', and this alerts us to the fact that the printed versions of the plays were aimed at a different market: the plays were performed in the public playhouses, to a socially mixed audience. The written texts were clearly aimed at those with the education, the disposable income and the leisure time to read them.

After the theatres were closed in 1642, the plays vanished from the stage for nearly 300 years, although they seem to have survived in some form even after the playhouses were shut down: Cunningham quotes a reference to impromptu performances of plays like *Tamburlaine* and *The Jew of Malta* as holiday entertainments, and this reference dates from 1654 (Cunningham, 1999, p. 33). The twentieth century saw some revivals, but they were few and far between, starting with an all-male production by the Yale University Dramatic Association in 1919 that mangled the texts badly to produce a playable two and a half hour show. Another university performance was directed in Oxford in 1933 by Nevill Coghill, probably the first revival in England since Marlowe's time, albeit an amateur one. Tyrone Guthrie's version, staged at the Old Vic in 1951, was the first professional revival of the play, and it featured the famous actor-manager Donald Wolfit in the title role, a barnstorming performer who certainly had the voice and the presence the part demanded. Five years later, in 1956, Guthrie revived the production with Anthony Quayle as Tamburlaine for performances in Toronto and then an unsuccessful run in New York. Once again, the two parts were edited and spliced together. In an introduction to his published version of the text, Guthrie suggested that the recent memory of the Second World War made the play seem more relevant to modern audiences. There is 'something attractive and contemporary in Marlowe's orgy of sadism by the light of meteors, in the inflamed power-dream of this genius that never reached maturity', he writes (cited in Geckle, 1988, p. 54). The resonance was certainly picked up by some – a review by J.C. Trewin refers to the play's 'Belsen-horrors' (cited in ibid., p. 59). In general, the reviewers found the spectacle, cruelty and violence of the plays a shattering experience. When the production failed in New York in 1956, Guthrie's rationale was that American audiences, having no tradition of rhetorical acting, found it incomprehensible: once again, the play's uncompromising style was identified as its 'failure'.

A number of productions of *Tamburlaine* were staged during the 1960s and 1970s, culminating in the National Theatre production of 1976–7 directed by Peter Hall and starring Albert Finney which was chosen to mark the much-delayed opening of the mainhouse Olivier theatre. Cuts to this version were less severe than in previous ones, and the show was visually spectacular, with nearly half the production budget being spent on costumes (Geckle, 1988, p. 69). Finney and Hall capitalized on the traces of comedy that remain, particularly in the first few scenes of Part One. The comic strain in the play as we have inherited it is undeniably there, but faint, and certainly not substantial enough to hang a production on. When Terry Hands directed Anthony Sher in the title role at the Royal Shakespeare Company's Swan Theatre (1992), the humour, where present, was heavily accented in Sher's virtuoso performance, and leavened the production a good deal, although the actors were forced in places to *ad lib* in order to raise laughter from the audience, or else inflect their lines for a distinctly modern twist. Sher's incredulous 'are *you* the witty king of Persia?' on first encountering the feeble Mycetes is one of the best examples (2.4.23); Mycetes's reaction was changed from the invocation 'O gods' to a thoroughly modern, despairing 'O God!' (2.4.41). Again, the audience laughed on cue. However, as so often in such cases, the comic touches were reliant less on the text itself than on the director or the actors' audacious manipulation of it.

Nevertheless, the overwhelming impression the play leaves is of an endless, enervating sequence of unrelenting military confrontation, conflict and carnage. According to Michael Billington, there is 'no question that the play is about the insanity of global conquest; the implication is that we have lived through too much twentieth century tyranny to view the piece simply as a flamboyant Elizabethan immorality play' (Billington, 1992). Another reviewer made a similar connection between Tamburlaine and modern dictators, suggesting that Sher played Tamburlaine 'as a demonic Hitler figure, possibly with a touch of Saddam Hussein' (Rutherford, 1992). What such descriptions do not take full account of is Sher's charisma, wit and panache as a performer. Whether slyly mocking Mycetes, swinging across the stage on a rope like Errol Flynn to knock the towering, stilt-mounted Bajazeth to the floor, or dangling upside down from a rope to deliver his victory speech over the defeated Turkish emperor, he continually provoked the audience to laughter and gasps of amazement, sometimes in spite of the horrific deeds perpetrated by the character he was portraying. It is somewhat fanciful, but not entirely inappropriate, to imagine that Ned Alleyn, the original Tamburlaine, may well have provoked an analagous response in

his audiences. Richard Levin, writing before the Hands/Sher production, concludes in his study of Elizabethan perceptions of the plays that,
if Marlowe had intended to present Tamburlaine and his triumphs in
an ironic light, then the plays must be counted as artistic failures, since
they seem to have provoked largely favourable responses to him (Levin,
1984, p. 66).

As we have seen, twentieth-century revivals of the plays have been
rare, and standard practice has been to cut the texts very heavily in order
to produce a composite, single performance from the two parts. The
1992 RSC production edited out around 2000 lines, or 44 per cent of
the text (Dawson, 1997, p. xl). Part Two was the chief victim: the subplot depicting the Christian king Sigismond's attempt to double-cross
the Moslem king Orcanes was cut, and much of acts 3 and 4 were edited
and re-ordered to bring a greater coherence and focus to the narrative.
Even in a severely truncated form, however, the play can appear monotonous. In general terms, the same pattern of action is repeated, as
Tamburlaine proceeds to conquer every challenger. As each new enemy
approaches, Tamburlaine indulges in a stream of threats and 'vaunts', or
boasts, which are met with a corresponding salvo of rhetoric from the
opposition. Each side having asserted its confidence of victory, the play
proceeds to a battle (often off stage, as was customary at this time), and
Tamburlaine emerges triumphant to deliver a glorified 'told you so' speech
over his defeated (and often dead) enemy. The cycle complete, the play
moves swiftly on to document the demise of the next doomed challenger. On stage, even when fired by the showmanship of a great actor
like Anthony Sher and the visual flair of a director like Terry Hands
(RSC, 1992), the effect can be stultifying. Certainly, reading the plays
can be difficult without a specific focus to guide the reader through
the often overbearingly rich language and the slow trajectory of the
through-line of the action. This is not a play that charts dynamic interaction between 'characters', or which represents the journey and evolution of a particular 'character' from one particular state to another. In
this sense, the two plays do not have the immediate appeal of *Hamlet*,
Macbeth or Marlowe's own *Edward II* simply because they do not abide
by the rules of drama as we tend to understand them today. However,
there is much to be learned by exploring the plays within their original performance context, for part of their fascination today resides in
their potential, via the evidence of their popularity, to provide some
insight into aspects of Elizabethan culture. Furthermore, as contemporary
theatre critics in particular have suggested, the play has some provocative
things to say about the nature of political power.

Timur the Lame

The figure of Tamburlaine and the tales of his conquests were a source of great fascination (and no little anxiety) to the Elizabethans. W.L. Godshalk notes that 'this same story, or one of its variants, may be found in as many as one hundred Renaissance sources' (Godshalk, 1974, p. 105). The Turkish empire controlled most of eastern Europe and about one-third of the known world by the turn of the century. The infidel was perceived as a real threat to Christendom and the civilization of western Europe. Emily C. Bartels has undertaken a thorough investigation of the complexities of Europe's perceptions of the East in her study of Marlowe, *Spectacles of Strangeness* (1993): although the East is exoticized to an extent in contemporary documents (in particular, in terms of the wealth the Orient was reputed to possess), it differs from the depictions of the Americas, or of Africa, whose indigenous populations were seen as alien, savage and bestial, and often associated with the demonic. Contemporary accounts, Bartels argues, 'produced an East at base more civilized, more organized, and more knowable than Africa and the Americas' (Bartels, 1993, p. 55). The Turks, 'the most prominent and threatening figures on the Eastern horizon', emerged on the one hand as 'barbaric, war-mongering, anti-Christian infidels', and on the other as 'masterful military tacticians' (p. 57). Thus Tamburlaine emerges in contemporary accounts as an instrument of God, 'raised . . . to chasten the kings and proud people of the earth', as George Whetstone describes him in *The English Mirror* (1586) (cited in Thomas & Tydeman, 1994, p. 95), but one whose military brilliance is edged with a savage cruelty. In the source that would have been most familiar to the Elizabethans, John Foxe's *Acts and Monuments* (first published 1563, although Marlowe would have used the 1570 edition), Tamburlaine is seen as the heroic conqueror of the savage heathen Bajazeth. This is a kind of propaganda in the context of Elizabethan England, a reassurance that even the seemingly all-conquering Turks could be defeated.

In Marlowe's plays it is commonplace to find Tamburlaine's enemies describing him as inhuman and monstrous. To Cosroe he is 'Barbarous and bloody' and 'Bloody and insatiate' (I.2.7.1, 11). Elsewhere, the Soldan of Egypt denounces him as a 'Merciless villain, peasant ignorant / Of lawful arms or martial discipline' (I.4.1.64–5), and there is indeed a wild savagery in Tamburlaine that seems to contravene the codes of ethics that govern warfare as it is waged by his enemies. Cosroe, in his death throes, wonders at their barbarism: 'The strangest men that ever Nature made! / I know not how to take their tyrannies' (I.2.7.40–1). The 1992

RSC production emphasized the sadism of Tamburlaine and his men in the depiction of Cosroe's death: having been cut down by Tamburlaine, Theridamas, Techelles and Usumcasane all joined in to finish him off, kicking and stabbing him repeatedly. However, more shocking than this is the killing of Tamburlaine's own son in act 4 scene 1 of the second part. Disgusted and, as he perceives it, dishonoured by the cowardly Calyphas, he executes him in front of his enemy Orcanes, for whom this is conclusive proof of Tamburlaine's savagery: 'Thou showest the difference 'twixt ourselves and thee / In this thy barbarous damned tyranny', Orcanes declares (II.4.1.138–9). The 1992 RSC production made the execution all the more horrific by having Tamburlaine embrace Calyphas from behind as Calyphas knelt centre-stage, kissing him on the top of the head before garrotting him – a killing considerably more brutal and protracted than the stabbing that most editors suggest in their stage directions at this point. Furthermore, Calyphas was played less as a coward than as a conscientious objector by Jasper Britton, aligning a greater degree of audience sympathy to him than might otherwise have been the case: it is certainly possible that an Elizabethan audience would have had a greater understanding of Tamburlaine's sense of honour defiled than we would tend to today.

Modern productions will inevitably make Tamburlaine's actions seem more shocking than they may have been 400 years ago, and it is important to bear this in mind when trying to guess how contemporary audiences would have responded to Marlowe's hero. No doubt the execution of the virgins of Babylon is intended as an unequivocal demonstration of his cruelty, and it probably would have been interpreted in that way by an Elizabethan audience: the unusually explicit stage direction which depicts Tamburlaine entering '*all in black, and very melancholy*' (II.5.1.63.*s.d.*) mitigates very little when he is able to indulge in the black humour of his punning order to Techelles:

> Techelles, straight go charge a few of them
> To charge these dames, and show my servant Death,
> Sitting in scarlet on their armed spears.

> [I.5.1.116–17]

This was the most harrowing moment of the 1992 RSC version, a production which staged each violent episode explicitly and graphically. A rehearsal note makes clear that the director Terry Hands wanted the virgins 'to be played by two children 10–12 years old', and it was a shockingly effective piece of casting. Zenocrate screamed in horror and despair as they were led away, vainly trying to snatch one of the girls back before she was pushed to the ground by Tamburlaine. His subsequent panegyric to the 'divine Zenocrate' was book-ended by this moment and the screams of the virgins as they were executed off stage, casting the whole speech into a cold, ironic shadow.

We are left with a deeply ambivalent figure. As I have already noted, Richard Levin's scrupulous survey of contemporary references to *Tamburlaine* suggests that audiences generally reacted favourably to him when the play was first performed (Levin, 1984, p. 66). The theatre critic Irving Wardle, reviewing the 1992 RSC production, described the Elizabethan Tamburlaine as a 'Rambo-like hero to the xenophobic ballad-makers of the 1590s who had declared war on London's immigrant population'. He concludes, somewhat hysterically, that 'Applauding him is like applauding National Front graffiti' (Wardle, 1992). Wardle is making a perhaps over-simplistic connection to the Dutch Church libel, but it is important to bear in mind that the wholesale slaughter of heathens, even at the hands of another heathen, may well have appealed to a typical Elizabethan in a way that would be lost on us today. Even setting this aside, there is clearly something about Marlowe's Tamburlaine that invites the audience to engage with some degree of complicity in his barbarous acts. Responses to both the RSC production (1992) and the National Theatre revival (1976–7) testify to this. J.S. Cunningham describes Tamburlaine's progress, as charted by Albert Finney, as one that 'blended wit, opportunism, a strutting confidence, and engagingly mischievous provocations to mirth'; he 'excited an expectant delight from the outset, admiration of his temerity and verve ever ready to broaden into partisan laughter' (Cunningham & Warren, 1978, pp. 157, 156). We have already seen that Anthony Sher's portrayal, founded as it was on the actor's ability to build a rapport with his audience in a space that allowed for such actor–audience dynamics, met with comparable success. In the same way that *The Jew of Malta* invites the audience to conspire with the anti-hero Barabas against his enemies, *Tamburlaine* presents us with a figure from whom we may find it difficult to disengage.

Playing the king

I have already discussed how Elizabethan dramatists, fascinated by the nature of the medium in which they worked, frequently exploited and explored the nature of theatre in their plays (see chapter 2, pp. 56–60).

The 'metatheatrical' dimension of their work emerges most clearly in the ways in which they experiment with the relation between actor and audience, from the relatively straightforward deployment of asides and soliloquies, to the complexities of the 'play within a play' device that features in Thomas Kyd's *The Spanish Tragedy* (first performed around the same time as *Tamburlaine*), a trick Shakespeare was to put to best use in *Hamlet* fourteen or fifteen years later. In Shakespeare's play, Hamlet himself is preoccupied with the gap between performer and role, particularly in relation to his own unwillingness to avenge his father's murder. In his first substantial speech, (literally) haunted by the death of old Hamlet, he dismisses outward shows of grief as 'actions that a man might play' (1.2.84). Later, he is stunned and shamed by an actor's impersonated grief: he contrasts this with his own reaction to his 'real' bereavement, berating himself as 'A dull and muddy-mettled rascal' (2.2.544). That passionate actor is in fact performing in a style that may be very close to Edward Alleyn's, and reciting a tale that is also recounted in Marlowe's *Dido Queen of Carthage*. Earlier in the same scene, hearing that the players are coming to perform at court, his response is seemingly innocuous, and yet subtly pointed: the remark 'He that plays the King shall be welcome' could be interpreted as another self-recrimination, implying he lacks the qualities required to fulfil the role of king. Hamlet perceives himself as woefully miscast as a king, and that perception opens wide the gap between performer and role.

The fascination of much of the first part of *Tamburlaine* resides in the way in which it stages the performance of power (it is something we shall meet again, in a more complex form, in *Edward II*). Mycetes, the Persian ruler, is established very quickly as one unsuited to the role of king – he is the antithesis of Tamburlaine, whom we shall shortly meet and whom we have already been introduced to via the prologue. Mycetes, aggravated by the bandit Tamburlaine who is threatening his borders, finds himself 'aggrieved / Yet insufficient to express the same, / For it requires a great and thund'ring speech', a speech which Mycetes is evidently incapable of delivering (I.1.1.1–3). The 'high astounding terms' that we have been told are characteristic of Tamburlaine are beyond him. The 1992 RSC production made an unashamed play for humour in its portrayal of a weak and silly king, fey, nervous, whining and heavily reliant on his attendant lords, a Mycetes who is all threat and no action. Indeed, even his threats are hollow, for he undermines them as he utters them – 'I might command you to be slain for this' he warns, in response to his brother Cosroe's sly mockery. 'I mean it not, but yet I know I might' (I.1.1.23, 26). Even this much requires moral support: he turns to one of his lords, imploring him to endorse his feeble threat: 'Meander, might I not?' (I.1.1.24). Striving for an imperious tone, he only betrays more anxiety. Cosroe's cynicism and barely disguised contempt for his brother hollow out Mycetes still further. Another of Mycetes's pleas for endorsement – 'Is it not a kingly resolution?' (I.1.1.55) – is met by a heavily ironic response: 'It cannot choose because it comes from you' (I.1.1.56).

Tamburlaine cuts a striking, if incongruous, figure at his first entrance (I.1.2). Surrounded by his retinue, his soldiers 'loaden with treasure', he makes his entrance in a shepherd's garb – a marked contrast, of course, to the royal attire Mycetes displays in the preceding scene. Zenocrate refers to him as 'shepherd' (I.1.2.7), building on the first scene's descriptions of him as a 'sturdy Scythian thief' and 'paltry Scythian' (I.1.1.36, 54). However, in a boldly theatrical gesture, Tamburlaine declares himself 'a lord, for so my deeds shall prove, / And yet a shepherd by my parentage' (I.1.2.34–5), and underlines the distinction by discarding the 'weeds that I disdain to wear' to display 'This complete armour and this curtle-axe [cutlass]' which are 'more beseeming Tamburlaine' (I.1.2.41–3). One recent editor of the play underlines the significance of the moment by inserting a stage direction: 'TAMBURLAINE *tears off his shepherd's garb to reveal a suit of armour*' (Burnett, 1999, p. 11). Much is made by Tamburlaine's enemies of his humble origins. To the Soldan of Egypt he is a 'base-bred thief' (I.4.3.12) and 'presumptuous beast' (I.4.3.15); Callapine describes him as 'this thief of Scythia, / This proud usurping king of Persia' (II.3.1.15–16), and Orcanes refers to him as 'shepherd's issue, base-born Tamburlaine' (II.3.5.77). The King of Amasia condemns him as a 'base-born tyrant' (II.5.3.18). Their contempt, fuelled by a kind of snobbery, sets them up ever higher so that Tamburlaine can bring them crashing down in their military confrontations.

Set against his political opportunist brother Cosroe, and now the imposing figure of Tamburlaine, Mycetes emerges even more distinctly as someone woefully inadequate to carry the title and role of king. There is some mileage in drawing a parallel between these figures and the relation between Edward and the usurper Mortimer in *Edward II*: when Cosroe is crowned by the Persian lords, his speech anticipates the kind of rhetoric employed by Mortimer: 'I willingly receive th'imperial crown / And vow to wear it for my country's good', he declares (I.1.1.157–8). The power games we encounter in *Tamburlaine*, however, are in some ways more complex, with internal struggles, alliances and betrayals triangulated by the constant threat Tamburlaine himself poses to all comers. Techelles's depiction of Tamburlaine as a 'princely lion' emphasizes Mycetes's fool-

Anthony Sher as Tamburlaine (right) and Gordon Case as Usumcasane in the RSC
production of *Tamburlaine* (dir. Terry Hands), The Swan, Stratford-on-Avon, 1992.
(Reproduced by courtesy of the photographer, John Bunting.)

ish underestimate of the Scythian's power when he refers to him as 'a
fox' come to 'pull my plumes' (I.1.1.31–3). Techelles's reference to
Tamburlaine 'with frowning brows and fiery looks / Spurning their crowns
from off their captive heads' ironizes the actual crowning of Cosroe that
the audience has just witnessed at the end of the preceding scene
(I.1.1.56–7). In a similar vein, and still working with the symbolism of
the crown with which the text constantly toys, Meander's declaration
to Mycetes's troops that 'Fortune herself doth sit upon our crests' (I.2.2.73)
sounds dizzily precarious compared to Tamburlaine's boasts about fortune. In the 1992 RSC production, Mycetes's chiding of his men (the
audience), who have failed to strike up the drum in response to
Meander's command, is met by a silence, and then finally a couple of
bungled, muffled taps. Almost immediately, Tamburlaine enters to the
accompaniment of a powerful, tribal drumbeat, and the stage fills with
soldiers chanting and performing one of their many martial dances (see
plate above).

The notes made by Welcome Msomi, the composer/choreographer for that production (compiled in the promptbook), explain that the dances were modelled on Zulu chants. This was a clever strategy, providing an accessible analogue (if only via a familiarity with rugby team chants) to the practice of 'vaunting' – an exchange of military boasts. It forms a crucial part of the confrontations between Tamburlaine and his enemies, and is an essential component of the performance of kingship and authority. This exchange of boasts and threats has a long tradition, rooted as it is in the practice of 'flyting' – a 'cursing match in verse' as J.A. Cuddon usefully defines it (1992, p. 345) – which can be traced back to the tenth-century Old English poem *The Battle of Maldon*. It is the vaunts that most fully embody the 'high astounding terms' that the Prologue describes as Tamburlaine's characteristic language. This is typical:

> Our quivering lances shaking in the air
> And bullets like Jove's dreadful thunderbolts
> Enrolled in flames and fiery smouldering mists
> Shall threat the gods more than Cyclopian wars;
> And with our sun-bright armour as we march
> We'll chase the stars from heaven and dim their eyes
> That stand and muse at our admirèd arms.

[I.2.3.18–24]

A number of his adversaries rise to the challenge of verbal combat, notably Bajazeth in Part One. The 1992 RSC production depicted Bajazeth and Tamburlaine threatening each other with noises as well as with their scripted vaunts, roaring at one another like animals facing each other down. Bajazeth was the most powerful of Tamburlaine's adversaries in this production, a fearsome sight in an ivory-tusked headdress, mounted on golden stilts with which he prowled around the stage with unnerving agility. In act 3 scene 3, as their lords march into battle, their two female counterparts, Zenocrate and Zabina, also indulge in an exchange of tirades, effectively acting out Tamburlaine and Bajazeth's roles for them while they are off stage:

> *Zabina.*   [*To Zenocrate*] Base concubine, must thou be placed by me
>   That am the empress of the mighty Turk?

> *Zenocrate.*   Disdainful Turkess and unreverend boss,
>   Call'st thou me concubine, that am betrothed
>   Unto the great and might Tamburlaine?
> *Zabina.*   To Tamburlaine the great Tartarian thief!

> [I.3.3.166–71]

In respect of vaunting, Mycetes is again found wanting: working up to something like a vaunt in act 2 scene 2, he gives up halfway and hands over to Meander: 'Tell you the rest, Meander; I have said' (I.2.2.13). Meander does his best, but even his exhortation delivered to the troops fizzles out with a concession that Mycetes has made towards the traitorous Cosroe – that 'His Highness' pleasure is that he should live / And be reclaimed with princely lenity' (I.2.3.37–8).

Elsewhere, we find that Tamburlaine's displays of authority are not necessarily dependent upon what he says. His appearance, and what he is able to communicate non-verbally, can be powerful weapons. Tamburlaine's physical appearance is crucial to his performance of power. Theridamas, when he first encounters Tamburlaine, is struck by his heroic appearance:

> His looks do menace heaven and dare the gods;
> His fiery eyes are fixed upon the earth,
> As if he now devised some strategem,
> Or meant to pierce Avernus' darksome vaults
> And pull the triple-headed dog from hell

> [I.1.2.156–60]

This description is endorsed and elaborated by the Persian lord Menaphon, reporting to Cosroe in the following scene. The lengthy speech includes a more detailed, less impressionistic physical description:

> Of stature tall, and straightly fashionèd,
> Like his desire, lift upwards and divine;
> So large of limbs, his joints so strongly knit,
> Such breadth of shoulders as might mainly bear
> Old Atlas' burden; . . .
> His lofty brows in folds do figure death,
> And in their smoothness amity and life;
> About them hangs a knot of amber hair

Wrapped in curls, as fierce Achilles' was . . .
His arms and fingers long and sinewy,
Betokening valour and excess of strength;
In every part proportioned like the man
Should make the world subdued to Tamburlaine.

[I.2.1.7–11, 21–4, 27–30]

In Tamburlaine's eyes Menaphon sees 'A heaven of heavenly bodies in their spheres / That guides his steps and actions to the throne / Where honour sits invested royally' (I.2.1.16–18). The notion that his very countenance heralds life or death finds its most concrete expression in a strikingly explicit stage direction in I.3.2, a direction which dates back to the first printed edition of the play. Immediately following the conversation between Agydas and Zenocrate, during which the Median lord has been shocked to hear Zenocrate's profession of love for Tamburlaine, whom Agydas despises, Tamburlaine himself approaches:

TAMBURLAINE *goes to her, and takes her away lovingly by the hand, looking wrathfully on Agydas, and says nothing.*

[I.3.2.65.*s.d.*]

Agydas needs no verbal warning: he has already read Tamburlaine's expression, and he describes how it has stricken him with terror: 'Upon his brows was portrayed ugly death' (I.3.2.72). When Techelles enters to 'salute' Agydas on Tamburlaine's behalf, he carries a naked dagger, and Agydas is in no doubt about what it signifies. 'I prophesied before and now I prove / The killing frowns of jealousy and love', he says (I.3.2.90–1), and fifteen lines later he stabs himself.

Marlowe invokes Achilles, great warrior of classical antiquity, directly, and elsewhere alludes to a range of classical gods and heroes in descriptions of Tamburlaine. As we have seen, the historical Tamburlaine bears a name which is a corruption of Timur the Lame, a moniker coined by his enemies. Nevertheless, the Tamburlaine that Marlowe depicts is clearly a physically powerful man, and some of his sources support the notion: Petrus Perondinus, for instance, writing in 1553, pictures him as 'of noble bearing, heavily bearded and broad-shouldered, deep-chested, his limbs . . . well-formed and indicative of general good health, except for one of his feet, which was misshapen and caused him to limp visibly' (Thomas & Tydeman, 1994, p. 118). The figure Marlowe portrays may also owe something to the actor who first played him, Edward Alleyn, who was noted for his commanding physical presence. Directors in the twentieth century have cast the role accordingly, from Donald Wolfit (Old Vic 1951), through Albert Finney (National Theatre 1976–7), to Anthony Sher (RSC 1992), who had clearly undergone some intensive physical training to prepare himself for the part.

One of the most common signifiers of political power used in the plays is the crown. Harry Levin notes that the term is 'bandied back and forth from scene to scene, no less than fifty times' (Levin, 1952, p. 39). Cosroe talks of their impending victory over Mycetes in terms of claiming Mycetes's crown:

> Come, Tamburlaine, now whet thy wingèd sword
> And lift thy lofty arm into the clouds,
> That it may reach the King of Persia's crown
> And set it safe on my victorious head.

[I.2.3.51–4]

Almost immediately afterwards, we see Mycetes enter '*alone with his crown in his hand, offering to hide it*' (I.2.4.s.d.). Tamburlaine follows him on stage, and an argument over the crown ensues in a scene shot through with humour: Tamburlaine's cheeky 'Is this your crown? . . . You will not sell it, will ye?' (I.2.4.27, 29) is one of those moments that lends itself easily to a comic spin. Certainly in the 1992 RSC production, Anthony Sher capitalized on it, his sly wit playing on the complicity with the audience that he built and sustained through much of the first half of the performance. However, ten lines later the scene is over, and the next scene opens with Tamburlaine presenting Cosroe with Mycetes's crown. A moment ago, it was the subject of a playground quarrel (Terry Hands, directing Sher, played the scene out as a literal tug of war); now it signifies victory and authority. It is worth noting how Tamburlaine foregrounds his own involvement in the claiming of the crown, and its exchange – when he declares Cosroe 'invested . . . / Even by the mighty hand of Tamburlaine' (I.2.5.2–3), he delivers to the Persian a coded message that it is he, Tamburlaine, who is the true victor. Cosroe is canny enough to acknowledge his ally's centrality; he is being strategically astute when he names Tamburlaine 'regent of Persia' with 'equal place in our affairs' (I.2.5.8, 14); but, finally, it will do him no good. His promise that 'none shall keep [i.e. protect] the crown but Tamburlaine' will prove ironic (I.2.5.7): before the end of act 2, Cosroe will lose his precious crowns to Tamburlaine himself. Almost as soon as Cosroe has left the stage, his supposed ally breaks his truce and marches against the Persian army to challenge Cosroe for the same crown he has just handed over to him. This short sequence is remarkable for its astute depiction of a critical moment in Tamburlaine's career, all the more notable for the fact that such flashes of what we might go so far as to call 'naturalism' are rare in the two plays. The birth of what will become Tamburlaine's unstoppable will to power takes place in the wake of a victory fought and won on behalf of another. As Menaphon declares that Cosroe will 'ride in triumph through Persepolis' (I.2.5.49), and the new king of Persia sweeps off stage with his retinue, Tamburlaine repeats the line, and his tone as he muses on it, bizarrely, is almost whimsical: 'Is it not brave to be a king, Techelles?' he asks. 'Why, say, Theridamas, wilt thou be a king?' (I.2.5.51, 65). Theridamas at first responds by shrugging it off with a joke: 'Nay, though I praise it, I can live without it' (66). The others respond more eagerly, however: Techelles replies to the offer, 'Ay, if I could, with all my heart, my lord' (68), and as speculation hardens into a plan of direct and immediate action, Tamburlaine laughs, ''Twill prove a pretty jest, in faith, my friends' (90). He dispatches Techelles to challenge Cosroe to fight them, 'That only made him king to make us sport' (101).

This exchange between Tamburlaine and his followers is open to different interpretations – where I have described Tamburlaine as 'whimsical', David H. Thurn describes him as 'rapt, dazzled by a fantasy that seems nearly palpable for a breathtaking moment' (Thurn, 1989, p. 13); and in performance, too, there are of course a number of interpretative options open to the cast. Nevertheless, however it is played or read, it remains a pivotal scene, marking as it does the moment when Tamburlaine focuses on the centrality of the crown as a symbol of all he desires: he has become, as Cosroe calls him, 'that fiery thirster after sovereignty' (I.2.6.31). Certainly, by the time we reach act 2 scene 7 the musing and amused tone is gone, and the crown has become the central symbol of all happiness for Tamburlaine: he describes it as 'the ripest fruit of all, / That perfect bliss and sole felicity, / The sweet fruition of an earthly crown' (I.2.7.27–9). The hyperbolic tone of the speech has led a number of critics to conclude that Marlowe is ironizing Tamburlaine here, undercutting his aspirations by allowing him to equate a crown with eternal bliss. Again, the text remains open for a range of different interpretations.

The vaunts that precede combat are an essential part of the staging of power and authority, and the humiliation of the conquered enemy is equally important. The treatment of Bajazeth, the Turkish emperor, is the clearest and most protracted example. At the opening of act 4 scene 2 he is brought forward caged, drawn by two Moors. He is let out of the cage so that Tamburlaine can use him as a footstool to climb into his throne, a detail which seems to have been lifted from John Foxe's *Acts and Monuments* (1570), although Foxe portrays him as using Bajazeth to mount his horse. Foxe also describes Bajazeth as being forced to feed like a dog beneath Tamburlaine's table, and how, caged, he was 'led about and showed through all Asia, to be scorned and laughed at' (Thomas & Tydeman, 1994, p. 136). Zabina, we hear, is not Zenocrate's slave, but her handmaid's slave (I.4.2.68–70). The scene is an agonizingly protracted exercise in humiliation, the most devastating display of Tamburlaine's power to overthrow any mortal challenge.

'The scourge and terror of the world'

One of the recurring motifs that cluster around Tamburlaine himself is the notion of his role as the so-called scourge of God: his last line in the plays is the self-regarding pronouncement, 'For Tamburlaine, the scourge of God, must die' (II.5.3.248). The significance of the epithet is underlined by the fact that it appears on the title-page of the first edition of the plays, printed in 1590. The concept of the scourge finds its origin in a passage from the Old Testament book of Isaiah (10.5–16). Significantly, it is an idea that Calvin seems preoccupied with in his commentary on the passage, which depicts God using a heathen Assyrian to punish the disobedient children of Israel. Although the Assyrian is triumphant, and revels in his victory, he is himself finally struck down by God. It became a familiar idea during Elizabethan times, with war often understood as God's scourge. Roy Battenhouse cites a number of contemporary references to the concept in his study of the play (Battenhouse, 1964, pp. 108–13). These include religious commentaries such as Calvin's, a popular history of the Turks by Richard Knolles, and proselytizing works such as Philip Mornay's *The Trueness of the Christian Religion* (1587). While all these references to God using a scourge occur in the strictly Christian context, we will see that Marlowe uses them in a much more elastic framework, eluding attempts to pin him down in terms of specifically Christian theology.

Marlowe's key sources picked up on the notion of Tamburlaine as scourge of God: a collection of stories compiled by the Spanish writer Pedro Mexìa (1497–1551) entitled *Silva de Varia Lecìon* (1540) is one of the chief sources, although Marlowe's actual text is likely to have been at two removes from Mexìa's work, having been through a French translation (by Claude Gruget in 1552) before being translated and abridged by Sir Thomas Fortescue as *The Forest or Collection of Histories* (1571) (Thomas & Tydeman, 1994, p. 74). There, the infamous king of the Goths Attila the Hun's reputation as 'Scourge of God' is mentioned in relation to Tamburlaine, who is reported to have asserted: ' "Supposest thou me to be any other than the ire of God?" ' (ibid., 1994, p. 82). The story goes on to propound the familiar notion of the scourge as one of those 'instruments wherewith God chastiseth sin'. Mexìa (or Fortescue) also notes, however, that these instruments cannot themselves 'escape the heavy judgement of God . . . Further in this life God assuredly at some time doth punish them, besides that in another world, Hell and damnation is certainly allotted' (pp. 82–3). This is the wisdom by which Callapine works when he declares his faith 'That Jove, surcharged with pity of our wrongs, / Will pour it down in showers on our heads, / Scourging the pride of cursed Tamburlaine' (II.3.1.36–8). Whether Marlowe's Tamburlaine suffers such a fate is something to which we shall return.

Cunningham draws a useful distinction between the scourge who inflicts suffering on God's people and so unwittingly brings about God's will, and the scourge as 'one who identifies God's enemies and punishes them on His behalf' (Cunningham, 1999, p. 72). Tamburlaine is certainly aware of his supposed role. Victorious over Bajazeth, he declares, 'let the majesty of heaven behold / Their scourge and terror tread on emperors' as he uses his defeated enemy as a footstool (I.4.2.31–2). In Part Two, when Babylon falls, he refers to himself as 'The wrathful messenger of mighty Jove' (II.5.1.92). Here we can see Tamburlaine acting more directly against the so-called heathens; when he orders his soldiers to burn the Moslems' holy books, he announces:

> There is a God full of revenging wrath,
> From whom the thunder and the lightning breaks,
> Whose scourge I am, and him will I obey.

> [II.5.1.182–4]

However, Tamburlaine's self-regard by no means guarantees his voluntary submission to Fate, God or gods. Tamburlaine reflects on Jove's example at several key moments in the play. In one respect, Jove (Jupiter) is a crucial precedent for Tamburlaine, since the ancient myths tell how Jove dethroned the titan Saturn in order to become supreme ruler. There are other aspects of the myths surrounding Jove that are relevant, too: reminding his followers of the Roman god's practice of disguising himself as a mortal and walking the earth 'in a shepherd's weed' (the garb is significant, mirroring Tamburlaine's), he suggests that 'by those steps that he hath scaled the heavens / May we become immortal like gods' (I.1.2.198–200) – simply by following Jove's route back to the heavens. In Part Two, Tamburlaine sees himself as 'arch-monarch of the world, / Crowned and invested by the hand of Jove' as well as 'The scourge of God and terror of the world' (II.4.1.150–1, 154). Until 'by vision or by speech, / I hear Immortal Jove say "Cease, my Tamburlaine"', he says, 'I will persist a terror to the world' (II.4.1.199–201).

While Tamburlaine does fairly consistently defer to Jove, no other gods seem to command his respect, be they Christian, Moslem or classical. In the first part he sets himself up against the Roman god of war: 'Though Mars himself . . . / And all the earthly potentates conspire / to dispossess me of this diadem,' he declares, 'Yet will I wear it in despite of them' (I.2.7.58–61). Tamburlaine places his faith in his earthly allies: 'So now it is more surer on my head, / Than if the gods had held a parliament', he says, after receiving their unanimous acclamation (I.2.7.65–6). For them, Tamburlaine himself takes on divine status; Techelles refers to him as 'mighty Tamburlaine, our earthly god' (II.1.3.138). No mortal has been able to check his inexorable rise to power. The god Mars has yielded to him, too, it seems, and even the god he says he obeys is not beyond the reach of his boasts: when Zenocrate pleads for her home city of Damascus, he refuses: 'were Egypt Jove's own land, / Yet would I with my sword make Jove to stoop' (I.4.4.75–6). As the first part of the play begins to wind down to its conclusion, Tamburlaine's megalomania continues to grow:

> The god of war resigns his room to me,
> Meaning to make me general of the world:
> Jove, viewing me in arms, looks pale and wan,
> Fearing my power should pull him from his throne . . .

> [I.5.1.451–4]

The cosmology of the two parts of *Tamburlaine* is certainly not consistent, stubbornly resisting attempts to systematize it. Quite apart from the fact that classical gods such as Jove and Mars mingle with the more orthodox figures of Christ and Mahomet, the relation of the gods to Fate and destiny is muddied. Early in the first part, Tamburlaine declares that 'I hold the Fates bound fast in iron chains, / And with my hand turn Fortune's wheel about' (I.1.2.173–4); later, he notes that Death and the Fatal Sisters do homage to his sword (I.5.1.457). Others acknowledge his good fortune – this is what Agydas means when he describes him as 'happy Tamburlaine' (I.1.2.256). According to Cosroe, 'Nature doth strive with Fortune and his stars / To make him famous in accomplished worth', meaning that all these elements vie with each other to assist him (I.2.1.33–4). Tamburlaine seems to have an unswerving faith in his own destiny, declaring his faith in his 'smiling stars' (I.3.3.42), and referring to the time 'when holy Fates / Shall 'stablish me in strong Egyptia' (I.4.4.137–8).

By contrast, his enemies are well aware of their own corresponding misfortune, often recognizing their doom as if reflected in the mirror of Tamburlaine's success. Cosroe's strong resolve and determination to fight his ally turned enemy is strangely mixed with fatalism – he talks gloomily of 'the loathsome circle of my dated life' (I.2.6.37), even as he leads his army into battle. Even proud Bajazeth is in despair:

> . . . we may curse his power,
> The heavens may frown, the earth for anger quake,
> But such a star hath influence in his sword
> As rules the skies, and countermands the gods
> More than Cimmerian Styx or Destiny.

> [I.5.1.230–4]

The confusion over cosmologies deepens when we start to take account of characters' calls for divine intervention. Whether the appeal is to a classical god or to a figure such as Mahomet, the calls appear to fall on deaf ears. Orcanes, led on stage as a prisoner of war, calls on Dis (Pluto, the god of the underworld) to 'Come once in fury and survey his pride, / Hailing him headlong to the lowest hell!' (II.4.3.41–2). In Part One, as Bajazeth and his wife Zabina are bound, the Turkish emperor, humiliated beyond endurance, is incredulous at his own divine protector's failure to act: 'O Mahomet, O sleepy Mahomet!' he cries (I.3.3.269). Zabina joins in the lament: 'O cursèd Mahomet that mak'st us thus / The slaves to Scythians rude and barbarous!' (I.3.3.270–1); and finally, as the two of them descend into suicidal despair, Zabina cries:

Then is there left no Mahomet, no God,
No fiend, no Fortune, nor no hope of end
To our infamous, monstrous slaveries?

[I.5.1.239–41]

Shortly afterwards, Bajazeth brains himself against the bars of his cage, and Zabina, seemingly driven insane at the sight of her dead husband, follows suit. It is one of the most striking instances of the play offering evidence for the indifference, or non-existence, of the divine.

A more intriguing interaction of god and man occurs in the sub-plot that develops early in Part Two between Orcanes, king of Natolia, and King Sigismund of Hungary. When Sigismund breaks the oath on which he and Orcanes have erected an unsteady truce, the Moslem Orcanes challenges Christ, if he exists, to revenge the treachery that has been perpetrated by the Christian. 'To arms, my lords, on Christ still let us cry', he calls; 'If there be Christ, we shall have victory' (II.2.3.63–4). In defeat, Sigismund acknowledges that 'God hath thundered vengeance from on high / For my accursed and hateful perjury' (II.2.3.2–3). There is a cynical kind of irony in the depiction of a victorious Moslem army that seems to owe its success to the intervention of an angry, vengeful Christian God. In a world where prayers seem to fall on deaf ears on every other occasion, whether those ears be classical, Moslem, or Christian, it seems in keeping with the tone of the play to make the exception in this case. The god in question responds, finally, to the call of a non-believer and punishes his supposed disciple for taking his name in vain.

It may be possible to impose a greater sense of coherence onto the second part of the play. In the fifth act, when Tamburlaine sacks the city of Babylon, he orders that the Moslem holy books be burned, and he is mocking and dismissive of Mahomet: 'Now, Mahomet, if thou have any power, / Come down thyself and work a miracle' (II.5.1.186–7). In Part One, Zenocrate expressed her fears for Tamburlaine, lest he incur the wrath of the gods: 'Ah mighty Jove and holy Mahomet', she cries, 'Pardon my love, O pardon his contempt / Of earthly fortune and respect of pity' (I.5.1.364–6). Although there is no evidence of any such retribution in the first part of the play, a number of critics have pointed out that Tamburlaine's sudden sickness ('But stay – I feel distempered suddenly') follows almost immediately after the burning of the Koran (II.5.1.217), and have cited this as evidence of divine punishment for his blasphemy. Tamburlaine is characteristically defiant, claiming that

'Sickness or death can never conquer me' (II.5.1.221), but the next time we see him, Tamburlaine will enter in his human-drawn chariot, not in triumph, but mortally ill, surrounded by his physicians.

The text devised for the 1992 RSC production was subtly altered to reinforce the impression of Tamburlaine as over-reacher, aspiring to godlike status, and being punished as a consequence of his presumption. According to the 'original' – the first printed text that forms the foundation for editions of the plays – Tamburlaine burns the Moslem holy books, exhorting the soldiers to

> Seek out another godhead to adore,
> The God that sits in heaven, if any god,
> For he is God alone, and none but he.

[II.5.2.199–201]

In the RSC production the lines were changed to read:

> Seek out another godhead to adore,
> The God that sits in heaven, if any god,
> Sits there alone, on earth there is none but me.

This added weight not only to the sense of Tamburlaine's presumption, but also to the idea that the 'distemper' that strikes him down almost immediately afterwards might have been a divine power's response to his audacious challenge. As he staggered, Anthony Sher toppled at the brink of the pit in which he had burned the Koran, and by cutting the following scene and the first half of the next, Hands made Sher's next line his outraged protest, 'what daring god torments my body thus / And seeks to conquer mighty Tamburlaine?' (II.5.3.42–3). A rapid decline toward death followed. Peter Hall adopted a comparable strategy in his production: J.S. Cunningham notes that 'Tamburlaine glanced up, when struck ill, as if to acknowledge Mahomet's intervention', although he concludes that the tone remained ambivalent, refusing to make an unequivocal connection between the blasphemy and his sickness. Cunningham and Warren agreed that this 'kept faith with Marlowe's own refusal to allow us the solace of such a simple allegorising of the event' (Cunningham & Warren, 1978, p. 158).

Throughout the two parts of the play, Tamburlaine seems to have held the power of fortune, and over life and death, in the palm of his hand. A more appropriate metaphor is coined by Tamburlaine himself,

as he draws his sword in front of the virgins of Babylon, sent to plead
for mercy. Asking them what they see at the weapon's point, they reply,
'Nothing but fear and fatal steel, my lord' (I.5.1.109). Tamburlaine replies:

> Your fearful minds are thick and misty, then,
> For there sits Death, there sits imperious Death,
> Keeping his circuit by the slicing edge.

> [I.5.1.111–12]

It is a bold and chilling metaphor: Death is 'imperious' but his 'circuit'
(drawing a parallel between the sword's sweep and the circuit of a judge)
is limited to the swing of Tamburlaine's sword. We have already seen
that there are numerous references to Tamburlaine's power over destiny,
and we have seen that his authority goes almost entirely unchallenged.
A notable exception comes near the beginning of the second part, when
Zenocrate dies. Tamburlaine's furious railing, 'Raving, impatient, desperate and mad' as he describes himself, is fearsome and at the same
time pitiful in its hopelessness:

> What, is she dead? Techelles, draw thy sword,
> And wound the earth, that it may cleave in twain,
> And we descend into th'infernal vaults
> To hale the Fatal Sisters by the hair
> And throw them in the triple moat of hell
> For taking hence my fair Zenocrate.

> [II.2.3.96–101]

Finally, he vents his towering frustration by razing to the ground the
city where she has died. Her body he orders to be embalmed until he
can be buried with her, a futile and grotesque attempt to outwit the
one power that has defeated him. When he does fall into what will
prove a fatal illness, the figure that has served him at his sword's edge
turns on him:

> See where my slave, the ugly monster Death,
> Shaking and quivering, pale and wan for fear,
> Stands aiming at me with his murdering dart
> Who flies away at every glance I give,
> And when I look away comes stealing on.

> [II.5.3.67–71]

Although a single coherent thesis on destiny and the relation between God and humanity seems elusive, a number of critics have struggled to impose particular interpretations on the two plays. One attempt to determine a moral system locates them within the so-called *de casibus* tradition. The term *de casibus* translates as 'of' or 'about falls', since the stories in that tradition focused specifically on the misfortunes of their protagonists. The idea of history, and how it differed in Elizabethan understandings, will be taken up more fully in the discussion of *Edward II*. For now, it is important to know that the Elizabethans understood history to move in endlessly repeated cycles: in terms of the careers of monarchs, these cycles usually involved a fall from authority and good fortune to a position of abjection and misery. The collection of tales known as *The Mirror for Magistrates* (first published in 1559 and frequently reprinted) is the best example, and George Whetstone's very similar *English Mirror* (1586) is one of Marlowe's probable sources for *Tamburlaine*. The didactic agenda of both is clear: each work is intended as a 'looking glass' in which the powerful will see their predecessors punished for vice and misrule.

Roy Battenhouse's full-length study of the plays, *Marlowe's Tamburlaine: A Study in Renaissance Moral Philosophy* (first published in 1941), interprets the first part as the depiction of Tamburlaine as scourge of God, 'brought to the highest worldly success', and the second as the story of 'this proud atheist . . . brought to his deserved overthrow' (Battenhouse, 1964, p. 253). Battenhouse, known for his examinations of Shakespeare's plays through a moralizing, Christian lens, concludes that the plays 'offer one of the most grandly moral spectacles in the whole realm of English drama' (p. 258). He casts it as a tragedy of 'uncontrolled, misdirected, and diseased passions' (p. 239). But, as George Geckle points out, if the play is intended as an explicit moral lesson in the consequences of challenging the divine, it seems odd that the play does not state its agenda more explicitly. In view of the play's tendency to depict appeals to deities for protection or revenge elsewhere, this seems like a significant challenge to Battenhouse's conclusion (Geckle, 1988, p. 29).

Other critics have challenged the notion that *Tamburlaine* works as a *de casibus* tragedy; Irving Ribner argues instead that it is to be seen as a history play, one that attempts to deal with 'politics rather than ethics' (Ribner, 1953, p. 251). According to Ribner, the play's unusual approach to Fate and the implication of divinities in the lives of human beings is conditioned by its location within a classical, pre-Christian historical framework, where 'human action [is] based upon human will in a world ruled only by fortune, a fickle fortune whom the hero of history can master and bend to his will' (p. 254). In this system, there is no place for a divine plan. Accordingly, 'Marlowe's is a classical fortune, the capricious, lawless element in the universe which can be controlled and directed only by human wisdom and power' (p. 258). From this perspective, then, Marlowe's play is defiantly anti-Christian. There is certainly some evidence to support a reading of *Tamburlaine* as a re-affirmation of its author's supposed atheism, since almost invariably the calls for divine intervention seem to be ignored by a heaven indifferent to human plight. On the other hand, those who have argued that the play works within a moral and religious framework can point to the blasphemy of burning the Moslem holy books as evidence that Tamburlaine is punished, the sudden sickness that finally lays him low acting as Mahomet's revenge. It then remains to be explained why it is the Moslem, not the Christian, deity that intervenes.

What we can be certain of is that the endings of the two parts offer very different conclusions. While the first part ends with Tamburlaine consolidating his power and establishing a new order by his marriage to Zenocrate (a comedic ending), the second finds him defeated, finally, not by his mortal enemies but by the natural limitations of human endeav-our: age, disease and death (a tragic ending). Since it is a fairly safe assumption that Marlowe did not conceive the project as a two-part play in the first place, it would be unwise to read it as a carefully shaped moral tale that raises Tamburlaine up only to destroy him at the close of Part Two. It may be that Peter Hall is right when he describes it as an immoral play in a morality play structure, which 'sets out to prove that there is no God, no Jove, no Mohammed, no Nirvana'; that 'Man, for all his aspirations, ends up with Hitlers, Mussolinis, Tamburlaines' (cited in Cunningham & Warren, 1978, p. 160). Terry Hands chose not to end the play with Tamburlaine's dying assertion of his role (and the end of his performance) as the scourge of God. Instead, the focus was on his military achievements. A huge map used as a backdrop from the opening scene of Part Two had been displayed as a visual repres-entation of his many conquests. His final line cut, Anthony Sher's Tamburlaine slipped away with the repeated line 'and shall I die and this unconquered? Unconquered?' With his proud map used first to dis-play his conquests, and then to document the extent of his failure ('and shall I die and this unconquered?'), it finally becomes his funeral shroud, as God, or fate, or death, claims back its instrument.

CHAPTER 4

OF GODS AND MEN:
Doctor Faustus

'Devilish exercise'

Doctor Faustus is probably the most frequently performed of Marlowe's plays today; it also happens to be the one that has received most critical attention, not least on account of its complex history as a text – or rather as a series of different texts. Its narrative is simple. Doctor Faustus sells his soul to Lucifer in exchange for a period of 24 years, during which time the devil Mephistopheles will serve him and grant him all manner of wealth, power, and (supposedly) access to forbidden knowledge. Faustus fritters his time away in futile and frivolous pursuits, and, after a torturous final evening during which he realizes the enormity of his folly and the inevitability of his fate, the play ends with devils carrying him off to hell.

In one sense, it is the most archaic of Marlowe's works, predicated as it seems to be on an understanding of the world that takes for granted the existence of the supernatural realm. Indeed, physical reality and the spiritual cohabit the stage in a way that roots the play in the medieval tradition of mystery and morality drama, as we shall see. At the same time, it is also important to investigate how the play has retained its fascination for a modern audience in an age that has largely dispensed with the set of beliefs in which it is rooted. In act 1 scene 3, Faustus questions his devilish companion about the nature of heaven and hell: 'Where are you damned?' he asks him, and Mephistopheles replies: 'In hell.' Faustus pursues his questioning: 'How comes it then that thou art out of hell?' and the reply is: 'Why, this is hell, nor am I out of it' (A.1.3.75–8; B.73–5). The debate continues in act 2 scene 1 after Faustus has signed away his soul.

Faustus.	First will I question with thee about hell.
	Tell me, where is the place men call hell?
Mephistopheles.	Under the heavens.

Faustus.	Ay, but whereabout?
Mephistopheles.	Within the bowels of these elements,
	Where we are tortured and remain
	for ever.
	Hell hath no limits, nor is circumscribed
	In one self place, for where we are is hell,
	And where hell is must we ever be.

[A.2.1.119–26; B.118–25]

Our own time is often described in the West as a post-Christian age. But in the wake of the barbarism of the last century, which has seen slaughter on a scale so vast that it dwarfs earlier history, the notion of hell all around remains one that resonates powerfully.

Moreover, the myth of the man who sells his soul to the devil is one that has proved particularly resilient in Western culture, as well as passing into common parlance. The phrase 'selling one's soul' is a familiar, largely secularized expression. The concluding chapter, 'Marlowe in our time', traces some of the reverberations of this powerful myth, showing how the concept has seeped into an array of forms and genres. The range of references extends from the work of the great German playwright Goethe (1749–1832) to the mythology that emerged around the American blues singer Robert Johnson (1911–1938) who died, like Marlowe, tragically young, amidst stories of pacts with the devil. The controversial religious subject matter of *Faustus* certainly piqued the interest of the Master of the Revels (the state censor for the theatre) in early performances of the play. He seems to have decided that the play transgressed the act 'to restrain abuses of players', an act that outlawed the use of the holy Name of God or of Christ Jesus, or of the Holy Ghost or of the Trinity in stage plays (Chambers, 1945, IV, pp. 338–9). There is clear evidence of changes made to the text, or one version of it, on this account. Even in its censored version, however, the play remains remarkable for the way in which the immediate, imminent presence of the supernatural erupts into the physical realm, both in the direct representation of spiritual beings on stage, and in conversations between Faustus and Mephistopheles.

One more issue needs to be addressed before we move on to study the play in depth. *Doctor Faustus* has survived in two early versions. The first, which has been designated by scholars as the A-text, was first printed in 1604, with the so-called B-text making its first appearance in 1616. There are substantial differences between the two, with the B-text being nearly 600 lines longer (much of it comic business that scholars in the past have dismissed as interpolations), and with thousands of individual variants in words, phrases and punctuation. This makes preparing to write about *Doctor Faustus* a daunting experience. Precisely because of the textual problem, one walks around it, sizing it up from different angles, trying to find the best line of approach. Eric Rasmussen talks about his experience in editing the play for the Revels series, noting how he and David Bevington began with the intention of presenting the A-text, with the B-text additions printed in an appendix. But as work progressed, Rasmussen reports, they discovered that the 'fundamental differences between the original and the revised version proved so compelling that we abandoned our plans for a single-text edition' (Rasmussen, 1997, p. 459). In my own study of the play, my conclusion has been similar. In the light of what textual scholarship has been able to establish and, equally, in consideration of what has been left undecided, it seems to me that there are only two ways of writing about the play: the first is to write a chapter on each version; the second is to try to find a way of exploring the two alongside each other. Since much of the debate that follows depends on comparisons across the two versions, I have chosen the second option. The chapter is intended to work for those who are reading the play in its two versions, or at least with an awareness of and interest in the significance of the textual problem. Equally, since the discussion that follows clearly signposts references to the play with an 'A' or a 'B' before the act, scene and line numbers, those studying one of the texts in isolation will find it easy to locate the passages cited. (The edition I refer to is David Bevington and Eric Rasmussen's version mentioned above.) Bearing in mind all that has been said about authorship, and particularly in relation to *Faustus*, it is important to reiterate that the phrase 'Marlowe's play', which I will continue to use from time to time, is shorthand for a much more complex notion than those two words tend to imply.

The Faust legend and Marlowe's *Doctor Faustus*

The source for Marlowe's play was a book entitled *The History of the Damnable Life and Deserved Death of Doctor John Faustus*, written by an author we know only as 'P.F., *Gent.*' This was itself a translation of a German book first published in 1587, the *Historia von D. Johann Fausten* (it is worth noting that P.F.'s translation is, in parts, fairly liberal). The original version seems to have been something of a bestseller (in early modern terms) across Europe, skilfully playing on aspects of theology that were hotly contested at the time, and simultaneously offering a taste of the guilty pleasure of occultism. Johann Faust is a figure who occupies that grey area between history and myth. The archives at Heidelberg University do record the admission of a student of this name in 1509. There are a number of references to him in various documents in the first half of the sixteenth century, with different accounts of his exploits, some more outlandish than others. It may be this Faust who is described in a priest's letter (in 1513) as 'a certain soothsayer by the name of George Faust, the demigod of Heidelberg, a mere braggart and fool' (cited in Palmer & More, 1936, p. 87). He is thought to have died around 1540. The story of a magician and astrologer who sold his soul to the devil in exchange for knowledge and power proved a provocative one in every age of religious fervour and dissent and there were echoes of Faust in the tales told about a number of other famous magicians, coming both before and after: Simon Magus in the first century, Paracelsus in the early sixteenth, as well as the Italian Giordano Bruno and John Dee. Both Bruno and Dee were roughly contemporary with Marlowe, and both made a significant impact on English culture at the time, the former working in England between 1583 and 1585, and the latter being known as a favourite at the court of Elizabeth. In a culture that witnessed the death of at least 3000 people (predominantly women) convicted of witchcraft between 1542 and 1746 (Laurence, 1996, p. 218), the fear and fascination engendered by the occult were evidently very near the surface.

Just as Marlowe found it necessary to make some radical changes when adapting his sources for the story of *Edward II*, as we shall see later, so there were aspects of *The Damnable Life* that posed problems, albeit mostly of a very different kind. It seems likely that some of the changes P.F. made to his German source were due to fears of censorship: the German *Historia* is a heavy-handed, moralizing tale that sets up an arrogant and presumptuous Faustus for a long, spiritual fall. Michael Keefer has pointed out that a number of the episodes in the *Historia* can be traced back to Martin Luther's writings:

> Luther told a string of carnivalesque anecdotes – about a
> sorcerer who devoured a peasant together with his horse
> and wagon, a monk who offered another peasant a penny
> for all the hay he could eat and then consumed half a
> wagon-load before being beaten off, and a man who made

it seem that his leg had been pulled off by his Jewish
creditor and thus frightened him away.

[Keefer, 1991, p. xxxvii]

Keefer also notes that 'Luther was convinced that all magicians have a
pact with the devil' (p. xxxvii). The Lutheran flavour survives in the
English Faust-book, and although the didactic tone is attenuated somewhat, it still resides in the gist of the narrative. Chapter 62's title ('Here
followeth the miserable and lamentable end of Doctor Faustus, by the
which all Christians may take an example and warning') gives a clear
indication of P.F.'s stance. Marlowe's play does seem to be aware of the
sensitivity of some of the material, although, as so often with Marlowe's
work, it seems much more inclined to explore and exploit the controversial issues, particularly in terms of orthodoxy and heresy. It is less
cautious than the *English Faust-book*, and it is certainly harder to pin
down in terms of its moral perspective, although there are aspects (such
as its anti-Catholicism) which are concrete. The source is also revealing in the ways in which it may have shaped Marlowe's work: although
a number of critics have expressed dissatisfaction with the mixed mode
of the play, finding that the comic material sits uneasily alongside the
serious freight of the text, the *English Faust-book* is peppered with the
kind of tricks that crop up in both versions of Marlowe's play: chapter
titles include 'How Faustus served the drunken clowns', 'How Doctor
Faustus ate a load of hay' and 'How Doctor Faustus in the sight of the
Emperor conjured a pair of hart's horns upon a knight's head that slept
out of a casement'. This last incident (A.4.1.74–99; B.119–69) and the
trick played on the horse-courser (A.4.1.109–95; B.4.6.57–125) are both
taken directly from the *English Faust-book*. The tale of Faustus eating a
'monstrous' amount of hay is recounted by a Carter in B.4.5.24–32,
and his scene with the drunken clown figures also occurs only in the
B-text (B.4.6.57ff).

Marlowe seems to have done his best to shape the chronicle structure of the *Faust-book* into something that has a coherent and dramatic
pattern, although both the A-text and the B-text in places seem to sprawl,
peter out, or else skip like scratched records. Following the short
Prologue, Marlowe begins the action with Faustus seated 'in his study'
(A.1.1.0.*s.d.*), poring over his books. Having rapidly dismissed several
fields of scholarship, including divinity, with varying degrees of impatience and contempt, Faustus turns his attention to necromancy – black
magic. The first appearance of a good angel and a bad angel alerts us

to the way in which the play follows the medieval drama's tendency to allow the physical and spiritual worlds to coexist on the stage. It also warns us, in terms of the play itself, that Faustus is endangering his soul by pursuing his desire for forbidden knowledge. Spurred on by the magicians Valdes and Cornelius, Faustus determines to learn more of their art. In the second scene, a light-hearted subplot is initiated as Wagner, Faustus's servant, baffles two scholars with his twisted logic before revealing that Faustus is dining with Valdes and Cornelius; the scholars express their concern over Faustus's fate in such company. Underlining the point, the scene immediately following depicts Faustus's first conjuration. Drawing a circle and chanting a Latin spell, he summons Mephistopheles. Unable to bear the sight of the devil in his own shape, however, Faustus bids him return in the shape of an old Franciscan friar; the remark that 'That shape becomes a devil best' is an anti–Catholic jibe (A&B.1.3.27). When Mephistopheles returns, Faustus proceeds to question him about heaven and hell, before offering to make a pact with Lucifer: he will give his soul in exchange for an agreement that Mephistopheles will serve him for a period of 24 years. The final scene of act 1 (A&B.1.4) finds Wagner conjuring up two devils to torment the clown figure Robin, and coercing him into giving himself up to serve Wagner – a clear analogue to Marlowe's relationship with Mephistopheles.

Act 2 opens with Faustus once again in his study, summoning up the courage to complete the pact offered to Lucifer, which he proceeds to do, despite the best efforts of the Good Angel to dissuade him. He signs the bond in his own blood, heating it with a flame supplied by Mephistopheles when it coagulates, his blood apparently 'unwilling' to write the fateful letters. Mephistopheles offers Faustus a display of devils, who crown him and dress him 'in rich apparel' (A&B.2.1.82.*s.d.*). But what Faustus seems to thirst for most is knowledge hidden from mortal man, and he is frustrated by the evasive and prosaic answers to his questions about the nature of the earth, heaven and hell. We may begin to wonder what Faustus has gained from his bargain with the devil, if he is denied the wisdom for which he has raged from the opening moments of the play. The second scene of act 2 continues the comic foil to the main plot, with the stablemen Rafe and Robin discovering a book of spells. Act 2 scene 3 finds Faustus thrown into doubt over the decision he made so recklessly, but he is convinced that 'My heart's so hardened I cannot repent' (A&B.2.3.18). Frustrated by another fruitless interrogation of Mephistopheles, Faustus attempts to repent again, only to be confronted by the figures of Lucifer and Beelzebub, who put on for him a spectacular pageant of the seven deadly sins, which

Faustus declares 'feeds my soul!' (A.2.3.166). Act 3 opens with Wagner delivering a chorus-style summary of Faustus's journey through the skies in a dragon-drawn chariot (in the B-text the speech is given to a Chorus rather than Wagner), and sets the scene to follow: Rome on St Peter's Day. A scene of slapstick comedy and vitriolic satire of Catholic church-men ensues, as the solemn feast is disrupted by the invisible presence of Faustus and Mephistopheles. The B-text features its most signific-ant additional material at this point: disguised as cardinals, Faustus and Mephistopheles rescue Bruno, a rival pope elected by the German emperor, who has been taken prisoner by Pope Adrian. The familiar comic undercurrent returns in the concluding scene of act 3, with Rafe and Robin tormenting a vintner, and conjuring an exasperated Mephistopheles, who transforms them all into animals.

The fourth acts of the two versions differ most radically, although both are built around Faustus's visit to the palace of Emperor Charles V of Spain. The A-text begins with a chorus speech (missing in the B-text) which tells of the spread of Faustus's fame across 'every land'. At the emperor's request, Faustus summons the figures of Alexander the Great and his paramour. He then proceeds to humiliate a knight who insulted him by conjuring a pair of horns on his head, and, after the emperor has left, he plays a trick on a horse-dealer: selling him his animal for 40 dollars, Faustus warns the hourse-courser not to ride him into water. Faustus falls asleep in his chair (we are, all of a sudden, back in Wittenburg – the poor continuity may be due to the displacement of a scene), and a moment later the horse-courser returns, drenched, to tell the audience that, unable to resist the temptation to investigate Faustus's prohibition, he rode into a pond. The horse promptly turned into a bale of hay, leaving him half-drowned. Coming across Faustus asleep, the horse-courser attempts to wake him, tugging Faustus's leg which, bizarrely and grotesquely, comes away from his body. The courser, terri-fied, exits. Faustus seems none the worse for the attack ('Faustus has his leg again', he declares (4.1.186–7)). The following scene, 4.2, may well be displaced, since it seems to sit more happily amongst the earl-ier scenes, such as Faustus's visit to the court of Charles V. In any case, we now find Faustus using conjuring tricks to impress the Duke and Duchess of Vanholt, this time to offer the Duchess a dish of grapes in midwinter – another of his petty parlour games. The B-text extends the business with the humiliation of the knight (given a name, Benvolio), and his attempt to avenge himself on Faustus. It also develops the comic business with the horse-courser, offering Faustus further opportunities to perform his conjuring tricks on the clown figures of the play.

The final act opens with Wagner, alone, performing his Chorus function once more, this time setting the scene for Faustus's doom: 'I think my master means to die shortly, / For he hath given to me all his goods' (A.5.1.1–2). For the pleasure of three scholars Faustus conjures the ghost of Helen of Troy, according to Greek legend the most beautiful woman in the world, and the cause of the ten years' war that resulted in the destruction of the Trojan city. As they depart, an Old Man enters, and pleads with Faustus to repent. Faustus is dissuaded by Mephistopheles's threats, confirming his vow with Lucifer, which he again endorses with a signature in his own blood. In return, he receives Helen as his paramour. As he leaves the stage with her, the Old Man is menaced by devils, which are unable to touch him because of the strength of his faith. Act 5 scene 2 is the final scene in the A-text. Faustus talks with the scholars again, confessing his pact with the devil. They leave, promising to pray for him, and Faustus ekes out his last hour in spiritual torment, finally being dragged from the stage by Mephistopheles and his devils amidst thunder and lightning. A chorus rounds out the play with a warning to all those who would 'practise more than heavenly power permits' (A&B.Epilogue.8). In the B-text there is a short scene preceding the Epilogue which depicts the scholars discovering Faustus's dismembered body 'All torn asunder by the hand of death' (B.5.3.7).

The text: one play or two?

Doctor Faustus raises a number of very significant issues about the context of the theatre industry in which Marlowe worked. As I have already noted, its volatile nature as a text is a troublesome challenge to a straightforward understanding of the relationship between an author, a text, a playing company and the audiences, both theatrical and (later) literary. *Doctor Faustus* is by far the most slippery of Marlowe's plays in terms of its publication history. The debates over its position in the Marlowe canon have been protracted and remain inconclusive. Some claim with confidence that it is his last play, although these arguments are often based on suppositions of the 'maturity' of its style, or even the same kind of romantic thinking that finds it pleasing to represent *The Tempest* as Shakespeare's final play. There is indeed something aesthetically satisfying in understanding Prospero's renunciation of his magic as an analogue for the playwright's farewell to the stage in *The Tempest*, and in associating Faustus's end with Marlowe's own untimely death, but both views are based on the fallacy that life imitates art. There is in fact strong evidence to suggest that *Doctor Faustus* may have premièred as early as 1588–9, and this would place it before both *Edward II* and *The Massacre at Paris*; it is possible that it also predates *The Jew of Malta*. A number of plays dating from 1591 and 1592 contain passages that read as either imitations or parodies of Marlowe's style and subject matter in *Doctor Faustus*. Incidentally, one of the plays that seems to draw significantly on *Faustus* is a play called *The Taming of a Shrew*, which was a source for Shakespeare's much more famous text. The early version of the *Shrew* play probably dates from 1590 (Smith, 1979, p. 116).

The textual problem in *Faustus*, mentioned at the beginning of the chapter, remains central. The so-called 'A-text' was first printed in 1604, and reprinted in 1609 and 1611. The 'B-text' followed in 1616 and was reprinted at least six times over the next fifteen years. As the summary of the plot indicates, the third and fourth acts differ most profoundly, with the B-text extending the action considerably. Although the B-text omits 36 lines of the A-text, it includes over 600 'new' lines. The multitude of individual variants in words and typography are often trivial, but occasionally potentially crucial, as we shall see. Over the years, editors have sometimes been at a loss as to how to deal with the differences, probably because of a classical training which is preoccupied with the establishment of the one 'genuine' text. They have even conflated the two texts to produce what one of them, W.W. Greg, billed as a 'Conjectural Reconstruction' of the 'original' (Greg, 1950, title-page). Although the A-text has gradually superseded the B-text as the favoured version, editors of the play (like Rasmussen and Bevington) have most recently chosen to issue the two texts in one volume, recognizing that, in effect, we have two distinct plays. By presenting both, we can get a clearer idea of the different theatrical experiences that each version offered then, and may offer now in revival.

The very fact that we can present two versions of one play illuminates significant aspects of early modern theatre production. Even using the earliest text (1604), we know that what we have is the result of a collaboration: the theatrical manager Philip Henslowe paid two playwrights, William Bird and Samuel Rowley, £4 for additions made to the play in 1602 (though what those additions are we cannot know for sure). The collaborative nature of performance in the Elizabethan theatre is hard to overemphasize. A number of editors, most recently David Bevington and Eric Rasmussen, have followed Greg's supposition that 'Marlowe "planned the whole" and then farmed out certain scenes to another dramatist who worked with only an imprecise knowledge of what Marlowe was up to' (Bevington & Rasmussen, 1993, p. 71). The sudden shifts from tragic to comic mode that punctuate the play's sequence of scenes have often been noted, and even interpreted by some as evidence that they were written by different authors and then poorly spliced together. However, while these transitions may challenge some critics' notions of aesthetic balance and harmony, it is quite possible that they would have been perfectly acceptable to an Elizabethan audience unencumbered by such prejudices. Furthermore, a number of critics have argued that the B-text of *Doctor Faustus* has fallen victim to the censor. Michael Keefer points out that the Act of Abuses referred to above 'imposed heavy fines for profane references to God in stage plays', and *Faustus* would obviously have been a potential transgressor (Keefer, 1991, p. xiii). However, it is also important to recognize that the B-text we have inherited has not been thoroughly expurgated in this respect. In fact, the evidence suggests that the B-text is a compilation of several different revisions of the chimerical 'original'.

The critical debate over the two quartos, and the disputes over which is the more 'legitimate' version, is revealing inasmuch as the consensus tends to shift as fashions change in literary criticism. Leah Marcus (1996) pinpoints those critics who have expressed some dissatisfaction with the comic scenes: their objections tend to be founded on a perception of these passages as vulgar and lurid, and they generally conclude that the A-text (mostly free of such 'interludes') must be the more accurate version of the 'original'. Those preferring the B-text point out that it has a more coherent succession of scenes, and argue correspondingly that the A-text is, in terms of its structure, an incoherent jumble (Marcus, 1996, pp. 43–5). In general, Marcus finds that in the decades leading up to the late 1960s there was a general preference for the smoothness, polish and theatrical effect of the B-text. Crucial in the recuperation of the B-text after the A-text had dominated most of the play's publication history through the nineteenth and early twentieth centuries was the work of W.W. Greg. His contention that the A-text was an abridged version of the 'original' was massively influential. However, with the rise of critical movements challenging the 'establishment' (whether literary, cultural or societal), there was a shift towards reading texts of the early modern period for incoherence and dissidence, and the A-text crept back into favour. Marcus also suggests that the A-text's playing down of theatre spectacle, and a closer concentration on psychology and introspection, suited the mood both of the avant-garde theatre of the time and this 'emerging generation of young scholars of the Vietnam era' (ibid., p. 44). At the turn of the millennium the

A-text is firmly in favour. However, it is perhaps in keeping with a postmodern aesthetic that it is now often considered most appropriate to publish the two versions together and steer away from qualitative debates over the relative merits of each one.

Faustus as tragic hero

Doctor Faustus represents a transition between dominant modes of drama, straddling as it does the medieval tradition and the emergent genre of Elizabethan tragedy. Medieval drama is populated chiefly by virtues, vices, angels and devils (entities that would today be understood largely as mythical figures and abstract terms), and in these plays it is man who is the abstraction. The 'Everyman' figure (the closest we get to a 'hero') is not an individual 'character', but an allegorical representation of sinful humankind. *Doctor Faustus* features devils and angels, as well as the seven deadly sins, and manifestations of mythical figures such as Helen of Troy. Faustus is attended by a Good Angel and an Evil Angel who appear to warn him and tempt him respectively of the implications of his pursuits at crucial moments: when he is first motivated to investigate necromancy further in the first scene, when he wavers in his resolve at the beginning of the second act, and when he is moved to repent in act 2 scene 3. The spiritual battle is being played out in a way that resembles the Morality play form – good and evil are personified and clearly represented by actors on the stage.

At the same time, while predicating its action and its significance on the reality of the supernatural, Marlowe's play can be seen, paradoxically, as deeply sceptical. 'Come,' says Faustus to the devil Mephistopheles, 'I think hell's a fable' (A&B.2.1.130). Whether or not we conclude that Faustus is foolish to scoff at the notions of damnation and hell while talking to one of its inhabitants, we can recognize the text's daring in the way it allows Faustus room for such radical scepticism. Some critics, spurred on by contemporary 'evidence' of the kind I have cited, choose to frame the play as a daring expression of Marlowe's own atheism. The close association of author and text is problematic, as we have already seen, and perhaps a more helpful approach would be to try to understand the text (rather than its author) in the context of its composition, production and consumption in Elizabethan England. A clearer conception of the way in which the play is implicated in (and intervenes in) the theological controversy and wider

crisis of religious belief in early modern culture might help us towards
a fuller understanding of its significance, and we will return to this in
due course.

Although it certainly incorporates elements of the medieval tradition, particularly in its form, the title-page of both A-text and B-text
refers to it as a 'tragical history'. Its interstitial status is perhaps one of
the reasons for the extraordinary range of readings that have proliferated in literary and theatrical investigations of the play. Earlier in the
twentieth century, a number of key Marlowe scholars opted to interpret the figure of Faustus as a tragic hero in Aristotelian mode, and
from this approach emerged the idea of the Marlovian hero as essentially a tragic figure doomed by his ambition, by his determination
to push back the boundaries of human experience or achievement.
Intent on establishing an overall pattern to his work, critics such as Harry
Levin (whose study of Marlowe, published in 1952, was entitled *The
Overreacher*) argued that all of Marlowe's tragic heroes are victims of this
same fault, usefully encapsulated in the Prologue to *Doctor Faustus* by
the reference to the Icarus myth. According to Greek legend, Icarus,
son of Daedalus, flew with his father from the island of Crete on wings
that his father had constructed for them. When Icarus, ignoring his father's
instructions, flew too close to the sun, the wax holding the wings together
melted, and he fell into the Aegean Sea and drowned. Hence the lines
towards the end of the Prologue:

> Till, swollen with cunning of a self-conceit,
> His waxen wings did mount above his reach,
> And melting, heavens conspired his overthrow;

> [Prologue: A.20–2; B.19–21]

Later in the play, the Chorus recounts some of Faustus's exploits:

> Learned Faustus,
> To find the secrets of astronomy
> Graven in the book of Jove's high firmament,
> Did mount him up to scale Olympus' top,
> Where, sitting in a chariot burning bright
> Drawn by the strength of yoked dragons' necks,
> He views the clouds, the planets, and the stars,
> The tropics, zones, and quarters of the sky,

From the bright circle of the hornèd moon
Even to the height of *Primum Mobile*;

[B.3.Chorus.1–10]

The passage (which also features in a slightly truncated form in the A-text) inevitably recalls the reference to the 'overreacher' Icarus, made in the play's Prologue. The traditional reading, then, draws upon a pattern of tragedy that is familiar from the Greek tragic model of *hubris*: the presumptuous human is punished for the pride he displays in daring to challenge (in the case of Faustus) God's law.

The Brazilian theatre practitioner and theoretician Augusto Boal (1931–) has traced the Aristotelian model of tragedy through its various stages in his seminal work *Theatre of the Oppressed* (1974). Although this kind of *schema* has been analysed many times before, Boal interprets it from a very specific perspective, one that follows Brecht in being predicated on the notion that all theatre is political. Around the time that Boal emerged as a key practitioner in Brazil in the 1960s, the country was in the grip of General Castello Branco's harsh military dictatorship, and, in a climate of repression and tough censorship, Boal's unwavering commitment to a Marxist social ethic led to his arrest, torture and imprisonment. After his release he continued his work in exile, chiefly in Argentina. In the meantime, the growing popularity of his work, in particular his seminal *Games for Actors and Non-Actors* (1989), meant that his theories eventually had a global impact. Knowing his background, it should not surprise us that Boal understands theatre as a weapon that must be fought for: 'the ruling classes strive to take permanent hold of the theater and utilize it as a tool for domination . . . But the theater can also be a weapon of liberation' (Boal, 1979, unpaginated Foreword). His ideas relate fairly closely to the critical perspectives we have already explored which situate the theatre in terms of its relations to the state and the ruling class, as well as ideological formations more generally. What he concludes from his study of Aristotle can be helpful in interpreting both Marlowe's work and his personality – or the stories of his personality that circulate. At the same time, we should read Boal's interpretation of Aristotle with a degree of circumspection, since it has been criticized by many as a rather perverse misreading of the *Poetics*.

According to Boal, the Aristotelian model begins with the 'stimulation' of the *hamartia* (the hero's 'tragic flaw'), and is followed by *peripeteia* (consequent radical change in destiny), *anagnorisis* (character's recognition

111

of the flaw and the error it has caused), and *catastrophe* – the tragic con-clusion. What follows for the audience is *catharsis* – 'the spectator, terrified by the spectacle of the catastrophe, is purified of his hamartia' (Boal, 1979, p. 37). Boal goes on to illustrate the political conservatism of this kind of model, which serves to purge a society of its anti-social elements:

> Let there be no doubt: Aristotle formulated a very powerful purgative system, the objective of which is to eliminate all that is not commonly accepted, including the revolution, before it takes place. . . . It appears in many and varied shapes and media. But its essence does not change: it is designed to bridle the individual, to adjust him to what pre-exists.

[ibid., p. 47]

There is a good deal here to quibble over. Boal does not do justice to the complexity of the *Poetics* in his polemic, and he implies that the *Poetics* created 'rules' for playwrights, when in fact Aristotle was merely analysing existing works: he was being diagnostic rather than prescript-ive. However, the force of Boal's argument, if only in a rhetorical sense, makes it worthy of our attention. The principle he is proposing – that tragedy aims to shut down the impulse to transcend existing circum-stances – is a powerful one, even if we disagree in a technical sense with his interpretation of Aristotle.

It is interesting that even the most romantic of myth-makers who lionize Faustus, and Marlowe, essentially reiterate Boal's point. The essay-ist William Hazlitt, writing around 1820, refers to Faustus as 'a per-sonification of the pride of will and eagerness of curiosity . . . devoured by a tormenting desire to enlarge his knowledge to the utmost bounds of nature and art' (cited in MacLure, 1995, pp. 78–9). A number of critics since have sought to cast Faustus in a similar mould, and Harry Levin takes the logic one step further, drawing parallels not only between Faustus and other Marlovian heroes such as Tamburlaine and Barabas, but also between Faustus and Marlowe himself. Levin picks up on T.S. Eliot's use of the term 'negative capability', a phrase first coined by the poet John Keats, but used by Eliot to define Shakespeare's 'capa-city for effacing his own personality behind his varied and vivid *dra-matis personae*'. If Shakespeare is unique for his 'negative capability', Levin argues, then Marlowe may be singled out for his 'positive capability':

'where Shakespeare is everybody, Marlowe is always himself' (Levin, 1964, p. 26). The temptation to interpret Marlowe's own personality in relation to the characters he created, particularly Faustus, has proved an irresistible one for many critics. As we saw at the beginning of the chapter, there is a tendency among the romantically minded to link Faustus's rejection of God with Marlowe's atheism. Levin's argument is slightly more sophisticated, but displays a similar inclination towards myth-making. For Levin, Marlowe is classified as one afflicted by an 'Icarus complex'. Levin continues: 'The disposition to isolate one's self on a higher plane, while attracting the admiration of others, is not an infrequent pattern of motivation . . . Since Icarus was the archetype of the overreacher, Marlowe was by temperament a tragedian' (Levin, 1952, p. 183). Paul H. Kocher prefers to see the impulse more in terms of religious heterodoxy, interpreting Faustus as a testimony to Marlowe's 'unremitting warfare with Christianity' (Kocher, 1946, p. 330). The consensus of critical opinion on *Faustus* has certainly toed the Aristotelian line, and this has implications for both popular representations of Marlowe (the radical atheist ultimately paying the price for his subversive impulses) and our understanding of Faustus himself. Whether Faustus is cast as Prometheus (the titan of Greek mythology who incurred the wrath of the gods for daring to bring fire to humankind) or Icarus, the upshot of his fate is the same: if we accept Boal's model of tragedy, the conclusion in either case is one of containment of a threat to the status quo.

Setting aside the Aristotelian model of the tragic hero, and the way it has been reinterpreted by Boal's work, there are other grounds on which we might challenge the interpretation of *Doctor Faustus* from this rigidly character-based perspective. I have argued in chapter 2 that the tendency to interpret the *dramatis personae* of an early modern play from a modern perspective, taking no account of the difficulties involved in bridging that 400-year gap, is a flawed strategy (see pp. 57–61). Having said that, it is undeniable that there are traits and tendencies in the 'character' of John Faustus that allow us to construct some semblance of interiority and even psychological consistency. The opening scene is a useful illustration: in a cleverly condensed, compact snapshot of his behaviour throughout the play, we find Faustus flitting from Aristotle's works ('Sweet *Analytics*, 'tis thou hast ravished me!' (A&B.1.1.6)), through Claudius Galenus ('Galen'), the Greek physician of the second century AD, and on to the sixth-century emperor Justinian, famed for his codification of law, concluding with Jerome's Bible, all in the space of 50 lines. The first, breathless tour through various diverse fields of study – logic, medicine, law and divinity – seems to establish Faustus's impressive intellectual credentials. But at the same time, we cannot ignore the speed with which he dismisses each in turn: logic is beneath him ('A greater subject fitteth Faustus' wit', A&B.1.1.11); since medicine cannot raise a man to life again, it is not worthy of his esteem ('Physic, farewell!', A.1.1.27; B.25); and the law is 'too servile and illiberal for me' (A.1.1.36; B.34).

His dismissal of divinity – religious knowledge – is not as swift, though it is equally vehement when it does come. Matching two disparate quotations from separate books of the Bible, he points out that, on the one hand, 'The reward of sin is death' (translating Romans 6.2), but on the other, quoting 1 John 1.8, 'If we say that we have no sin, / We deceive ourselves, and there's no truth in us' (A.1.1.44–5; B.42–3). Faustus, apparently putting two and two together and coming up with something other than four, concludes that 'Why then belike we must sin, / And so consequently die' (A.1.1.46–7; B.44–5). Some have suggested that this is an illustration of Faustus's foolishness, in spite of his supposed great learning: since the next verse of 1 John 1 is 'If we confess our sins, he is faithful and just to forgive us our sins, and to cleanse us from all unrighteousness', it is clear that Faustus's conclusion is poorly founded. The B-text provides another explanation by including a speech in which Mephistopheles tells Faustus that 'When thou took'st the book / To view the Scriptures, then I turned the leaves / And led thine eye' (B.5.2.99–101). This has implications for the extent to which Faustus has control over his own fate, and the power God and the devil have over the choices he makes, as well as the exact nature of the relationship between divine and infernal influences. On the other hand, we could read Faustus's reaction to these scriptures as evidence of a scepticism on the part of Faustus himself, with the threading together of the two quotations showing our scholar laughing at the illogic of scriptural 'authority'. The range of different answers to these questions keys us into the way the text, or texts, function as sites where divergent theologies engage in battle, both with each other and, at the same time, with an emerging radical scepticism.

Our focus on Faustus himself, and the temptation to believe that we can lay a firm conceptual hold on him by interpreting him as a three-dimensional 'real' character, tends to underestimate the significance of those *dramatis personae* that we would, equally instinctively, dismiss as allegorical. While recognizing the dangers of generalization, it is fair to say that many members of Marlowe's original audience would have understood the spiritual realm as equally real as, or more real than, the physical, material realm. A few accounts of contemporary, or nearly contemporary, performances exist, and the descriptions of audience behaviour provide some evidence to support this idea. The first is an intriguing passage in William Prynne's *Histriomastix*, a polemic against playhouses published in 1633, where Prynne refers to

> The visible apparition of the Devil on the stage at the Belsavage Play-house, in Queen Elizabeth's days (to the great amazement both of the actors and spectators) while they were there profanely playing the History of Faustus (the truth of which I have heard from many now alive, who well remember it) there being some distracted with that fearful sight. . . .

[cited in Chambers, 1945, III, pp. 423–4]

Thomas Middleton writes in *The Black Book* (1604) of a performance of the play 'when the old Theatre cracked and frighted the audience', and another report of uncertain date describes a performance in Exeter:

> as a certain number of Devils kept every one his circle there, and as Faustus was busy in his magical invocations, on a sudden they [the actors] were all dashed, every one hearkening other in the ear, for they were all persuaded, there was one devil too many amongst them; and so after a little pause desired the people to pardon them, they could go no further with this matter; the people also understanding the thing as it was, every man hastened to be first out of doors.

[cited in ibid., p. 424]

John Aubrey, writing around 1673, associated the story with Edward Alleyn himself, and so with the earliest performances of the play (ibid.). These tales suggest a degree of superstition that would be part of a mindset still very heavily conditioned by orthodox Christianity, and the associated beliefs that had sprung up around official doctrine. However, the stories need to be contextualized – Prynne's in particular can be recognized relatively easily as serving his own agenda, which was to shut down the playhouses altogether. Through the lens of a fanatical Puritanism, playhouses were seen as places of riot, debauchery and sexual licence. Prynne himself made the mistake of offending Queen Henrietta Maria by criticizing the appearances of women in some court masques after she had herself appeared in a rehearsal at court of *Shepherd's Pastoral*; Prynne was arrested, had his ears cut off, and was imprisoned, though he would live to fight another day. While Prynne's story is relatively easy to contextualize, Middleton's reference is made very much in passing, and the account of the Exeter performance is impossible to date, besides which it seems very much anecdotal (Aubrey's association of the supposed incident with Alleyn himself is fanciful). Even if we could establish that audiences did respond in some kind of hysterical fashion to a performance of *Faustus*, one must take account of the fact that being a member of a theatre audience can in itself entail a sense of 'performance' – audiences tend to respond not only to one another's reactions, but also according to their own anticipations, and what they may feel is expected of them: anyone who has attended a screening of a horror film in a packed cinema will be familiar with the phenomenon.

However, while it is important to recognize that the accounts of devilish manifestations at performances of *Faustus* may be unreliable for all sorts of reasons, it is still likely that an acceptance of the supernatural realm would have remained a dominant (and certainly more than a residual) part of the culture of Marlowe's time. That said, we would be unwise to assume that such unquestioning belief was universal. As Wilbur Sanders makes clear, in quoting Thomas More (1520), Thomas Nashe (1594) and Edward Jorden (1603), there was certainly an undercurrent of scepticism: discussing these writers, Sanders concludes that 'The progressive weakening of old superstition is often signalled by a new kind of flippancy about the devil' (Sanders, 1968, p. 196). Today, the good and bad spirits that populate medieval plays, and who appear also in *Faustus*, would tend to be interpreted unhesitatingly as metaphorical figures. Even the representation of the human presented in *Faustus* is something that is, in one sense, far removed from our own understanding. In the universe the play depicts, the human is dualistic, made up of conflicting, opposing principles, whether that be understood in terms of the will to do good and the will to do evil, or the body (with its earthly desires) and the soul (with its heavenly aspirations). The division between the two halves is what opens up the human being to the possibility of damnation and salvation. Although the theology that underpins the play is hard to determine with precision – hence the proliferation of scholarly investigations into it – it is undeniable that the play is deeply engaged with these issues.

'I do repent, and yet I do despair'

We have already established that Marlowe lived and worked in a climate of bitter religious controversy, and it seems likely that he was himself, at least for a time, very actively involved at points where bitterly opposed factions met and fought. Battle was engaged between Protestantism and Catholicism, as we have already seen. At the time Marlowe was writing, England was predominantly Calvinist: movements within the Reformation camp meant that the Puritans were turning their face against the ritual and liturgy of some of the more moderate Protestant traditions, which they denounced as papist. The Pope, whom the Catholics identified as the spiritual descendant of St Peter, the founder of the Christian church, was regarded by many Protestants as the anti-Christ. Jonathan Dollimore's seminal work *Radical Tragedy* (1984, revised 1989) explores how, in the literature and especially the drama of the Elizabethan/ Jacobean period, the notion of providence – the idea that God is in ultimate control of human fate, including the individual fates of each one of us – comes under scrutiny. When considering the expectations of an Elizabethan audience, it is a fair (though by no means indisputable) assumption that the narrative of *Doctor Faustus*, once the hero has signed the pact with the devil, would have been shaped according to the spectators' understanding of Faustus's capacity for repentance and salvation, and it is likely that there would have been significant differences in opinion amongst the members of that audience. Much of the drama of both the A-text and the B-text is built around the vacillation between hope and despair. However, the complexity of differing, and mutually incompatible, beliefs about damnation is also brought to light by a *comparison* of the two versions of the play. It has even been contended that one of the main reasons for the alterations to the play for the edition we know as the B-text was to adapt it according to the prevailing orthodoxy.

It is generally agreed that, of the two versions, the A-text is the more unforgiving, and the debate crystallizes around one line in act 2 scene 3. In the A-text, as Faustus is tempted to turn back to God, the Evil Angel slams him down: 'Too late'; to which the Good Angel responds: 'Never too late, if Faustus can repent' (A.2.3.78–9). In the B-text the line contains a tiny but crucial alteration: 'Never too late, if Faustus will repent' (B.2.3.80, my emphasis) – and in that one word inheres a huge theological gulf. The B-text locates agency within the human subject (Faustus), implying that, if he is willing to repent, then he will find forgiveness and salvation. The A-text, however, poses the dilemma as something that may be beyond Faustus's control: although we might choose to interpret the word 'can' as simply another way of asking the same question — 'will he repent? Can he bring himself to repent?' — it may also carry the existential sense of 'is it possible for him to repent (even if he wanted to)?' On the other hand, bearing in mind the roots of the word 'can', which carry the sense of 'knowing how to' (hence the Scottish 'ken' and the term 'canny'), the distinction between the two versions may be between being willing to repent, and being aware of the path to redemption.

The centrality of the doctrine of predestination in Europe at this time is due largely to the work of Jean Calvin (1509–1564), who published his *Institutes of Christian Religion* in 1536. First translated into English by Thomas Norton in 1561, it was to prove hugely influential in Protestant England and, more widely, across Europe. According to Calvin, God's omniscience meant that he had foreknowledge of the fall of mankind; hence every human being was predestined either for damnation or salvation, with the majority falling into the category of reprobate — the damned. For these souls, nothing they said or did could alter their predetermined fate. But this concept of God, which might strike us today as perverse, is even more disturbing than it first appears. According to the *Institutes:*

> Whereas therefore the reprobate do not obey the word
> of God opened unto them, that shall be well imputed to
> the malice and perverseness of their heart, so that this be
> therewithal added: that they are therefore given into this
> perverseness because by the righteous but yet unsearchable
> judgment of God they are raised up to set forth his glory
> with their damnation.

[3.24.14; Calvin, 1961, p. 981]

Alan Sinfield also quotes Calvin's *Institutes* in his discussion of *Faustus*, tracing Calvin's line on predestination back to Luther and Luther's citation of Romans 9.18: 'Therefore hath he mercy on whom he will have mercy, and whom he will he hardeneth.' Calvin's position seems to be a reassertion of this version of God, a divinity seemingly both arbitrary and beyond questioning: ' "When God is said to visit in mercy or harden whom he will, men are reminded that they are not to seek for any cause beyond his will" (*Institutes* 3.22.11)' (Sinfield, 1992, p. 233).

In the light of this, what are we to make of Faustus's resolve to renounce his magic and repent in act 2 scene 3? Here, the Good Angel encourages him to believe that God will pity him, and the Evil Angel intervenes at once, snapping, 'Thou art a spirit. God cannot pity thee'. Faustus retaliates with desperate repetition: 'Be I a devil, yet God may pity me; / Ay, God will pity me if I repent' (A&B.2.3.12–15). The Evil Angel's parting shot is, perhaps, the Calvinist response: 'Ay, but Faustus never shall repent' (A&B.2.3.17). The angels then leave the stage, and a performance of the moment that follows would either depict Faustus offering grim assent to the Evil Angel's words, or else find him on his knees struggling to pray and repent before the final, terrible realization: 'My heart's so hardened that I cannot repent' (A&B.2.3.18). In the first case, Faustus confronts the Calvinist God who has damned him to his fate before he was born; in the second, the centrality of human agency is restated, and the potential for tragedy restored. A soul that is destined to be damned is simply a pitiable spectacle, containing very little one could call tragic or even dramatic. Only when we understand Faustus as one who chooses his alliance with the devil, realizes the consequences of his actions, and then chooses to believe that God is incapable of extending forgiveness to him, do we have potential for real dramatic engagement. A couple of the most renowned lines in the play beautifully encapsulate Faustus's position in relation to salvation and damnation. Presented with the figure of Helen of Troy, Faustus pleads:

Sweet Helen, make me immortal with a kiss.

[*They kiss.*]

Her lips suck forth my soul. See where it flies!

[A.5.1.93–4; B.96–7]

The first line ironizes Faustus's predicament: he seeks immortality as his doom approaches, but, characteristically, seeks it in a very earthly, transient pleasure. The second line mingles ecstasy and despair, the heavy stresses in the middle of the line rendering a powerful impression of regret and a yearning to linger in that inevitably fleeting moment. Even on the brink of damnation, Faustus looks to mortal love, or satisfaction of his lusts, for salvation.

The further we delve into the two texts, the more complex becomes the triangular relationship between the two versions and the theological conflicts with which they engage. In neither version does the fact that Faustus has conjured Mephistopheles seem to count as a spiritual crime that would damn him; as Mephistopheles says (the speech is virtually identical in both texts):

> For when we hear one rack the name of God,
> Abjure the Scriptures and his Saviour Christ,
> We fly in hope to get his glorious soul,
> Nor will we come unless he use such means
> Whereby he is in danger to be damned.

[A.1.3.48–52; B.45–9]

Faustus's perspective, however, seems not to accord with Mephistopheles's, for within 40 lines of the devil's pronouncement, he offers a very different interpretation (again, the lines are duplicated in the B-text):

> Seeing Faustus hath incurred eternal death
> By desp'rate thoughts against Jove's deity,
> Say he surrenders up to him his soul,
> So he will spare him four-and-twenty years . . .

[A.1.3.90–3; B.87–90]

Faustus, it seems, is convinced that his soul is already forfeit, a conviction he restates at the beginning of the second act:

> Now, Faustus, must thou needs be damned,
> And canst thou not be saved.
> What boots it then to think of God or heaven?

[A.2.1.1–3]

Bevington and Rasmussen choose to omit a question mark that is printed in the A-text at the end of the second line – 'And canst thou not be saved?' They suggest that it 'probably should be regarded as an accidental anticipation of that in 1.3' (Bevington & Rasmussen, 1993, p. 138n.). They also point out that question marks are often intended as exclamation marks in texts of this period. Although the status of such typographical details is notoriously tricky, the question marks are crucial; Bevington and Rasmussen choose to omit the question marks in the A-text but allow them to stand in the B-text, and render quite a different meaning:

Now, Faustus, must thou needs be damned?
And canst thou not be saved?
What boots it then to think on God or heaven?

[B.2.1.1–2]

Although the conclusion is the same – surrender – the B-text, as presented in this edition, offers a ray of hope that the A-text shuts out, suggesting that the A-text may be the more rigidly Calvinist of the two. However, these kinds of deductions, once again, remain frustratingly inconclusive. The fact that different critics have identified each of the texts as more Calvinist than the other should alert us to the pitfalls of trying to pin down each version in doctrinal terms. As Faustus's fate begins to seal around him, for instance, in the B-text (but not the A-text) we find Mephistopheles gloating over the part he has played in his damnation:

'Twas I that, when thou wert i'the way to heaven,
Dammed up thy passage. When thou took'st the book
To view the Scriptures, then I turned the leaves
And led thine eye.

[B.5.2.98–101]

The Good Angel goes on to assure Faustus (now it is too late) that 'Hadst thou affected sweet divinity, / Hell or the devil had had no power on thee' (B.5.2.113–14). To reinforce the point, a throne 'descends' at this moment, a signifier of the heaven Faustus has refused (or been shut out of), and then disappears again at the end of the Good Angel's speech: 'The jaws of hell are open to receive thee', he is told (B.5.2.120). The final appearance that the angels make in the B-text, which seems to underline the certainty of Faustus's doom, does not occur in the earlier version.

The Calvinist, determinist universe has troubling implications for our understanding of the relationship between God and the devil. If God has established from the beginning of time that some are to be saved and some are to be damned, then it is difficult not to see this entrapment of Faustus as one ultimately determined by the divine will, using Mephistopheles as its instrument. Just as the Old Man who comes to counsel Faustus as he hurtles towards his doom cannot be harmed by the devils, destined as he is for salvation – 'His faith is great',

Mephistopheles tells Faustus, 'I cannot touch his soul' (A.5.1.79; B.5.1.82) – so there is nothing that can save Faustus. 'Faustus' offence can ne'er be pardoned', Faustus asserts. 'The serpent that tempted Eve may be saved, but not Faustus' (A.5.2.15–16; B.44–5). In a performance of the A-text, there is some room to interpret Faustus as one who is deceiving himself, committing the ultimate sin of despair that would put his sins beyond the bounds of God's forgiveness. The B-text, however, stipulates the physical presence of Lucifer, Mephistopheles and Beelzebub on stage (they enter, to the sound of thunder, at the beginning of act 5 scene 2). When Faustus tries to beg for God's mercy, he cries, 'O, he stays my tongue! I would lift up my hands, but see, they hold 'em, they hold 'em' (A.5.2.32–4; B.61–3), and, with the devils present, it is clearly possible to stage the moment with them physically holding him back. In the A-text these horrors remain demons of Faustus's mind, and we can understand his predicament as one he is interpreting – and so perhaps misinterpreting – as irredeemable. By contrast, the B-text is more emphatic about his fate by virtue of having the devils present on stage, and it continues in the same vein as Faustus rushes to his grim end. The final sequence is drawn out and elaborated in the B-text: a stage direction reads, '*Hell is discovered*', and the Bad Angel proceeds to describe the 'vast perpetual torture-house' beyond its jaws (B.5.2.122). Faustus protests that 'I have seen enough to torture me', but, with a relish that is familiar from the moralizing of the *Faust-book*, the Bad Angel replies: 'Nay, thou must feel them, taste the smart of all. / He that loves pleasure must for pleasure fall.'

While the B-text does extend Faustus's torment in his last moments, it also edits some of the A-text's lines, probably showing the scars of the censor's cuts; so, the A-text's justly famous lines:

> O, I'll leap up to my God! Who pulls me down?
> See, see where Christ's blood streams in the firmament!
> One drop would save my soul, half a drop. Ah, my Christ!

> [A.5.2.77–9]

become in the B-text:

> O, I'll leap up to heaven! Who pulls me down?
> One drop of blood will save me. O, my Christ!

> [B.5.2.150–1]

In both, the vision of salvation is swiftly replaced by something even more terrifying than the perspective on hell he has been offered – in the B-text it is 'a threat'ning arm, an angry brow', and 'the heavy wrath of heaven' (B.5.2.155, 157); in the other version it is a more explicit vengeful deity:

> . . . and see where God
> Stretcheth out his arm and bends his ireful brows!
> Mountains and hills, come, come and fall on me,
> And hide me from the heavy wrath of God!

[A.5.2.82–5]

It is an intensely theatrical moment. Nigel Alexander describes the ingeniously devised climax to the 1968 RSC production directed by Clifford Williams:

> Faustus finished his final speech grovelling in abject terror
> on the ground. The clock finished striking. Nothing
> happened. After a long moment Faustus raised his head
> and looked round the totally empty stage. He started to
> laugh. As he reached the hysteria of relief, the back wall
> of the stage gave way and fell forward in sections revealing
> an ominous red glow and a set of spikes like the dragon's
> teeth of the Siegfried Line. The denizens of hell emerged
> with a kind of slow continuous shuffle until Faustus was
> surrounded by a circle of these skeletal figures – including
> the seven deadly sins. He was then seized and carried
> shrieking through the teeth of hell mouth which closed
> leaving the wall of Faustus's study again intact.

[Alexander, 1971, p. 341]

Faustus's final words, as the devils take the stage to lay hold of him, are a desperate pledge, all too late, that he will burn his books. His last gasp is, 'Ah, Mephistopheles!' (A.5.2.123) – perhaps a curse, perhaps a sudden and final vain hope that his devilish companion may save him – this companion who has been 'sweet Mephistopheles' (A.2.1.148; A.5.1.70; B.5.1.73), 'my Mephistopheles' (A.2.3.30; B.2.3.28), and 'my good Mephistopheles' (A&B.3.1.1). Some productions, notably Barry Kyle's version for the RSC in 1989, have even chosen to add homoerotic overtones to the relationship between the two of them, emphasizing the sense of betrayal at the climax of the play.

The B-text includes a short scene depicting the aftermath, deriving its detail fairly directly from the *Faust-book* source:

> But when it was day, the students, that had taken no rest that night, arose and went into the hall in the which they left Doctor Faustus, where notwithstanding they found no Faustus, but all the hall lay besprinkled with blood, his brains cleaving to the wall; for the devil had beaten him from one wall against another. In one corner lay his eyes, in another his teeth, a pitiful and fearful sight to behold. Then began the students to bewail and weep for him, and sought for his body in many places; lastly they came into the yard where they found his body lying on the horse dung, most monstrously torn and fearful to behold, for his head and all his joints were dashed in pieces.

[cited in Thomas & Tydeman, 1994, p. 237]

Jonathan Dollimore points out that Faustus, at the point of his destruction, is located at the intersection of the forces of good and evil: between them, God and Lucifer destroy him. 'God and Lucifer seem equally responsible in his final destruction', Dollimore writes, 'two supreme agents of power deeply antagonistic to each other yet temporarily co-operating in his demise' (Dollimore, 1989, p. 111). This kind of interpretation of the implications of Faustus's fate seems to have informed a 1963 production of the play staged by the Polish director Jerzy Grotowski (1933–1999). Grotowski's montage adaptation of the original posits Faustus as a martyr, one who 'must rebel against God, Creator of the world, because the laws of the world are traps contradicting morality and truth' (Grotowski, 1964, p. 121). Taking its cue from Faustus's select-ive quotations ('the reward of sin is death . . .'), the conclusion drawn by Grotowski's programme notes is that 'Whatever we do – good or bad – we are damned . . . God's laws are lies, He spies on the dishonour in our souls the better to damn us' (p. 121). In the final scene, the speeches that in the original depict Faustus pleading for mercy, for time to stop, and then for the earth to swallow him, become the 'last, and most out-rageous provocation of God' (p. 129); Faustus's death and damnation become a martyrdom, as Faustus demonstrates how God 'ambushes' man – arguing that if he were truly merciful and omnipotent, he would rescue him at the moment of his damnation. The climax shows Faustus 'in a rapture', his 'ecstasy . . . transformed into his Passion'; he is 'ready for his martyrdom: eternal damnation', and his final cries are 'the piercing, pitiable shrieks of an animal caught in a trap'. Faustus is carried off by the two actors playing Mephistopheles to his eternal damnation, 'as a sacrificial animal is carried, as one is dragged to the Cross' (p. 133). Grotowski stages explicitly the Calvinist theology of predestination and makes Faustus the martyr of a spiteful deity.

'By their folly make us merriment': *Faustus* as comedy

I have already explained that *Doctor Faustus* has a particularly complex textual history. The scenes in the play that seem to function as comic, burlesque interludes have been read by some as interventions in the 'original' text – farcical skits introduced to liven up the serious main plot of Faustus's damnation. In terms of performance, the comic scenes are often the first to be edited when the text is cut for production. John

Ian McKellen as Faustus (left), Emrys James as Mephistopheles in the RSC production of *Doctor Faustus* (dir. John Barton), Aldwych & Tour, 1974. (Photographer: Joe Cocks. Reproduced by courtesy of the Shakespeare Centre Library: Joe Cocks Studio Collection.)

Barton, directing Ian McKellen as Faustus in Edinburgh (premièred 26 August 1974) and then in London, excised most of the comic business on the basis that, though these interludes succeed in showing 'the abuse of necromantic powers in trivial pranks, in practice they tend to trivialize the tone of the play itself' (cited in Tydeman, 1984, p. 50). However, such swift dismissal of the comic scenes in *Faustus* betrays a failure to take into account how much notions of genre have ossified in the 400 years since the play was first performed: our impulse to fence off the tragic (and therefore, so the logic goes, serious) from the comic (and therefore trivial) does allow for exceptions, particularly in the Beckettian mode of the theatre of the absurd, and in the more populist form of black comedy. However, when looking back at early modern drama, the tendency to categorize and classify ('Shakespeare's tragedies', 'Shakespeare's comedies', and so on) persists, despite the fact that many texts stubbornly refuse to let us squeeze them into the boxes we construct for them. We should also remember that performances of the most 'serious' of tragedies in the playhouses would probably have been book-ended by jigs, clowning and other entertainments.

It is revealing that, as we trace the stage history of *Doctor Faustus*, we find that the text soon sheds its tragic trappings, and by the late seventeenth century it is being described as a 'comedy' by William Winstanley in his *Lives of the Most Famous English Poets* (1687); Winstanley refers to 'its Devils and such like tragical Sport' and notes that it 'pleased much the humors of the Vulgar' (cited in MacLure, 1995, p. 52). It was about this time that the play passed into pantomime mode, and Harlequin and Scaramouch, characters imported from Italian *commedia dell'Arte*, were incorporated into the action. John Thurmond's *Harlequin Doctor Faustus* (1724) is typical of these adaptations. The first scene depicts the signing of the contract, and is accompanied by spectacular stage effects:

> Lightning and Thunder immediately succeed, and
> *Mephostophilus* [*sic*], a Daemon, flies down upon a Dragon,
> which throws from its Mouth and Nostrils Flames of Fire.
> He alights, receives the contract from the Doctor, and
> another Daemon arises, takes it from him and sinks
> with it.

[Papetti, 1977, p. 118]

The scenes that follow are a sequence of comic set pieces punctuated by dances: in scene 6, for instance, Faustus allows a usurer to cut off his leg and then calls on Mephostophilus who 'causes several legs of different Colours, Forms, and Sizes, to appear'. The description continues:

> The Doctor no sooner has it, but he leaps upon the Table,
> and having admir'd and shewn his Satisfaction for his new
> Leg, in transport he tries its Use and Power by a brisk
> Dance.

[ibid., p. 121]

The scenes revolve almost entirely around the satisfaction of 'the Doctor's' carnal appetites, and are driven along by surreal illogic and a manic energy, as well as by spectacular theatrical effects apparently conjured by his magical wand. The ending is abrupt: Death and Time appear in order to announce his doom, and Faustus is struck dead. Finally, two devils appear, take up his body, and 'turn him on his Head', sinking with him into hell-flames; 'other Daemons, at the same time, as he is going down, tear him Limb from Limb, and his mangled Pieces, fly rejoicing upwards' (ibid., pp. 126–7). The climax of the pantomime was usually a lavish crowd-pleaser, and thousands of pounds were often spent on such spectacles. The final scene features Roman gods and goddesses congratulating each other on Faustus's deserved damnation and dancing a choral dance to finish the entertainment.

In shifting the ground of the Faustus story into unashamedly comic territory, this pantomime version also ditches the theological wrangling that remains at the knotted heart of the play. There is no mention of Christ, salvation or even damnation – the text refers to 'the dreadful Effect of his hellish Agreement' and to the Doctor's 'Black Soul' (p. 126), but nothing that is readily traceable back to Christian doctrine; the final scene carefully announces the setting as 'a Poetical Heaven' (p. 127). Clearly, Thurmond is leaving the play we associate with Marlowe far behind in his devising of this harlequin version, but the process by which the original is refashioned is revealing about both Thurmond's time and Marlowe's. The unashamedly spectacular and populist style of the pantomime was despised by many: Alexander Pope fired off one satirical salvo at these *Faustus* pantomimes in his *Dunciad* (1728) with a sardonic portrait of the actor Colley Cibber:

> His never-blushing head he turned aside . . .
> And looked, and saw a sable sorcerer rise,
> Swift to whose hand a wingèd volume flies;

All sudden, gorgons hiss, and dragons glare,
And ten-horned fiends and giants rush to war.
Hell rises, Heaven descends, and dance on earth:
Gods, imps, and monsters, music, rage, and mirth,
A fire, a jog, a battle, and a ball,
Till one wide conflagration swallows all.

[Pope, 1985, III.231–40]

However, entertainments like John Thurmond's *Harlequin Doctor Faustus* were hugely, if fleetingly, popular. More widely in the London theatres at this time, the drama was becoming increasingly focused on the bourgeoisie in both its audience and its subject matter. The taste was not for tragedies on the grand scale but for the topical and the domestic. In the case of *Faustus*, the heavy theological freight of the original was jettisoned, and the bare bones of its plot used to structure a spectacular entertainment.

Evidently, the *Doctor Faustus* that had been acted before Elizabethan audiences was a world away from the burlesque that took its name over a hundred years later. However, the comic potential that Thurmond and others found in *Faustus* should not be passed over too easily, for it draws attention to another aspect of the play that has attracted a significant amount of critical attention. Readings illuminated by the work of the Russian thinker Mikhail Bakhtin (1895–1975) have concentrated on the so-called carnivalesque aspects of *Faustus* (particularly in its B-text version). Bakhtin's most significant work is his book *Rabelais and his World*, which he wrote in the 1940s, but which was not published until 1965 (in the Soviet Union); it was first translated into English in 1968. Ostensibly a study of Rabelais' *Gargantua and Pantagruel* (1532), its scope is actually much wider, comprising as it does an investigation of the festive life of early modern Europe. It has been enormously influential in studies of early modern culture, including English culture, and of the drama in this period in particular. Briefly, Bakhtin's work focuses on what he describes as the 'second life' or 'second culture' that existed in this society, sustained by the common people. The celebrations and holidays associated with carnival are interpreted as challenges to the dominant class and culture in a society constructed on a strictly hierarchical basis. The significance of carnival, Bakhtin insists, extends beyond the period of festivity that traditionally preceded the period of Lent in the Christian calendar. Under the conditions of carnival, official ideology (which seeks to consolidate the status quo) is challenged, order is disrupted and hierarchies are reversed. Crucial elements of carnival include a focus on the materiality of the body – the emphasis is on those functions and aspects of the body and associated processes that Bakhtin defines as grotesque (the mouth, the anus, the buttocks, the genitals) and degrading (defecation, urination and copulation). All things that are traditionally seen as spiritual and exalted (and therefore to be endorsed by the dominant ideology) are debased. Liberating laughter that subverts, parodies and ridicules official culture is also a crucial element of the carnivalesque. Bakhtin identifies what he calls the concept of grotesque realism as the heritage of the culture of folk humour. 'The essential principle of grotesque realism', he writes, 'is degradation, that is, the lowering of all that is high, spiritual, ideal, abstract; it is a transfer to the material level, to the sphere of earth and body' (Bakhtin, 1984, p. 19). In the light of this kind of understanding, we may choose to challenge the common interpretation of the comic interludes as distortions of Marlowe's 'original' play, and instead see them as carnivalesque elements which are integral to the text.

While the play ostensibly deals with a 'tragical history' that involves complex theological issues, it may be that alongside the serious strand runs a seam that can be exploited to throw the dominant, Aristotelian trajectory of the plot off course. The critic Michael Bristol, whose *Carnival and Theatre* broke new ground in offering an extensive application of Bakhtin's theories to a study of Elizabethan theatre, refers to the comic scenes in *Doctor Faustus* as 'a kind of anthology of popular material in which Faustus's diabolical powers are an excuse for slapstick, practical jokes and irreverent disregard of theological matters' (Bristol, 1985, p. 150).

The clown scenes are packed with lewd and crude comedy: in act 1 scene 4, the first time Robin appears, there is advice on the distinction between male and female devils, who are differentiated in terms of their sexual organs ('all he devils has horns, and all she devils has clefts and cloven feet', A.1.4.56–7), and Robin also imagines being turned into a flea so that he can be 'here and there and everywhere' and 'tickle the pretty wenches' plackets' (A.1.4.66–7). Act 2 scene 2 is played out between the two clowns Robin and Rafe in the A-text, Robin and Dick in the B-text. Here we find that Robin has stolen one of Faustus's conjuring books:

O, this is admirable! Here I ha' stol'n one of Doctor
Faustus' conjuring books, and, i'faith, I mean to search
some circles for my own use. Now will I make

all the maidens in our parish dance at my pleasure stark naked before me, and so by that means I shall see more than e'er I felt or saw yet.

[A.2.2.1–6]

'Circles', like 'plackets', can be taken to mean vaginas. It is worth noting that the B-text is more coy in this scene: here it is Dick that is spoken of as dancing naked rather than 'all the maidens in our parish' (B.2.2.28). Some jokes remain about cuckoldry, and there is some more subtle sexual innuendo about wading 'deep into matters' (22–3), but the talk of plackets and Nan Spit is gone. In the wake of Faustus having demanded a wife – he claims he is 'wanton and lascivious and cannot live without a wife' (A&B.2.1.144–5) – and having been presented with 'a Devil dressed like a woman with fireworks' (A.2.1.151.*s.d.* – it is merely a 'woman Devil' in B.2.1.146.*s.d.*), the fireworks presumably signifying venereal disease, it is appropriate that Robin should display a similar preoccupation. His anticipation of seeing 'more than e'er I felt or saw yet' also serves to undercut Faustus's great ambitions, set against what we have seen him achieve so far: it is evident that Robin's aspirations do not extend beyond sex. As things turn out, Faustus's last conjuration raises the spirit of Helen of Troy to be his lover. When he kisses her, the image he uses to describe it fuses different kinds of appetites:

Sweet Helen, make me immortal with a kiss.
[*They kiss.*]
Her lips suck forth my soul. See where it flies!

[A.5.1.93–4; B.96–7]

In act 2 scene 2 Robin goes on to assure Rafe that he shall 'have' Nan Spit the kitchen maid, and 'turn her and wind her to thy own use as often as thou wilt, and at midnight' (A2.2.29–30). Both A- and B-texts feature variations on the popular riff of cuckoldry: Rafe frets over a gentleman who 'would have his things rubbed and made clean' and who 'keeps such a chafing with my mistress about it' that she has sent him on an errand (A.2.2.8–10). The conjuring of horns onto the head of the Knight (called Benvolio in the B-text) is in a similar vein (A.4.1.77–96; B.119–69).

As well as preoccupations with sex, one of the fundamental features of carnival, there is dialogue and business centring around food, drink,

and other bodily needs. In act 1 scene 4 the unemployed Robin is
sized up by Wagner, and Wagner reckons Robin to be so hungry that
he 'would give his soul to the devil for a shoulder of mutton, though
it were blood raw' (A&B.1.4.9–10). Robin protests, 'By'r Lady, I had
need have it well roasted, and good sauce to it, if I pay so dear'
(A.1.4.12–13). The two devils Wagner summons to chase Robin away
are called Baliol and Belcher (46); the latter's name has obvious carnivalesque associations. As for Baliol (whose name evolves into the less
interesting Banio in the B-text), Bevington and Rasmussen note that
Thomas Nashe puns on Belial and 'Belly-all' in his *Piers Penniless*
(Bevington & Rasmussen, 1993, p. 135 n. 46), and a similar pun is presumably intended here. Robin promises Rafe that he can 'make [him]
drunk with hippocras at any tavern in Europe for nothing' as one of
his conjuring tricks (A.2.2.25–6). The B-text is even more explicit in
its celebration of the pleasures of alcohol – Robin promises Dick 'white
wine, red wine, claret wine, sack, muscadine, malmsey, and whippin-
crust, hold belly hold, and we'll not pay one penny for it' (B.2.2.30–2).
If we look for corresponding moments in the main plot, although we
hear of some of Faustus's great exploits and journeys, what we *see* more
often than not are conjuring tricks that are not very much further up
the scale than those the clowns boast about. One of Faustus's stunts is
to conjure grapes, out of season, at the request of the Duchess of Vanholt
(A.4.2.16; B.4.6.21); 'I have heard that great-bellied women do long
for things are rare and dainty', Faustus remarks (B.4.6.11–13), and at
her request he dispatches Mephistopheles to return within seconds with
fruit plucked from a vine in some distant country. The B-text actually
underlines the ironic mimicry of the clowns' behaviour even more em-
phatically than the A-text, for just as the Duchess declares the fruit 'the
sweetest grapes that e'er I tasted' (B.4.6.34–5), the stage direction
announces that 'The Clown[s] bounce at the gate, within', and the Horse-
courser, the Carter, Robin and Dick stagger on stage drunk.

One of the most carnivalesque scenes (and certainly the most
explicit challenge to and disruption of social ritual, order and hierarchy) takes place in Rome, where Faustus and Mephistopheles, invisible, visit a banquet held by the Pope (act 3 scene 1 in the A-text, but
3.2 in the B-text). Here, Faustus snatches a 'dainty dish' from under
the Pope's nose (A.3.1.64; B.3.2.66), steals another, and then pilfers the
Pope's cup, too (A.72; B.74). He finishes it off by boxing the Pope's
ear when he crosses himself (A.80; B.87) and, as the friars attempt to
perform an exorcism, he and Mephistopheles beat them and attack them
with fireworks, chasing them from the stage. The depiction of the Pope

and his bishops indulging themselves with rich food and drink is fairly blatant, and predictable, anti-Catholic propaganda. But at the other end of the spectrum we find Robin drooling at the prospect of a shoulder of lamb, and Wagner conjuring his carnivalesque demons Baliol and Belcher. Whether it be the dire need of a man, starving, 'bare and out of service', or the gross over-indulgence of corrupt churchmen, the focus is on what Bakhtin calls 'the material bodily lower stratum'. The bizarre episode, occurring in both texts, in which the horse-courser pulls off Faustus's leg, is comic and grotesque (A.4.1.174.s.d.; B.4.4.37.s.d.). Rooted in medieval dramatic tradition, the comical dismemberment serves to prefigure Faustus's eventual fate. It might also be taken as an ironic comment on the tradition of preserving parts of saints' bodies in churches – Bakhtin notes that the practice of venerating such items as arms, legs, heads, teeth, hair and fingers in this fashion was a particular target of Protestant satire during the sixteenth century. Calvin himself wrote a pamphlet about these relics that is shot through with comic, ironic overtones (Bakhtin, 1984, p. 350).

The preoccupation of scholars with *Doctor Faustus*, particularly in relation to its textual status, is provoked by its indeterminacy, its refusal to be pinned down. Theatre practitioners find that *Faustus* offers huge potential in terms of stage interpretation, partly for the same reasons. This chapter has offered a number of possible approaches to the *Faustus* texts, not all of them mutually compatible. For instance, the perspective on the tragic genre posited by Boal sees the play as fundamentally conservative; a Bakhtinian reading, on the other hand, would insist that the play's carnivalesque elements render it (at least potentially) subversive. Although some critics have argued that Marlowe places the deep imprint of his own personality on his work (contrasting him with Shakespeare in this respect), the divergent readings of the play that we have touched on here tell a different story. It may be that the play was written as an unflinching, stony-faced parable of transgression and divine retribution; it may be that the author or authors intended to question a theology that portrays a human soul tormented and obliterated by a divinity that offers only the illusion of a way out. In any case, *Doctor Faustus*, in all its complexity and indeterminacy, remains the cornerstone of Marlowe's legacy as a playwright.

CHAPTER 5

UNHALLOWED DEEDS:
The Jew of Malta

The Jew of Malta and cultural difference

Christopher Marlowe's *The Jew of Malta* was the most popular play of his short career, first performed around 1589–90 and frequently revived in the following decade. It would re-emerge around 1633 to be performed both at the Cockpit theatre and at the court of King Charles I. Briefly, it tells the story of a villainous Jew named Barabas who, having had his wealth confiscated by the Christians who rule the island of Malta, takes his revenge on the Governor and his Knights. In the course of his plotting, he brings about the death of a number of innocent (and not so innocent) parties, including his daughter's two rival suitors, a friar, and the inhabitants of a nunnery. The latter crime, achieved by poisoning the nuns' food supply, also results in the death of his own daughter. When he is identified as the perpetrator of these crimes he is arrested, but he fakes his own death. With Cyprus under threat from Turkish forces, Barabas betrays Malta to Calymath, the Turkish emperor's son. Shortly afterwards, he decides to switch sides again, but Ferneze, the Governor of Malta, springs the trap on Barabas himself, who dies cursing. The Governor restores (Christian) order to the island.

The Jew of Malta is undoubtedly the most problematic of Marlowe's plays: the portrayal of a Jew in terms that are hard to see as anything other than anti-Semitic brings us up against the important issue of ethnic identity and racial prejudice, and whenever a director decides to stage a production of the play, a moral minefield opens up before him or her. Similarly, when we read and discuss the play it is important to be aware of the sensitivity and complexity of the issues it raises. When we look back 400 years to the first staging of the play, we can create some comfortable distance: we can say that a long time ago people had primitive attitudes towards such things as racial and cultural difference. If we agree that the play exhibits a casual attitude to and use of anti-Semitism (an opinion that has been disputed, as we shall see), then we can justify it by noting how anti-Semitism was prevalent at the time, that it was part of the dominant ideology. We can then, in a sense, disown the play, explaining it away by saying that everybody thought like that then, but reflecting that we are more enlightened now, and no longer discriminate against people on the grounds of their ethnic identity.

There are a couple of reasons why this may not be good enough. First of all, a play is always something more than an historical document, taking on new resonances in new social contexts whenever it is revived. It is important to try to grasp something of what the play would have signified to its first audience, but it is equally important to be sensitive to what the same play means (or can be made to mean) in our own culture. Thomas Heywood's Epilogue, spoken when the play was performed at the court of Charles I sometime around 1633, concludes: 'And if aught here offend your ear or sight, / We only act and speak what others write' (Bawcutt, 1997, p. 193). It seems likely that this was an awkward attempt to excuse a play that might by then have appeared old-fashioned in terms of its form (ibid., pp. 2–3). However, whereas Heywood's embarrassment was provoked by the play's crude style, in our own time the text is more likely to unsettle us because of its blatant and brutal anti-Semitic content. This chapter will read *The Jew of Malta* in the light of this tension between the past and the present: we will first consider the play within its original performance context, taking account of the ideological pressures that would have influenced both its production (by the author and the company of players who first staged it) and its reception (by the Elizabethans who attended those first performances). We will then go on to consider what the play might signify in our own time.

To consider the second reason why this distancing of ourselves from the play may be insufficient, we can look for a moment at a more familiar play, Shakespeare's *The Merchant of Venice*, to clarify the status of the play in relation to racism. *The Merchant of Venice*, acknowledged as having been heavily influenced by Marlowe's play, is often thought of today as a document that speaks out against anti-Semitism; in Germany and Nazi-occupied Europe in the 1930s and 1940s, it meant something very different. In September 1939, Shakespeare was the one playwright exempt from the ban on 'enemy' dramatists in the occupied territories, due at least in part to the usefulness of this one play. In 1933, *The Merchant of Venice* was produced 23 times, and another 30 times between 1934 and 1939. Needless to say, the portrayal of Shylock in every production was without exception a vicious one. Perhaps the most famous production featured Werner Krauss in the key role, in a production in Vienna in May 1943. This is an excerpt from a contemporary account of that production:

> The pale pink face, surrounded by bright red hair and beard, with its unsteady, cunning little eyes; the greasy caftan with the yellow prayer-shawl slung round; the splay-footed, shuffling walk; the foot stamping with rage; the claw-like gestures with the hands; the voice, now bawling, now muttering – all add up to a pathological image of the East European Jewish type, expressing all its inner and outer uncleanliness, emphasizing danger through humour.
>
> [Gross, 1994, pp. 296–7]

If a play by Shakespeare, who is supposed by many to be the great universal dramatist, can be appropriated for a particular ideological agenda, it seems likely that a play by Marlowe could be used in a similar way. Furthermore, it should be fairly clear that it is not enough to say that we are more enlightened than the Elizabethans were, and that racial prejudice is no longer an issue – the Nazi Holocaust in which six million Jews died is still relatively recent history, and racism remains a problem on a local, national and global scale at the turn of the millennium. The Balkans crisis is the most newsworthy instance at the time of writing, but is only one of a number of examples of continuing ethnic tension and oppression around the world. Plays such as *The Jew of Malta* and *The Merchant of Venice* therefore remain problematic whenever they are revived, both for the spectres they may raise, and for the current, potentially explosive issues they may ignite.

The genesis of prejudice and the mechanisms by which it operates are complex. Studies in what has come to be termed post-colonial theory have sought to identify its patterns. The full terms of the post-colonial debate are too complex to engage with here, but we can identify some of the key strands relatively briefly. Communities tend to identify themselves in contradistinction to what we could term the 'Other', onto whom that community can project its fears and aggressions. This pattern of behaviour is discernible in all societies. We see it operating in colonialism, where it is used as a justification for the oppression and exploitation of indigenous population: the reasoning is that if the natives are something other than human, then there is no reason to treat them humanely. We find it, too, in attitudes towards immigrant populations, where it may be used as a justification for advocating deportation or segregation. The Other is usually distinguishable by some physical sign – skin colour, culture or mode of dress – something that marks out the Other as differing from the norm (which historically has been white, eurocentric and male). The Other becomes a focus for aspects of the self that the subject chooses to ignore or reject: in this way, the Other is identified as idle, greedy, sensual, violent, for instance, and their behaviour is understood to be determined by their group identity – their race or ethnicity – rather than by individual circumstances. It is interesting to note how often Barabas is referred to as 'Jew' in the play, rather than by name. This is indicative of the process whereby the Other's status is determined via the perception of a group, rather than on an individual basis. The post-colonial theorist Homi K. Bhabha talks about the stereotype as 'a form of knowledge and identification that vacillates between what is always "in place", already known, and something that must be anxiously repeated' (Bhabha, 1983, p. 18). When we look at the way Barabas is represented in *The Jew of Malta*, we can see this vacillation in action: the frequency with which the stereotype of the evil Jew is invoked can be interpreted as a sign of the anxiety that lies behind the process of misrepresentation. In respect of this, it is interesting to note that most of the Christians refuse to use his name when they address him: 'Sirrah Jew', Don Mathias hails him at the slave market (2.3.162), and the knights tend to call him simply 'Jew' – 'Tut, Jew, we know thou art no soldier' (1.2.52). The exception is Ferneze, who alternates between the two forms of address. At the time his property is confiscated, Ferneze's dialogue with him is punctuated by an almost ritualized series of denials: 'No, Jew, like infidels . . .' (1.2.62); 'No, Jew, thou hast denied the articles' (93); 'No, Jew, we take particularly thine . . .' (97). When Ferneze does address Barabas by name, it tends to sound patronizing and condescending. For those (like Lodowick and Mathias at the end of act 1) who don't know him personally, he is identified as 'the rich Jew' (1.2.363, 380), bearing out his earlier insistence that he is a well-known figure in Maltese society. In any case, the identification of Barabas as 'Jew' makes it clear that he tends to be identified as a type rather than as an individual.

As we look more closely at the play itself, a more complete impression of a Barabas – or a Shylock – through Elizabethan eyes will emerge. Until we have a better understanding of the place of Jews in English and European society in the sixteenth century, we will not be able fully to appreciate the crucial ideological dimensions of *The Jew of Malta*. The history of Jews in Europe and in England in particular is a complex one, and to begin to imagine how Marlowe's audience would have responded to Barabas requires an acquaintance with at least some of that history. The myths, tales and propaganda purporting to be the truth about Jews in the early modern period were numerous, and some of them are quite astonishing. A number of them are directly relevant to *The Jew of Malta*. For instance, Barabas's Jewish identity would immediately mark him out as a villain for an audience of Marlowe's contemporaries. Barabas is the name of the thief who was released in place of Jesus by Pontius Pilate, and the biblical Barabas had consequently taken on some kind of Satanic status in early Christian doctrine. During medieval times, Jews had been traditionally associated with the devil – they were thought to be a cursed race, the curse originating from the idea that they were responsible for the death of Christ. One of the Christian knights in *The Jew of Malta* justifies stripping Barabas of his wealth with the phrase "Tis not our fault, but thy inherent sin' (1.2.110), a clear reference to this belief. Later in the play, Katharine tells her son not to speak to Barabas, since he is, by virtue of being a Jew, 'cast off from heaven' (2.3.160); and Barabas himself, when pretending that he wishes to convert, declares that 'I am a Jew, therefore am I lost' (4.1.57).

'A scattered nation': the Jews in European history

In 1096, the First Crusade had set out from western Europe to reclaim the Christian holy places in the Middle East from their Arab conquerors. On their way through France and Germany, the Crusaders slaughtered the Jews in the middle-European cities. There were large-scale massacres in Worms, Cologne, Prague and other places. At Regensburg, the Jewish population was forcibly baptized in the River Danube. (It was part of Christian doctrine that Israel would be redeemed by conversion to Christ. At the end of Shakespeare's *The Merchant of Venice* we hear that part of Shylock's sentence for his crime will be an enforced conversion to Christianity.) When Jerusalem was reclaimed by the Crusaders, a further massacre of Jews and Moslems followed. In 1189 the start of the Third Crusade, led by Richard Plantagenet (also known as Richard Coeur de Lion – the Lionheart), brought about another cycle of persecution of the Jews. As the king prepared to leave with his knights, word spread that he had ordered the slaughter of Jews to mark the departure, and hundreds of them were burned in their houses. At York, the Hebrew congregation took refuge in the castle and were besieged. Rather than face torture and death at the hands of the mob, 150 of them committed suicide (Litvinoff, 1989, pp. 63–4). From the castle the crowd proceeded to York Minster, where records of money owed to local Jews were found and burned. In a grim irony, Richard the Lionheart, ransomed from captivity in the Holy Land, owed his freedom in large part to the money of wealthy Jews in England.

There were common myths in circulation about Jews crucifying and murdering children. Such a reference actually crops up in Marlowe's play: the two friars, Bernardine and Jacomo, are discussing the deaths of the nuns, and are standing over Abigail's body. Abigail has just informed Bernardine with her dying breath that her father brought about the deaths of Lodowick and Don Matthias.

> *Jacomo.*   Oh, brother, all the nuns are dead! Let's bury
>   them.
> *Bernardine.* First help to bury this; then go with me,
>   And help me to exclaim against the Jew.
> *Jacomo.*   Why, what has he done?
> *Bernardine.* A thing that makes me tremble to unfold.
> *Jacomo.*   What, has he crucified a child?
> *Bernardine.* No, but a worse thing.

[3.6.44–50]

Such tales can be dated back to the first half of the twelfth century: according to the *Anglo-Saxon Chronicle* of 1137, when a child's body was discovered in a wood in Norwich, Theobald of Cambridge, a monk who had converted from Judaism, disseminated the notion that Jews used Christian blood as an ingredient in their Passover bread. Although no-one was ever convicted of the child's murder, the idea that Jews indulged in the ritual slaughter of Christian children soon took hold. Chaucer picks up the story of Little St Hugh of Lincoln in his *Prioress's Tale*: in 1255, the boy Hugh had disappeared, and the local community was accused of his murder. Eighteen Jews who refused to make a plea were presumed guilty and hanged (Litvinoff, 1989, p. 60). Such stories proliferated through the centuries, all across Europe. The supposed patron saint of choirboys, Domingo del Val, never existed, but the legend goes that he was crucified by Jews in the thirteenth century. These ritual murders were often connected with a particular ceremony – the Jews were reputed to engage in some kind of Satanic, inverted parody of Christian holy communion. There were tales of Jews stealing the Eucharistic host (the wafer ritually consecrated as the body of Christ) and abusing, striking and burning it. The conclusion of such stories was familiar: Christ's blood would stream from the Eucharist and the Jews would instantly be converted at the sight of such a miracle. The Croxton *Play of the Sacrament*, a 'miracle play' dating from the late fifteenth century, survives as a dramatization of the legend. Some Jews steal the sacrament and set about it with their daggers, torturing it as if it were a physical body (orthodox Christian doctrine at this time held that the consecrated host was in fact the body of Christ). The host, pierced, begins to bleed. One of the Jews, a man named Jonathas, tries to put it in boiling oil, but it sticks to his hand. His fellow Jews attempt to free the host from his hand, but only succeed in pulling Jonathas's hand off; shortly after, it is thrown into the cauldron with the host still attached. The contents of the cauldron turn to blood, and when the host is finally retrieved and thrown into an oven, the oven cracks, and blood seeps from it – this is meant to evoke the bleeding of Christ on the cross. When a vision of the crucified Christ appears, the Jews beg forgiveness and convert. Jonathas has his hand miraculously restored. Incidentally, Barabas's opening speech, with its detailed description of his hoard of wealth and precious stones, seems to echo a passage spoken by Jonathas in the *Play of the Sacrament* (Adams, 1924, p. 246).

By the time Marlowe was born, Jews had in fact been officially banned from England for over 300 years. From 1217, Jews in England had been forced to wear a yellow badge in the shape of stone tablets – representing the Ten Commandments – to indicate their ethnic identity. In 1287, Edward I imprisoned the leaders of the English Jewish community, who were ransomed for the sum of £12,000 (Litvinoff, 1989, p. 69). During the reigns of Edward and of Henry III, the Jewish population were literally bought and sold – having no rights of citizenship, and surviving under the protection of the monarch, they were tantamount to the king's possessions. They did not enjoy rights of inheritance, all their property being confiscated by the state on their death. They were also heavily taxed, and tortured if they refused to pay. In 1290, Edward I expelled the entire Jewish population from the nation – perhaps as many as 15,000. The sale swelled the royal coffers, since most of their property was claimed by the throne, including all moneys owed to them by English citizens. Although a handful converted – or claimed to convert – to Christianity in order to remain, to all intents and purposes the Jews were now banished from English shores, not to be readmitted until 1655 when Cromwell allowed a Jewish settlement. In other parts of Europe, some Jewish communities survived, although their members remained almost invariably marginalized and ghettoized. In 1347, when the plague hit Europe, the Jews once again found themselves targeted as the cause. The plague was a weapon of Satan, and the Jews were Satan's agents. The rumour circulated that Jews were poisoning the water supply (among the crimes Barabas boasts of we find his claim to 'go about and poison wells', 2.3.179), and thousands of Jews were killed in the wake of the report, many burned at the stake, others in their homes.

Protestantism inherited the tradition of persecution of the Jewish people from Catholicism. In 1543 Martin Luther, the reformer and founder of the Protestant faith, wrote a violent polemic against the Jews, *On the Jews and Their Lies*, in which he declared that 'We are at fault in not slaying them'. He called on faithful Christians to 'Set fire to their synagogues and schools and bury or cover with dirt whatever will not burn'. It was fortunate that Protestantism splintered early enough to prevent Luther's words from taking on doctrinal status. Around the time of the early sixteenth century, too, European Christians began to find a use for the Jews in their midst: although it was certainly not the case that all Jews were wealthy, many were, and they were valued for the fact that their religion allowed them to take money on usury, that is to say, loan money and charge interest. The Christian church had decreed that credit and loans were against God's law: edicts such as the Second Lateran Council of 1139 had established that any Christian discovered taking money on usury should be denied the sacraments. There was no such ban for those practising Judaism. With the emergence of embryonic capitalism in the sixteenth century, there was a heavy demand for the facility of credit for banking and for ventures in industrial and other enterprises, and Jews consequently were in increasing demand as credit brokers in European cities: the use that Antonio makes of Shylock in *The Merchant of Venice* is typical. In the second half of the sixteenth century, we find European nations gradually readmitting Jewish populations, partly, no doubt, because they had now identified a specific use for them. In truth, it was not just Jews who lent money at interest – the demands of capitalist economics were inevitably more pressing than the strictures of church dogma. In 1571, a law was passed in England that allowed interest to be charged at the rate of 10 per cent. Consequently, there was a shift in the way Jews were seen in relation to usury, and they were identified instead with over-inflated rates of interest. By 1624, the English parliament had formally retracted the divine interdict on the practice of usury. Jews in European society at this time, then, were marginalized and denied full citizenship, but allowed to remain on the edge of Christian society. Venice, for instance, was to a limited extent what we would understand as a multicultural society. Jews in Venice during the sixteenth century suffered heavy taxes (the justification being that they were wealthy and could afford it), and were confined to one specific area of the city called the ghetto (this is where the modern use of the term comes from). They were forced to take out a permanent lease on the area at an amount fixed at a third above the normal rate. The ghetto is a clear illustration of the way in which the Venetian authorities, though quite prepared to allow the Jews to participate in the economic life of the city, were nevertheless determined to restrict their participation in its social life.

Although the Jewish population had been deported from England in the thirteenth century, a few remained. Often, they survived by professing to be Christians while covertly continuing to practise their own religion. One significant Jew in English society during Marlowe's time was Roderigo Lopez, a Jew of Portuguese descent. He had supposedly converted, and had been appointed as Queen Elizabeth's personal physician in 1586. Jews in Europe were often credited with particular skills as physicians; unfortunately, this also placed them in close proximity to a related art, that of poisoning. When Lopez apparently began to lobby for peace with the great enemy nation of Spain, he antagonized the Earl of Essex, who consequently framed him in an alleged plot to assassinate the Queen. Lopez was hanged, drawn and quartered at Tyburn in June 1594. Standing on the gallows before a crowd of spectators, Lopez insisted that he loved the Queen as much as he loved Jesus Christ. The crowd's response was scornful laughter and abuse. *The Jew of Malta* was revived in February 1594, which probably coincided with the time of Lopez's trial, when it proved immensely popular – due no doubt, at least in part, to the scandal of the Lopez affair. It was revived again in June and July 1594.

Barabas as villain and victim

The title-page of the 1633 quarto of the play – the earliest surviving version – introduces it as 'The Famous Tragedy of the Rich Jew of Malta'. It should be fairly evident from even a cursory reading that it is not a tragedy in the classical mode. It is full of (admittedly very black) comedy; the progression of the plot is so dependent upon coincidence and unlikely happenings that structurally, too, it borders on farce at times. These twists in the narrative increase the sense of Barabas's ingenuity while simultaneously working to set him up for his (quite literal) fall at the end of the play, but the laughter they will provoke in the theatre cannot be unintentional. The uneven tone of the play has led some critics in the past to conclude that the extant text is actually one that has been modified by a later playwright. Although it is true that there is a well-defined and rather sudden change of gear between acts two and three, the idea that this should cast its authorship in doubt is one that betrays a too rigid adherence to notions of genre that did not constrain the Elizabethan dramatists.

It should also be clear that we are not dealing here with characters as we might instinctively talk about dramatic characters today. *The Jew of Malta* represents the drama at a point of transition. The traces of popular morality drama do not leap from the page or from the stage as they do from *Doctor Faustus*, which is populated by good and bad angels, devils, and even features a parade of the allegorical figures of the seven deadly sins. However, it still works to a large extent within the morality play framework. The genre of the so-called morality play dominated the fifteenth and early sixteenth centuries – the five extant texts are *Mankind*, *Wisdom*, *The Pride of Life*, *Everyman* and *The Castle of Perseverance*, but many more were written and performed during this period. The morality dramatized the conflict between good and evil, played out on earth, with the figure of Everyman or Mankind, representing humanity, on a spiritual journey, aided and abetted by allegorical figures of good and evil such as angels and devils, and personifications of virtues such as Mercy, or vices such as Lechery. A number of critics have analysed Barabas's relation to the Vice figure of that genre, and in this sense the most direct ancestor of Barabas is perhaps the figure of the devil Titivillus in *Mankind* (c.1471). Titivillus tempts and torments the Mankind persona, who falls from grace but is eventually redeemed via the intercession of Mercy. One of the interesting aspects of Titivillus in relation to Barabas is the way in which he interacts with the audience, exploiting that relationship for sharp satirical effect, the object of that satire being the audience as often as it is Mankind. There are also features of Marlowe's Machevil that bear comparison with the Vice figure, or even with Satan in *Conflict of Conscience* (printed 1581), as David Bevington has pointed out (Bevington, 1962, p. 222). The moralities tend to splice the supposedly universal spiritual dimension with the intensely parochial: the texts are peppered with references that include place names and names of local celebrities. Furthermore, the authors of these plays often indulge in streams of obscenities: if such frank references to bodily functions shock us today, this merely reflects the fact that a fifteenth-century rural community would be far more familiar with and therefore plainspoken about these things than a twenty-first-century Western audience would be. In Marlowe's work, the scatological and obscene strain is suppressed, though not entirely eliminated (there are a number of indecent jokes about the nature of the friars' relationship with the nuns, and Barabas leads the Turkish soldiers through the city's sewers when they capture Malta in the fifth act).

Although *The Jew of Malta* is populated by named individuals, and although these *personae* do seem to interact with each other in a human (if often inhumane) fashion, we are still some distance from 'naturalistic' representation. *The Merchant of Venice* is inevitably mentioned in parallel with *The Jew of Malta*, and this remark of Charles Lamb's is typical of the kind of judgement that has been passed in any such comparisons:

> Marlowe's Jew does not approach so near to Shakespeare's as his Edward II does to Richard II. Shylock, in the midst of his savage purpose, is a man. His motives, feelings, resentments, have something human in them: . . . Barabas is a mere monster, brought in with a large painted nose, to please the rabble . . .

> [Park, 1980, pp. 115–16]

Lamb usefully pinpoints *The Jew of Malta*'s double handicap: placed next to Shakespeare's *The Merchant of Venice*, and judged by the kind of criteria that have become commonplace in discussions of Shakespearean drama, Marlowe's play may appear shabby, disjointed, uneven and distasteful. Furthermore, when accepted definitions of Renaissance tragedy are applied to *The Jew of Malta*, the play's awkward refusal to remain in a serious register means that it strains against the customary rules and conventions, and it refuses to be crammed into that category. But to concentrate on the two central figures for a moment: according to Lamb, Barabas is a 'monster', Shylock is a 'man'. The unacknowledged assumption that lies behind this judgement is the idea that what a dramatist is doing when he writes a play is creating 'characters' – that is to say, characters that are recognizable as 'real'-seeming human beings. Typically, Shakespeare's plays are assumed to be populated by well-rounded characters, bristling with the kind of particular detail that marks them out as truly human and individual. At the same time, they are understood to embody something that is essentially human and therefore true of all people at all times and in all places: 'just representations of general nature', as Samuel Johnson would have it. More recent theoretical approaches to Shakespeare have begun to question these ideas about Shakespearean character, not least because, as we have already seen, the concept of what it means to be human has altered drastically since the sixteenth and seventeenth centuries. But, to continue with our consideration of the received wisdom about the two plays, Shakespeare's Shylock is seen not as a stereotypical stage Jew (as Barabas tends to be), but as a figure that we can sympathize with at certain points in the action, because of his 'humanness', because he is like a 'real person'; what is more, it is suggested that we can identify him as representative of human suffering and victimization in general, both individual and universal.

While we could challenge this idea by looking more closely at the way Shakespeare's portrayal of Shylock is bound up within the ideologies of his own age, it should be clear from a first reading of *The Jew of Malta* that Barabas demands a very different response from his audience. Whether or not Shakespeare did create characters to populate his plays that have this curious individual/universal quality, it will probably be generally accepted that Marlowe did not. We have already begun to see how Marlowe has constructed his Jew from stereotypes, prejudices and myths that were current at the time. Not only is he portrayed as avaricious, vicious and egocentric: he is also murderous, leaving in his wake the bodies of Lodowick and Mathias, Bernardine, Ithamore, Pilia-Borza and Belamira, and the inhabitants of a convent, including his own daughter, not to mention the knights and Turkish soldiers who die in the off-stage action as a result of his political intrigues.

It is fairly evident, even from the opening scene of *The Jew of Malta*, that Barabas will be drawn in terms of the Elizabethan Jewish stereotype. The new historicist critic Stephen Greenblatt refers to him as 'a social construction, a fiction composed of the sleaziest materials in his culture' (Greenblatt, 1994, p. 209). Even before the play proper begins, we are introduced to him by the figure of Machevil, the manifestation of the spirit of Niccolo Machiavelli, who introduces the play as 'the tragedy of a Jew' – a man, it would seem, very much after his own heart. Machiavelli was a fashionable and, in Protestant England, infamous figure at this time. An Italian politician, philosopher and writer, his key work *The Prince* (1513) was an investigation of the ways in which a ruler can advance his own interests and the interests of his state through processes of political manipulation. Marlowe's Machevil is in fact a travesty of the historical figure Machiavelli, embodying distorted misreadings of the Italian's writings that were by this time familiar in Europe, particularly in Protestant England, where his supposed immorality could be linked with his Catholicism: at this time, the Italian courts were largely perceived as places of decadence, corruption, degradation and spiritual bankruptcy. Setting the tone for the play to follow, Machevil here dismisses religion as 'a childish toy' and declares that he holds 'there is no sin but ignorance' (Prologue.14–15). Atheism was another charge frequently laid against Machiavelli by his opponents. As Simon Shepherd points out, Machevil's 'identity and reputation should cause scepticism about the reliability and truthfulness traditionally associated with the Presenter' – the narrator, or Chorus figure, of the drama (Shepherd, 1986, p. 53). Machevil claims Barabas as one of his acolytes: the Jew's wealth, he claims, 'was not got without my means' (Prologue.32). Clifford Leech makes the useful point that, in late sixteenth-century Protestant England, both Machiavelli and the Jew Barabas are 'outsiders', and speculates that 'Marlowe must have particularly enjoyed the association he was making' (Leech, 1986, p. 167). Significant to the way in which the whole play operates is Machevil's final sentence:

> I crave but this, grace him as he deserves,
> And let him not be entertained the worse
> Because he favours me.

[Prologue.33–5]

Here a recognized villain requests the indulgence of the audience to 'grace' Barabas – to honour him, in other words – 'as he deserves'. Machevil asks us not to be biased against Barabas because he 'favours' – which could either mean resembles or sides with – him, Machevil. The irony is encapsulated in that phrase 'as he deserves'. Barabas will quickly be established as a stage villain the likes of which the English stage had never seen before. An Elizabethan audience, it would seem, would be in no doubt as to what Barabas deserved. However, one of the most fascinating aspects of the play is the way in which the audience is manipulated into 'honouring' Barabas, as Machevil invites us to at the beginning of the play. We 'honour' him in both senses of the word, by siding with him and admiring him for his ingenuity and his audacity, even in the midst of his terrible crimes. Barabas demands our interest not only because he is fascinating in himself, but also because of the relationship he engineers between himself and the audience: the text allows him to address us, the audience, directly. We do not engage easily with any of the other characters because none of them is really likeable, and none of them is fleshed out in any great detail except Abigail, perhaps, and even she remains sketchy and largely functional.

We first see Barabas detailing his riches in a speech studded with exotic references and opulent descriptions of his jewels. We hear news of the success of Barabas's trading exploits as we learn of the return of various vessels laden with rich cargo. In the 1987 RSC production, Barabas was discovered at his accounts, his table heavily laden with piles of coins. On the floor in front of him was spread a huge map. As his fellow Jews were heard approaching, he made a desperate attempt to hide what he could, conveying both avarice and a sense of paranoia, an acute aware-ness of the precarious status of his wealth. It will soon become clear that his fears are justified. Barabas evidently has some status on the island, or at the very least a reputation ('Go tell 'em the Jew of Malta sent thee, man', he urges one of the merchants; 'Tush, who amongst 'em knows not Barabas?', 1.1.66–7). The scene helps to establish Barabas as a greedy man, vicious and egocentric, motivated purely by self-interest. At the end of the first scene he utters a Latin proverb that could be seen as his motto: *Ego mihimet sum semper proximus* – I am always nearest myself (1.1.188). This self-interest is manifested in particu-lar as monetary greed, and to some extent he can be seen as embodying that particular 'deadly sin'.

We get an inkling, too, of his deceptive nature, which even extends to his fellow Jews ('these silly men', as he calls them [1.1.178]): talk-ing to them about what might happen at the Senate, he seems to be seeking to reassure them – 'If anything shall there concern our state, / Assure yourselves I'll look – *(Aside) unto myself*' (1.1.171–2). The aside, stage-whispered for the benefit of the audience, will become a familiar technique as the play progresses, both a character note that helps define Barabas, and a tool in constructing a specific relationship between him and the audience. Barabas is motivated by a hatred of and disdain for Christians, but his contempt for his fellow Jews is also obvious to the audience. Though he is a force to be reckoned with on the island, he knows he is hated in return, at least by the Christians he encounters. Towards the end of the play, installed as governor after he has betrayed the island to the Turks, this is important, but for now it is no great matter to him:

> Rather had I, a Jew, be hated thus
> Than pitied in a Christian poverty.
> For I can see no fruits in all their faith

But malice, falsehood, and excessive pride,
Which methinks fits not their profession.

[1.1.113–17]

We also learn that Barabas's one great love beside his wealth is his daughter, Abigail, 'whom', he tells us, 'I hold as dear / As Agamemnon did his Iphigen; / And all I have is hers' (1.1.136–8). The line is ironic – the legendary king Agamemnon was forced to sacrifice his daughter for the Greek cause in the war against Troy. Before the end of the play, Barabas will kill Abigail for the sake of his own gain.

All the Jews in Malta have been ordered to attend a meeting at the senate-house. Barabas guesses, rightly, that the Turks are demanding an increase in the tribute paid to them by the inhabitants of the island. What Barabas does not yet know is that the Maltese have decided to raise the money by confiscating half the wealth of every Jewish citizen (historically speaking, this kind of excessive taxation of Jews by Christian authorities, as we have seen, was not uncommon). When this is proposed, it is framed first as an entreaty: with the excuse that recent wars have drained their resources, Ferneze declares that 'therefore are we to request your aid' (1.2.49). Very quickly, however, the matter is made more direct ('tis thy money, Barabas, we seek', 54), and a request becomes an ultimatum that is very close to blackmail, one that has already been set down in writing as a public decree:

Officer. (reads) 'First, the tribute money of the Turks shall all be levied amongst the Jews, and each of them to pay one-half of his estate . . . Secondly, he that denies to pay shall straight become a Christian . . . . Lastly, he that denies this shall absolutely lose all he has.'

[1.2.68–70, 73–4, 76–7]

Barabas refuses to hand over what is demanded of him, while his fellow Jews opt to surrender without a fight. Ferneze, Governor of Malta, consequently confiscates all Barabas's property and declares that his mansion shall be converted into a nunnery. The actions against Barabas are not only harsh and unfeeling, but actively vindictive. When Ferneze and his officers have left the stage, Barabas bemoans his fate in lamentations that recall the suffering of Job, a character in the Old Testament who is deprived of his property and possessions, his family and his health, in a test of his faith in God. Just as, in the book of Job, there are those who try to comfort him in his affliction, so here Barabas's fellow Jews try unsuccessfully to offer consolation. When they depart, Barabas scorns them:

> See the simplicity of these base slaves,
> Who, for the villains have no wit themselves,
> Think me to be a senseless lump of clay
> That will with every water wash to dirt!
> No, Barabas is born to better chance
> And framed of finer mould than common men,
> That measure naught but by the present time.

[1.2.216–22]

There is no sense of solidarity between Barabas and his fellow Jews. His only real allies are Abigail (for the first half of the play) and his slave Ithamore (until Ithamore betrays him in act 4 scene 2). Barabas sticks closely to that Latin tag, being 'always nearest [him]self'.

Throughout the play Marlowe switches between the central focus of Barabas and his roller-coaster fortunes on the one hand, and the political strand of the plot on the other, which is concerned with Ferneze and his Knights' defence of Malta against the barbarous Turks. In historical terms, the Moslem threat was a significant one: Suleiman the Magnificent had continued the steady, seemingly unstoppable march of the Ottoman empire with alarming rapidity, through the Middle East, North Africa, Greece and parts of Europe. Marlowe has drawn on historical sources for the setting of his drama, although it is important to note that he is playing fast and loose with the facts as we understand them. Around 1530, the Knight Hospitallers of the Order of St John of Jerusalem established a garrison on Malta, having been forced to abandon their stronghold on the island of Rhodes after repeated attacks by Turkish forces. In the battle for supremacy in the region, the Mediterranean islands were of crucial importance for the control of the sea routes. In 1551 and 1565, the Turks besieged the Knights garrisoned at Malta. However, contrary to Marlowe's version of events, the Turks were on both occasions beaten back, though significant losses were incurred by both sides. The idea of a city being captured by means of a secret tunnel is familiar from a number of accounts of sieges. N.W. Bawcutt has suggested that the use of the monastery as a trap to blow up the Turkish army might have been inspired by the account of a similar booby-trap sprung on Turkish forces during their siege of a town in Hungary – the story was familiar from John Foxe's *Acts and Monuments* (1583) (Bawcutt, 1997, p. 6). It is possible that Barabas himself might be based at least in part on the figure of Jao Micques (also known as Joseph Mendez-Nassi), a Marrano Jew who, according to Belleforest's *Cosmographie* (1575), persuaded the Turkish emperor Selim (who had succeeded his father Suleiman in 1566) to seize Cyprus from the Venetians.

Martin Del Bosco provides the other strand of the political plot. Vice-Admiral of Spain, Bosco's arrival in act 2 scene 2 prompts Ferneze to refuse to pay the money demanded by the Turks, and to stand firm against Malta's oppressors. But while Bosco may be a great warrior, he is, like so many in the play, a businessman too; in his case, it is the lucrative business of trading slaves. It is at the slave market that Barabas buys his slave Ithamore, who is to become one of the key players in the drama that follows, Barabas's sidekick, confidant and partner in crime. He also provides the audience with a useful index to Barabas's increasing viciousness.

Playing false: Barabas as performer

In a play written by William Rowley in 1609, *A Search for Money*, a character identified as a usurer is portrayed wearing 'an old moth-eaten cap buttoned under his chin, his visage like the artificial Jew of Malta's nose'. The description is a transferred epithet – that is to say, a phrase where the adjective ('artificial') is transferred from the appropriate noun ('nose') to another noun ('Jew'). This is, of course, an accident of grammar, but it usefully signals a dimension of the play that has enormous potential for the way it, and Barabas in particular, may be interpreted. What the transferred epithet can be made to suggest is that it is not only the false nose (worn presumably by Edward Alleyn when playing the role) that is artificial, but Barabas himself. As has already been indicated, Barabas operates by dissembling. As we have seen, asides, lies, assumed emotions and subject positions develop into the adoption of physical disguise, and even the ultimate pretence, a feigned death. Taking one step back from the play, we are reminded that this is a performance: it is safe to assume that the Elizabethans were more aware of the artificial nature of a play than we tend to be today. The performance conditions ensured this, and the playwrights were imaginative and unrestrained in their exploitation of that awareness. And so Barabas too is a fiction, a character *played* by an actor. His frequent asides and soliloquies, establishing direct contact between actor and audience, add emphasis to this important principle.

Barabas has no qualms about deception, pretence and disguise. While persuading a reluctant Abigail to enter the nunnery in order to retrieve some hidden treasure, he declares:

> As good dissemble that thou never mean'st
> As first mean truth and then dissemble it;
> A counterfeit profession is better
> Than unseen hypocrisy.

[1.2.290–3]

The syntax here is confusing, but what Barabas is saying is that conscious deception is as good as (or, by implication, better than) the intention to remain honest which consequently fails and lapses into deceit. And as far as Barabas is concerned, the nuns are hypocrites and Abigail's intentional disguise is better than the 'unseen hypocrisy' that they practise. Having persuaded her, and having seen her accepted by Jacomo and Bernardine as a convertite, the rest of the scene constitutes one of the play's great slapstick sequences (and there are several in this so-called tragedy), with Barabas alternating between the outward show of grief and fury at his daughter's apostasy, and whispered instructions to her concerning the gold (I have inserted some stage directions, in square brackets, to clarify how quickly he is switching tone and register):

[*Aloud to Jacomo*]	Blind, friar? I reck not thy persuasions.
[*Aside to Abigail*]	*The board is marked thus that covers it.*
	[*He makes a sign of the cross.*]
[*Aloud to Jacomo*]	For I had rather die than see her thus. –
[*Aloud to Abigail*]	Wilt thou forsake me too in my distress,
	Seduced daughter?
[*Aside to Abigail*]	*Go, forget not –*
[*Aloud, rhetorical*]	Becomes it Jews to be so credulous?
[*Aside to Abigail*]	*Tomorrow early I'll be at the door.*
[*Aloud to Abigail*]	No, come not at me! If thou wilt be damned,
	Forget me, see me not, and so be gone.

> [*Aside to Abigail*]   *Farewell, remember tomorrow morning.*
> [*Aloud to Abigail*]   Out, out, thou wretch!

[1.2.353–63]

When staged with dexterity and an eye for physical comedy, as they were in the 1987 RSC production, the switches from anger and contempt for the friars, grief and fury over Abigail and her supposed conversion, and the whispered instructions to find the gold are dazzling. The actors criss-cross the stage as the friars attempt to lead Abigail into the new nunnery, and Barabas pulls her back, each time whispering more details to her, swerving up and downstage of her to ensure Jacomo and Bernardine hear nothing. It is one of those scenes that exploit the relationship Barabas has been nurturing with the audience, where we laugh at his daring and his skill, and mock along with him the blind stupidity of the friars.

Highly performative too are the 'actual' mood swings Barabas experiences. Not only does Barabas perform emotions and attitudes in order to deceive other characters, we are also privileged to see how Barabas 'really' feels, and the switches are often as swift as the ones he performs for the benefit of others. (The terms 'actual' and 'really' are used reluctantly here: the distinction is between the emotions Barabas acts for the benefit of others on stage, and what he is genuinely thinking and feeling beneath his disguise; but it is crucial to remember that this is itself merely another 'layer' of the actor's performance.) When he first hears that his house has been confiscated to be converted into a nunnery, Barabas's mood slaloms from despair, to determination, to excitement, as a plan takes shape in his mind:

> My gold, my gold, and all my wealth is gone!
> You partial heavens, have I deserved this plague? . . .

He briefly contemplates suicide, in the space of four lines, and almost immediately rejects the idea:

> No, I will live, nor loathe I this my life;
> And since you leave me in the ocean thus
> To sink or swim, and put me to my shifts,
> I'll rouse my senses and awake myself.
> Daughter, I have it! . . .

[1.2.258–73]

Simon Shepherd points out that this sudden switch can be played in two ways: to rant, stop, think and then have an idea, or else to rant and suddenly have the idea (Shepherd, 1986, p. 174). The first method will bring us closer to what we would be more familiar with in the theatre today, psychological realism. However, as Shepherd points out, it will be 'a comically inept display of realistic thinking' because it is over so quickly. The second method will suggest that the despair is performed rather than felt, and so will destabilize our reaction to Barabas's predicament. Just as Barabas mocks his fellow Jews after they have attempted to comfort him, so he scorns any attempt the audience might make to establish some kind of sympathetic relationship with him. It is unsettling, working almost in the fashion Brecht tried to establish via his so-called *Verfremdungseffekt*, or alienation effect – as a theatrical technique that would encourage an audience to engage intellectually before it engaged emotionally with what was portrayed on stage.

Barabas is acutely aware of his part in the drama as a performer, aware that he is playing a role (the term *play* being particularly appropriate as a description of his behaviour). It is this capacity that enables him to step in and out of the frame of the action, while the other characters remain, relatively speaking, trapped in their roles: we might say they *act* rather than *play* their roles. There are few asides and soliloquies in the play that are not spoken by Barabas. The other key figure in the drama, Ferneze, has only one. While in conversation with other characters in the play, Barabas will suddenly turn to address the audience, allowing them some vital piece of information that those on stage are unaware of, or else presenting one face – polite respect, or shame and sorrow – to the characters he is addressing, while letting the audience see his true attitude and his scorn at the stupidity of those he is tricking. Marlowe supplies Barabas with a sidekick, and it would have been easy enough for Marlowe to have used Ithamore as Barabas's confidant. And although he does so on occasion, he more often feeds his thoughts directly to the audience, thus implicating us in his plot. For instance, we are intrigued and may find it hard to be unimpressed by the ingenuity with which he engineers the rivalry between Abigail's two suitors, Lodowick and Mathias, the rivalry which leads two friends to a duel in which they both die. In act 2 scene 3 Barabas convinces Lodowick that he intends to make arrangements for him to marry Abigail:

> Lodowick.   Well, Barabas, canst help me to a diamond?
> Barabas.   Oh, Sir, your father had my diamonds.
>   Yet I have one left that will serve your turn:

> [*Aside*] *I mean my daughter:* — *but ere he shall*
>   *have her*
> *I'll sacrifice her on a pile of wood.*
> *I ha' the poison of the city for him,*
> *And the white leprosy.*

Lodowick.	What sparkle does it give without a foil?
Barabas.	The diamond that I talk of, ne'er was foiled:
	[*Aside*] *But when he touches it, it will be foiled:*
	Lord Lodowick, it sparkles bright and fair.
Lodowick.	Is it square or pointed? Pray let me know.
Barabas.	Pointed it is, good sir, — [*Aside*] *but not for you.*
Lodowick.	I like it much the better.
Barabas.	So do I too.
Lodowick.	How shows it by night?
Barabas.	Outshines Cynthia's rays:
	[*Aside*] *You'll like it better far a nights than days.*
Lodowick.	And what's the price?
Barabas.	[*Aside*] *Your life and if you have it.* — Oh my Lord
	We will not jar about the price; come to my house
	And I will giv 't your honour — [*Aside*] *with a*
	vengeance.

[2.3.49–68]

The frequent and abrupt switches from the lines spoken to Lodowick to those spoken to the audience render the scene unplayable in 'realistic' terms. The fact that Barabas maintains the two relationships simultaneously, and refuses to keep them separate, enhances that sense of performativity; it is also a vital part of the process by which the audience are made complicit in his crimes.

There are other elements besides these tools of soliloquy and aside that emphasize the performative nature of the Barabas role. Barabas is himself a consummate actor. Most notable is the adoption of his disguise as a French musician towards the end of the play: the farcical register of that scene tells us not that he is a bad actor, but instead works as a testament to his skill, underlining how easily he can dupe Ithamore, Pilia-Borza and Belamira. He also successfully feigns his own death.

Barabas, then, turns in performance pieces displaying differing emotional states as they are required, and plays the different roles as circumstances demand. It is unhelpful to attempt to draw a line of psychological consistency through Barabas's varied states, as they erupt during the course

153

of the play. It is wiser to think of them more in terms of a series of set pieces. At the end of act 1 scene 2 he is the raging, grieving father of an apostate daughter; by act 4 scene 1 he is himself a groveling convertite before Jacomo and Bernardine. On most occasions he is defiant and abusive before Ferneze and his Knights, but he is willing to adopt a more politic attitude when it is necessary, such as in act 4 scene 3, when he knows that his only means of survival will be to betray the Turks and return Ferneze to power. 'Thus, loving neither, will I live with both,' he tells us, 'Making a profit of my policy' in true Machiavellian fashion (4.3.111–12). His protean emotional state at the time he hears of the fate of his house takes this a stage further – his 'real' self, it would seem, is as performative as the selves he adopts for the benefit of the other characters in the play. At other points, Barabas plays the part of director (such as in the scene mentioned above when he controls the traffic on the stage in order to instruct Abigail on where to find the gold) and the part of stage manager, as when we see him in the final scene quote '*Enter, with a hammer above, very busy*' (5.5.0.*s.d.*). The play is very much concerned with performance, then; and as the audience, our sense of Barabas as a performed character remains acute. Towards the end of the chapter I will consider how this fact might be made use of when the play is performed today. It may be that we can confront the anti-Semitic aspects of the play by filtering them through this performative dimension.

'Holy friars turn devils'

The representation of Barabas within the parameters of Elizabethan stereotype, then, is nothing more or less than what we would expect. A number of critics, in attempts to deflect attacks upon the play as a document of anti-Semitism, have pointed out that it satirizes the Christians as mercilessly as it does the Jews. The way the Jews are treated by Ferneze and his Knights would probably not have shocked or even surprised an Elizabethan audience: as far as the Elizabethans were concerned, Jews were something less than human. What might have shocked them, however, is the way the friars and nuns are satirized – and possibly Ferneze too. But attempts to imagine contemporary audience response are made more complex by the political and religious complexion of Elizabethan England. Reading the play today, we are not surprised to hear Lodowick and Mathias discussing Abigail's beauty:

A fair young maid scarce fourteen years of age,
The sweetest flower in Cytherea's field.
Cropped from the pleasures of the fruitful earth

[1.2.375–7]

But we might be more surprised to hear a friar lamenting her death in this fashion: as Abigail breathes her last and dies in the arms of the friar Bernardine, she implores him:

ah, gentle friar
Convert my father that he may be saved,
And witness that I die a Christian

To which he responds:

Ay, and a virgin too, that grieves me most.

[3.6.38–41]

Barabas also drops some heavy hints about mischievous goings-on between nuns and friars in 2.3.80–6, with puns about 'doing' (meaning having sex), reaping fruit and fullness of perfection (meaning pregnancy), but the most startling scene is act 4 scene 1 in which Bernardine and Jacomo fight for the right to convert Barabas and so inherit his wealth. Under the confidential terms of confession, Abigail, almost dead herself, has told the priest Bernardine that her father was responsible for the deaths of Mathias and Lodowick. The friars confront Barabas, who mocks them mercilessly. When it becomes clear that they know he is responsible for the deaths of the young men, he pretends to be overcome by remorse and begs to be allowed to repent and convert, offering his great wealth to whichever friar will receive him. Jacomo and Bernardine argue, each trying to convince Barabas that the other's order is too strict; then they fall to insults and eventually begin physically assaulting one another in their eagerness to win Barabas's soul and, more importantly, his money. The whole sequence actually mirrors the fight between Don Mathias and Lodowick over Abigail. Instead of the conventional encounter between two rivals for the love of a young woman, however, we have the tawdry spectacle of two friars, ostensibly vowed to a life of poverty and chastity, competing for Barabas's fortune. It is no wonder that Abigail finally despairs that 'I perceive there is no love on earth, / Pity in Jews, nor piety in Turks' (3.3.49–50). We are in a world where everyone, it seems, like Machevil himself, holds religion as a childish toy; it is used only for personal gain.

However, Marlowe takes the joke a stage further: Barabas pretends to side with Bernardine and he and Ithamore lure the friar back to their house and strangle him while he sleeps. In the meantime, they have arranged for Jacomo to return a short time later. Ithamore, spurred on to a grotesquely imaginative creativity by his participation in the murder of first the nuns and now Bernardine, takes over:

> Nay, master, be ruled by me a little. [*Stands up the body.*]
> So, let him lean upon his staff; excellent, he stands as if
> he were begging of bacon.

> [4.1.153–5]

When Jacomo approaches Bernardine and catches sight of his fellow friar in the gloom, apparently standing ready to attack him, he challenges him and then knocks him to the ground. The corpse falls, and Barabas and Ithamore rush on stage. They quickly convince Jacomo that he has killed Bernardine, Ithamore relishing the moment with his attention to gruesome detail: 'Ay, master, he's slain; look how his brains drop out on's nose' (4.1.177–8). The irony of the situation, and the force of Abigail's earlier judgement that there is 'no love on earth', is underlined by Barabas and Ithamore as they frog-march Jacomo off to be arrested. But what motivates Marlowe to write in this fashion about the Christian characters? When critics attempt to defend the play against charges of anti-Semitism on the grounds that it is as critical of Christians as it is of Jews, they are failing to situate the play properly within its original context of composition and performance. We need to remember that both Ferneze and his Knights, and the Spanish admiral Del Bosco, are not just Christians but *Catholic* Christians. We have already noted that England under Elizabeth was a Protestant nation forced to meet the Catholic challenge on a number of fronts, both international and internal. It would be fair to say that the Jews and the Turks are demonized more blatantly than the Christians, and it is significant that the play ends with a restoration of order under Christian rule, with Barabas the Jew dead and Calymath the Turk a prisoner. However, the satire of the friars in particular is sharp, and it is possible to perceive Ferneze as a greater Machiavellian than Barabas himself. Ferneze is certainly the subtler and ultimately more successful one. It should be clear how the kind of satire Marlowe unleashes on the Catholics might work as political propaganda, then. It would certainly fit with the marked anti-Catholic bias of *The Massacre at Paris*. Ithamore, like Barabas, is delineated in terms of stereotype. He is seen as savage, in some ways barely human, displaying a primitive excitement at the havoc his master wreaks on the Christians. When Barabas has poisoned all the inhabitants of the nunnery, Ithamore typically attempts to ape his master's actions: 'But here's a royal monastery hard by; / Good master, let me poison all the monks' (4.1.13–14). Barabas's reply is in line with the satire on the Catholic community: 'Thou shalt not need, for now the nuns are dead, / They'll die with grief' (4.1.15–16).

It does not take very long for Ithamore to betray his master. In keeping with the representation of him as a semi-savage, the prostitute Bellamira awakens his lust, and she and her accomplice Pilia-Borza, a petty thief, easily persuade Ithamore to blackmail Barabas into handing over huge sums of money to them. What we might loosely call the 'love scene' between Ithamore and Bellamira is a parody of courtly love conventions. Ithamore declares:

Left to right: Andrew Chisholm as Pilia-Borza, Jessica Lines as Bellamira, Lisa Curtis as Ithamore in the KAPAC production of *The Jew of Malta* (dir. Stevie Simkin), John Stripe Theatre, Winchester, 1997. (Reproduced by courtesy of the photographer, Peter Jacobs.)

> . . . but we will leave this paltry land,
> And sail from hence to Greece, to lovely Greece:
> I'll be thy Jason, thou my golden fleece;
> Where painted carpets o'er the meads are hurl'd,
> And Bacchus' vineyards o'er-spread the world,
> Where woods and forests go in goodly green,
> I'll be Adonis, thou shalt be Love's Queen.
> The meads, the orchards, and the primrose lanes,
> Instead of sedge and reed, bear sugar canes:
> Thou in those groves, by Dis above,
> Shalt live with me and be my love.

[4.2.94–104]

The choice of mythological references is significant: the reference to the golden fleece, which Jason and the Argonauts retrieved after passing through many great dangers, suggests that Bellamira is valued in material terms. Bacchus conjures up images of debauchery rather than tender love, and the familiar notion of Adonis as the beautiful youth would, for an Elizabethan, render this a grotesque and laughable comparison for the ugly Turk Ithamore to make. The final line of the speech is an ironic echo of Marlowe's own famous love poem, 'The Passionate Shepherd to his Love', barbarously inappropriate for the savage slave the play depicts.

Performed ethnicity

Marlowe satirizes his Catholics and uses familiar stereotypes when portraying his Turk Ithamore (although it should be noted that Selim-Calymath is a fairly neutral figure in these terms, operating primarily as part of the mechanism of the plot). But at the heart of the play, in terms of race and ethnicity, the problem of anti-Semitism remains to be dislodged, or at least challenged in some way. In reading the play, discussing it, and writing about it, these issues of prejudice can be brought out into the open. However, performance of the text does not allow such easy and open negotiation of the issues involved. Some other strategy is required. One way forward might be to think of Barabas's Jewish identity in relation to the performative dimension of his persona that we have already discussed. Might it be possible to see Barabas's ethnic identity in relation to this playfulness he displays in the deployment of his performed self or selves? Perhaps we can keep Barabas to some extent dissociated from his identity as a Jew, in a way that is more difficult or perhaps impossible with Shylock. This is not to say that Marlowe intended any such thing. We cannot know for sure, of course, but it seems more likely that he was working within the ideological parameters of his own time and his own society. Performance of a 400-year-old text, however, allows (or demands) a freedom of interpretation that might open up another option in the instance of *The Jew of Malta*. If we not only perceive Barabas as being aware of the role he is playing, but extend that game so that the actor playing the role is also permitted to be 'playful' in his presentation of it, there may be a way of turning the play's apparent anti-Semitism inside out.

The Jewishness portrayed in the performance of Barabas, then, might be perceived in the same way that we recognize other aspects of his performative nature: it is what we could term a *performed ethnicity*. Our ability to recognize Marlowe's Jew as a *constructed* one – and to retain that awareness as we track his progress through the play, whether watching a performance or reading the text – can throw a whole new light on the way we perceive this problem of anti-Semitism in Marlowe's play (for a full discussion of the notion of performed ethnicity, see Simkin, 1999). This is a difficult but crucial notion to grasp if we are to appreciate how *The Jew of Malta* may be used to challenge rather than simply reinforce racial stereotype and prejudice. It requires us to re-examine the assumptions we bring to a reading or a performance of a play written over 400 years ago. Our attention is constantly drawn to the fact that Barabas has taken on the contours of the Elizabethan Jewish stereotype, acting the role of the typical stage Jew in something that comes close to a parody of the conventions that operated at the time. It seems clear that when Alleyn played the part he wore an artificial nose, and he would probably have worn a red wig, too, as actors did when they played the role of Judas in the miracle plays. So the actor takes on the outward signs of Jewishness through these stage props. No doubt the actor's costume, probably a long gabardine coat, would have functioned as another signifier of Jewish ethnicity, but this opportunity of seeing his ethnic identity self-consciously performed emerges from the dialogue, too, both in things that are said about Barabas (such as the reference to him crucifying a child, part of the folklore surrounding Jews in Europe at this time) and particularly from Barabas's own soliloquies. There is an oft-quoted speech where Barabas describes his past history:

> . . . I walk abroad a-nights,
> And kill sick people groaning under walls:
> Sometimes I go about and poison wells;
>
>   . . .
>
> Being young I studied physic, and began
> To practise first upon the Italian;
> There I enriched the priests with burials,
> And always kept the sexton's arms in ure
> With digging graves and ringing dead men's knells
> . . .
>
>   I filled the jails with bankrupts in a year,
> And with young orphans planted hospitals,
> And every moon made some or other mad,
> And now and then one hang himself for grief,
> Pinning upon his breast a long great scroll
> How I with interest tormented him.

[2.3.177–9, 184–8, 196–201]

These lines are comic because of the dislocation between context and tone: the deeds he describes should horrify us, but when they are couched in casual phrases like 'as for myself', 'sometimes I go about', 'and now and then', and the final 'But tell me now, how hast thou spent thy time?', it is impossible to take them seriously. (Indeed, it is hard to imagine Marlowe expected his audience to take them seriously.) Barabas is highly self-conscious about his role as a stage villain, and often comments humorously and ironically on it. What is important to note is that Barabas's Jewishness and his villainy are virtually indivisible: for an Elizabethan, at least, they would presumably have been synonymous. There is a similar moment at the beginning of the second act. Barabas is on his way to his house – now a nunnery – to meet Abigail and, as he hopes, recover the treasure he hid there:

> Thus, like the sad presaging raven that tolls
> The sick man's passport in her hollow beak,
> And in the shadow of the silent night
> Doth shake contagion from her sable wings;
> Vexed and tormented runs poor Barabas
> With fatal curses towards these Christians.
> The incertain pleasures of swift-footed time
> Have ta'en their flight, and left me in despair;

And of my former riches rests no more
But bare remembrance; like a soldier's scar,
That has no further comfort for his maim.

[2.1.1–11]

Many of these lines seem to belong to a Chorus speech, rather than to a Barabas soliloquy: the actor playing Barabas here seems quite distinctly dissociated from his persona. Marlowe slips into third person commentary: Barabas talks of himself not as 'I' and 'me' but as a separate entity: 'Vexed and tormented runs poor Barabas / With fatal curses towards these Christians'.

Again, this approach seems to work on two levels. At the first level, Barabas reminds the audience that he is playing the role of a Jew, acting out the part of the kind of Jew the Christians expect to see. In performance, the actor might mime each sculpted pose and rehearsed movement as he shows off his skills as a dissembler:

We Jews can fawn like spaniels when we please,
And when we grin, we bite; yet are our looks
As innocent and harmless as a lamb's.
I learned in Florence how to kiss my hand,
Heave up my shoulders when they call me dog,
And duck as low as any barefoot friar,
Hoping to see them starve upon a stall,
Or else be gathered for in our synagogue,
That when the offering-basin comes to me,
Even for charity I may spit into 't.

[2.3.20–9]

He is evidently wise enough to understand that the Christians perceive him not as Barabas but as Jew, and he moulds his behaviour to their expectations. He is mindful of the submissive role that he is expected to play as a Jew – to 'heave up my shoulders when they call me dog', as he says; but behind the show of surrender is bitter hostility – 'And when we grin we bite'. At the second level, there is a self-consciousness about the part his persona is playing in the performance: this is, if you like, the actor commenting ironically on Barabas himself, rather than Barabas reflecting on his own dissembling within the world of the play. The staginess of Barabas's villainy, as Robert C. Jones has noted, is in sharp contrast to Ferneze's intrigues which are conducted without any of the asides and other stage business that Barabas indulges in (Jones, 1986, p. 89). And so the ironic detachment that the Barabas actor can employ is not such an easy option for the actor playing Ferneze, who remains more closely identified with his evil practice because of this lack of self-awareness. The idea of Barabas as a self-consciously performed ethnic stereotype is a potentially powerful one. We have already seen how the Other acts as a kind of evil inversion of the subject's self, an embodiment of all those features one would prefer not to recognize in one's own self. If we can recognize in reading and accentuate in performance this principle of performed ethnicity, there might be a way of flipping inside out the interpretation of the play we would assume to have been dominant in its original performance context – that is to say, identification of Barabas as a pantomime villain to be laughed and hissed at. The way forward from this principle is not a simple one, but it at least opens up possibilities for a new kind of engagement with the text in performance.

'The unhallowed deeds of Jews': crime and punishment

The final section of the play moves fairly swiftly, although it has in effect two denouements. After Barabas reluctantly hands over the gold to Pilia-Borza in response to Ithamore's threat of blackmail, he quickly devises a way of retaliating to Ithamore's act of betrayal. Another assumed persona (a comic French musician) gains him entry into their company and he leaves behind poisoned flowers which will kill all three of them, though not quickly enough to prevent Bellamira and Pilia-Borza revealing to Ferneze the full details of Barabas's crimes. Barabas and Ithamore (dying) are arrested immediately, and Barabas denounces all three of them as liars. When he demands justice ('Let me have law; / For none of this can prejudice my life'), Ferneze's response is a harsh, probably ironic: 'Once more, away with him! You shall have law' (5.1.38–40). Moments later, we hear that all four of them have died. Ferneze's subsequent speech could almost be bringing the play to its conclusion:

> Wonder not at it, sir, the heavens are just.
> Their deaths were like their lives, then think not of 'em;
> Since they are dead, let them be buried.

For the Jew's body, throw that o'er the walls,
To be a prey for vultures and wild beasts.

[5.1.55–9]

But a loose end remains: the Turkish threat. Ferneze gives the order
for the fortification of the town. According to the editor of the Revels
Plays edition of *The Jew of Malta*, some stage business occurs around
this point: '[BARABAS *thrown down*]' (5.1.59.*s.d.*). Other editors insert
a similar stage direction here. It is unclear how this might have been
represented on the Elizabethan stage, but it is obvious that when a moment
later, with the stage empty, Barabas leaps to his feet in cartoon fashion
and vows revenge on the town, we are to understand that he is outside the city walls. His chance for revenge occurs almost immediately,
with the arrival of Calymath and the Turkish army. Barabas shows them
a secret way into the town, through the sewers, and the fifth act opens
with Ferneze and his knights led on as prisoners of Calymath and his
Turkish soldiers. As a reward, Barabas is made governor of Malta. However,
he realizes that his position there is gravely compromised by the fact
that he has come to rule them by betraying them all to the Turkish
enemy. There is still room, it would seem, for a final twist in the play's
narrative (although in the past critics have responded unfavourably to
this seemingly rather *ad hoc* aspect of the play's structure).

It is Barabas's final piece of trickery that makes the Machiavellian
parallels most relevant. Left alone to ponder his good fortune, it rapidly
emerges as more of a predicament than a position of advantage:

I now am governor of Malta. True,
But Malta hates me, and in hating me,
My life's in danger . . .
No, Barabas, this must be looked into;
And since by wrong thou got'st authority,
Maintain it bravely by firm policy,
At least unprofitably lose it not;

[5.2.29–31, 34–7]

In a startling reversal of loyalties that even outdoes Ithamore's
betrayal, he strikes a deal with his old enemy Ferneze, offering to betray
Calymath, and to return the island to the Maltese governor. An invitation is issued to Calymath to attend a banquet, which he accepts. The

final scene opens with Barabas preparing a trap for Calymath – a trap door beneath Calymath's chair with a cauldron below. Everyone arrives for the banquet, but at the crucial moment Ferneze steps forward and springs the trap set for the Turk on Barabas himself. The play's final moments are closest to the model of tragedy that would become familiar in Elizabethan drama: Barabas overreaches himself and is overtaken by his own villainy. Having tumbled into the cauldron, he has a long dying speech (a dozen lines) which, considering he is being boiled alive in oil as he speaks, evidently has very little to do with realism. This is another convention, one that eschews what we would consider 'realistic' so that the play's protagonist can remind us of the catalogue of his crimes and, in Barabas's case, seal his eternal fate by dying with curses on his lips:

> Damned Christian dogs, and Turkish infidels!
> But now begins the extremity of heat
> To pinch me with intolerable pangs:
> Die, life: fly, soul; tongue, curse thy fill and die!

[5.5.85–8]

It has often been noted that the manner of his death mirrors the particular fate reserved for the avaricious in hell, according to such writings as Dante's *Inferno*. It was also the traditional punishment for convicted poisoners. Calymath tries to sue for peace but instead he is taken prisoner, and Ferneze's brand of order is restored.

For an Elizabethan audience, we can assume that this would have been a fitting conclusion to the play. Ferneze outwits the villainous Jew and the Turkish infidel. Barabas is not only seen to pay for his crimes by losing his life, but his eternal damnation is graphically staged, represented as it is in the exact manner of his death. The conclusion even bears the pleasing symmetry of revenge, with Ferneze repaying Barabas for the death of his son, Don Lodowick. By this time, the audience is far enough away from the early victimization of Barabas to remember only his crimes. In any case, as we have already discussed, it is unlikely that the treatment he receives at the hands of Ferneze and his knights would have inspired much sympathy in an audience of Marlowe's contemporaries. In our own time, our feelings might be more ambivalent. A number of critics have pointed out the blurred divisions between moral and immoral behaviour on the part of Ferneze, and today we are likely to be more suspicious of him. The 1987 RSC production capitalized on this by doubling the roles of Ferneze and Machevil. At the play's conclusion, Ferneze stepped back into the Machevil character, adopting the same Italian accent he had used for the Prologue to speak Ferneze's final two lines. Clearly the director's intention was to signal unambiguously to the audience how the roles had been assigned, establishing Ferneze, rather than Barabas, as the true Machiavelli. Nevertheless, the reception of the 1987 production, the most recent major revival of the play in Britain, was decidedly mixed. The decision to play it as broad farce, and to emphasize the hypocrisy of the Christians, could not excuse its anti-Semitism in the eyes of many critics. One columnist headlined her thoughts on the revival with the uncompromising line, 'A society that can laugh at the Jew of Malta by pretending anti-semitism is dead' (Phillips, 1988). For Elizabethans, Barabas's punishment fits his crimes, and his boiling alive is a cause for celebration; with the extermination of some six million Jews still relatively recent history, Ferneze's command, 'Make fires, heat irons, let the rack be fetched' (5.1.24), and Barabas's cry, 'But now begins the extremity of heat / To pinch me with intolerable pangs' (5.5.86–7), will have much more immediate connotations than punishments in hell. The anti-Semitism at the heart of *The Jew of Malta* cannot be argued away, or disguised with broad comedy when the play is revived. The willingness with which we imagine the Elizabethans accepted it must serve as a constant reminder of how ethnic prejudice, along with many other kinds of minority oppression, lurks all too close to the surface in any human society.

Postscript: *The Jew of Malta* in the Warsaw ghetto

In December 1997, a production of *The Jew of Malta* I directed using a cast of student actors offered an opportunity to explore precisely the issues that are central to the argument of this chapter. The purpose of the experiment was to try to recuperate an anti-Semitic text and use it to investigate how ethnic identities can be created, imposed and resisted (for a fuller investigation of the production, see Simkin, 1998; Simkin & Williams, 1999; and Williams, 1999). The production appropriated a familiar early modern theatrical convention, the play within a play motif, in order to investigate the notion of performed ethnicity discussed above. The setting for the production was the Nazis' establishment of a Jewish ghetto in Warsaw towards the end of 1939. The staging of Marlowe's play took place within this framing device, a performance

Tom Rennie as Barabas (left), Stewart Andrew as Ferneze in the KAPAC production of
The Jew of Malta (dir. Stevie Simkin), John Stripe Theatre, Winchester, 1997.
(Reproduced by courtesy of the photographer, Peter Jacobs.)

initiated by the Nazi authorities in an attempt to humiliate the Polish
Jews. The roles of the Christians – Ferneze and his Knights, and the
friars – were performed by German soldiers and the Jewish roles by
Jewish interns (with the leader of the Jewish community forced to play
the part of Barabas).

The creation of two contexts opened up a performative space
between the two sets of roles in the two plays – the 'outer' play set in
Poland in 1939, and the 'inner' play, Marlowe's *The Jew of Malta*.
Furthermore, the ways in which the two plot-lines (1939 and 1590)
separated and converged illuminated the issue of ethnic oppression: as
the Marlowe text played itself out, it was clear that another narrative,
centring on the struggle between the leader of the Jewish community
and the German officer, was unfolding. At certain points, the performance of the Marlowe play was interrupted or disrupted in various ways,
and at these points the 1939 action intruded on the Marlowe text: for
example, the 1939 Jew performing the role of Abigail, confronted with
a scene (3.3) in which she has to play a conversion to Christianity, initially refused. Physically restrained by two soldiers, she was forced to

complete the speech at gun-point, spitting out the lines in a sarcastic fury and tearing the book to pieces as she finished. The key role, however, was the head of the Jewish council, forced by the German officer (playing Ferneze) to act the part of Barabas. What the audience witnessed in this production was not simply Marlowe's anti-Semitic stereotype; instead, they observed an actor depicting an oppressed 1939 Jew being forced to play a viciously stereotyped Elizabethan Jew. The performer acted the 1939 role in familiar naturalistic mode. However, he was most assuredly *playing* (rather than acting) the role of Marlowe's Barabas. The awareness of that role as stereotype was fully exploited by the actor, whose ironic approach (in his 1939 role) worked to subvert that stereotype, either by playing up to it, or else exposing it with ironic detachment.

The re-appropriation of the Marlowe play for a more progressive politics was finally achieved by an act of sabotage on the text that had been left largely undisturbed up to that point (although lines were frequently read against the grain). While all around him the performers stripped to their 1997 street clothes, the German officer was left trying to hold the play together, unable to discard his own costume (a magnificent Elizabethan robe over a Nazi officer's uniform). As the performers reprised the play's most blatant anti-Semitic lines, throwing them back in the face of the Ferneze actor and frustrating his attempts to bring the play to an end with his scripted concluding speech, he was left helplessly repeating the lines from the 1633 prologue: 'But if aught here offend your ear or sight / We only act and speak what others write.' Just as Marlowe's Barabas is hoist by his own petard, so the production sprang a trap on Marlowe's text, attempting to catch it in the jaws of its own anti-Semitism. Finally, this approach to *The Jew* was intended not only to challenge understandings of Marlowe's play, but to raise significant questions about more frequently revived early modern plays featuring representations of ethnic 'Others' that require closer interrogation. For while theorists have for some time now been applying post-colonial perspectives to texts like *Othello*, *The Tempest* and *The Merchant of Venice*, the gap between the academic and the public theatrical communities is one still waiting to be bridged.

CHAPTER 6

TELLING STORIES: *Edward II*

Playing with history and telling stories

As we have already seen, one of the reasons why Marlowe is such a fascinating and important figure is that, as a playwright, he was a pioneer, breaking new ground in the form and the content of the drama during this volatile period. *Edward II* is a case in point: probably first performed during the winter of 1592–3, it was a key text in the establishment of a new genre in English drama, the 'history' play. We will find out a little more about this genre first; we will then analyse what we mean by the term 'history' (not as straightforward as it might first appear), before going on to look in some detail at the play itself. Of all the plays in the Marlowe canon, *Edward II* is considered by many to be his most satisfying piece of drama. It is the most frequently revived, after *Doctor Faustus*, and if it does not contain the potential to be as explosive in ideological terms as *The Jew of Malta*, it still has the capacity to provoke by its probing analysis of state politics, sexual politics and the intersection of the two.

Although Marlowe's play is significant in the establishment of its genre, recent scholarship has concluded that Shakespeare's first history plays probably predate *Edward II*; furthermore, there are a number of other lesser known works that cluster around the first years of this decade: George Peele's *Edward I* (1591), anonymous plays such as *Jack Straw* (1590–1), and, possibly, *The Troublesome Reign of King John* (1591–2) and *Woodstock* (1592?). Tracing the lineage back further still, the most well-known prototype for the history play is *Gorboduc*, written by two lawyers, Sackville and Norton, and first performed around 1561. *Gorboduc* is a fairly dull play, less a drama than a series of monologues and lengthy, leaden dialogues, and its audience was not the popular one that Marlowe was writing for, but Sackville and Norton's fellow lawyers at the Inns of Court. *Gorboduc* would also have been performed before Queen Elizabeth, and it seems likely, bearing in mind the political climate at this time, that the play was written with a specific purpose: to persuade the monarch to tidy up the issue of succession, which many at this time saw as a crisis waiting to happen. Consequently, its tone is grimly serious and its moralizing heavy-handed. The metre of the verse remains stuck in a slow and heavy groove, and its vocabulary is cold and abstract. Nevertheless, *Gorboduc* remains a useful reference point in the development of the history play genre. What is more, its political concerns are echoed (with far greater subtlety) in later plays, notably Shakespeare's *King Lear*.

It is Shakespeare who provides the most substantial single body of work within the genre of the history play, and much has been written about how his two tetralogies are deeply implicated in the politics of their time. The two sets of Shakespeare's history plays comprise the three parts of *Henry VI* along with *Richard III* (*c*.1589–94) and, making up the second set, *Richard II*, *Henry IV* Parts 1 & 2 and *Henry V* (*c*.1595–9). Shakespeare's chief source – and Marlowe's major source for *Edward II* – was Raphael Holinshed's *Chronicles of England, Scotland and Ireland* (first published about 1577). Aside from its length (the second, enlarged edition of 1587 ran to some three and a half million words), one of the most striking aspects of Holinshed's work from a modern perspective is its tendency to file so-called 'real history' alongside myths and legends (Lear himself makes an appearance in the *Chronicles*). Sober 'facts' rub shoulders with the most improbable tales. The heavy use of so-called scare quotes here indicates that the terminology requires closer attention, and before we pursue any further the idea of the history play, we should pause for a moment to consider those concepts I have designated as problematic.

What do we understand by the term 'history'? And, bearing in mind what we have established previously about how radically different our mindset is from that of the Elizabethans, we must also ask ourselves, what did someone like Marlowe understand by the term 'history'? Our first response might be to say that history consists of a collection of facts about the events of the past. The reason why it might not be as simple as this is that we need to investigate where these 'facts' come from: on what (or, more accurately, on *whom*) do we rely for our facts about the past? History does not exist: it is *made* (in both senses), and it is apt to play surprising tricks on those who would rely unthinkingly upon it. To take a familiar example: Alfred the Great, the ninth-century king of Wessex, is most famous (no doubt unjustly) for being scolded by a peasant woman for letting her cakes burn in the oven he had been asked to mind. However, this story is nowhere to be found in the earliest accounts of Alfred's career; it only emerged 100 years or more later. This is in some ways an extreme example; after all, we are dealing here with ancient history that is poorly sourced, and such history is bound to shade into the grey area of myth sooner or later. We will even find this beginning to happen when we examine Marlowe's sources for *Edward II*. But King Alfred's story is chosen to make the point that we should think carefully about what the term history can mean; it is one of those everyday but vitally important concepts that is too often left unexamined precisely because it is so familiar. To defamiliarize the idea of history, I would suggest a different and perhaps more useful way of understanding what history means: history is not about facts, but about *telling stories*. The totality of the past is, self-evidently, irrecoverable, and history will always and inevitably be partial and selective. Furthermore, there is no such thing as disinterested, objective history. History is told by people, and people have attitudes, agendas, social and political beliefs, and so on. All of these pressures and influences will colour, consciously or not, the way they tell the stories of history.

To take this a little further, we may return briefly to the story (or, rather, stories) of Marlowe's life and death we explored in an earlier section. According to Beard's *Theatre of God's Judgements* (1597), Marlowe was 'by practice a playmaker, and a poet of scurrility' and a blasphemer. As we saw in the biographical chapter, Beard claimed that, despite the nature of Marlowe's wound, he 'even cursed and blasphemed to his last gasp', and Beard takes it as 'a manifest sign of God's judgment' that Marlowe should die in such a fashion. The hand 'which had written those blasphemies' holds the dagger that stabbed him, 'and that in his brain, which had devised the same' (cited in MacLure, 1995, p. 42). Later accounts further embellished the story. Francis Meres contests that Marlowe was 'stabbed to death by a bawdy serving man, a rival of his in his lewd love' (cited in ibid., p. 46). Edmund Rudierd worked from Beard's story in discussion of Marlowe's case in his *The Thunderbolt of God's Wrath against Hard-Hearted and Stiff-Necked Sinners* (1618), turning the story into a warning against 'brain-sick and profane poets' (meaning playwrights, in this context) and the players 'that live by making fools laugh at sin and wickedness' (cited in Wraight & Stern, 1993, p. 307). This is history in the making: it is not simply a matter of gathering the details and recounting facts; it is rather a process of telling stories about an event in the past. Each account is a report of Marlowe's death; but, as we can see, the fact of his death is interpreted in different ways, whether as a warning against atheism, sexual immorality, or as a judgement on the theatre and those who work there. It is a notion we shall return to when we come to look at the story Marlowe told about the reign of Edward II in the play of that name.

What we always need to ask ourselves is, who is telling this particular history? Who is telling this story about the past? And what might their agenda be, conscious or not, as they construct their narrative? As the historiographer Keith Jenkins puts it, 'History is never for itself; it is always for someone' (Jenkins, 1991, p. 17). Until relatively recently, just about the only histories on offer have been told by men of the middle and upper classes. Now those stories find themselves challenged by fascinating explorations of history from the perspective of women, for example, or of the working class. Early modern drama is particularly interesting in relation to this question of who is telling the story of history, and there are a number of reasons for this. The major difference between, say, the year 2000 and the year 1600 is the idea of what history *should* be. G. Elton, writing in 1969, states that 'The study of history, then, amounts to the search for the truth' (Elton, 1969, p. 70). Although today the goal of objective 'truth' is generally recognized as being beyond our grasp, a readiness to acknowledge bias can in itself be seen, paradoxically, as a nod towards the goal of objectivity. However, in Marlowe's time, history was seen as a didactic tool, and the prime commitment was not to 'facts' but to the usefulness of the past in expounding political theory. The patterns of the past were laid over the present and, by implication, the future; for it is clear that the Elizabethans understood history as moving in cycles, these cycles usually involving the fall of a monarch from authority and good fortune to a position of abjection and misery. The collection of tales known as *The Mirror for Magistrates* (first published in 1559 and frequently reprinted) repeats this pattern over and over again, and the rationale is clear:

> For here as in a looking glass, you shall see (if any vice
> be in you) how the like hath been punished in other
> heretofore, whereby admonished, I trust it will be a good
> occasion to move you to the sooner amendment.

> (cited in Campbell, 1938, pp. 65–6)

Its agenda is explicitly stated: it aims to teach and to warn the powerful. The stories of history are recycled as object lessons in good and bad government.

As we noted in our discussion of Marlowe's England, a great many of his playgoers would have been illiterate, and the dramatized history of their nation would have been one of their only sources of information. It should be clear from this that the drama had immense political potential. Recent studies of plays like Shakespeare's tetralogies, as well as Marlowe's *Edward II*, have found that the significance of this was not wasted on those active in the theatres at the time, either on the writers themselves or on the authorities who stood to lose or gain whenever that political potential was activated. The most familiar example is evident in what has come to be termed the Tudor myth. The Tudor myth was based on the idea that the Tudor dynasty had redeemed the English nation from a curse initiated by that most heinous of crimes, a regicide – the murder of a king, Richard II. Henry VII had brought about a new, harmonious state by defeating the villainous King Richard III at the battle of Bosworth and bringing the Wars of the Roses to an end. Elizabeth I, who was to be the last of the Tudors, was the granddaughter of Henry VII, the first Tudor king. The representation of Richard III in the play of that name (and Richard is always a villain, no matter how impressive an audience may find him) epitomizes the agenda of *The Mirror for Magistrates* quoted above. The Tudors fostered the notion that they were bringing harmony and restoring the health of the nation after decades of unrest, and propagated the idea by various means, the most immediate being their crest which united the symbols of the two rival dynasties, the Yorkist white rose and the Lancastrian red, in their own symbol.

But how does our play, *Edward II*, relate to its historical sources? As mentioned above, Holinshed's *Chronicles* formed the bulk of Marlowe's source material; other incidents were taken from the work of Robert Fabian (*The Chronicle of Fabian*, 4th edition, 1559) and John Stow, whose *Chronicles of England* first appeared in 1580. Marlowe would probably have used its 1592 edition, *The Annals of England*. Here are some of the bare 'facts', as far as we can know them, about Edward's reign: born in 1284, he was crowned king in 1307, having spent seven years as Prince of Wales, the first heir apparent to bear that title. He married Isabella of France in 1308. His reign was characterized by periodic conflict with the powerful baronial class, culminating in the Ordinances of 1311. The Ordinances continued the political process initiated by the more famous Magna Carta to which King John had put his seal in 1215, and forced Edward to accept the constitutional reform that enabled the barons to shift power further away from the throne. He also suffered humiliating defeats in Scotland, most famously at Bannockburn, where his adversary was Robert the Bruce. On 25 January 1326 or 1327 he was forced to renounce the throne, handing power over to his son, who was under the protection of Mortimer; and on 22 September 1327 he was horribly murdered at Berkley Castle, near Gloucester. It is also worth tracing what we know of Edward's arch-enemy in the play, young Mortimer (there are two Mortimers in the play, and unless otherwise specified, the one referred to in this chapter is Mortimer Junior, who is the more significant). Born in 1287, he was appointed Lieutenant of Ireland in 1316. He was sent to the Tower by Edward in 1322, but escaped and fled to France within a year, joining forces with Isabella, Edward's estranged wife, in 1326. Having brought about the king's abdication, within the space of a few short years he was beheaded for the murder of Edward, on 30 November 1330.

We can see from these dates that one of the most radical things Marlowe does with his text is to compress, cut and vigorously reshape the narrative events. From a first reading of the play, the impression one gets is of everything happening in a relatively short space of time. In fact, from the return of Gaveston (Edward's male lover) in 1307 from his period of exile in France, to the death of Mortimer (Edward's nemesis and, in time, the queen's lover), we are spanning a period of 23 or 24 years. The first two acts cover two or three years each; act 3, dealing with the emergence of Edward's second favourite, Spencer, after the death of Gaveston, is the most concentrated, squeezing in about fourteen years; and acts 4 and 5 (the rise and fall of Mortimer) span about three or four years each. Marlowe has taken a sprawling mass of information and events and turned it into a drama that is crafted carefully both for its internal logical coherence and its theatrical excitement. To this end, Marlowe pays precious little attention to the conflicts with Scotland, Ireland and France that dogged the historical Edward II's reign, though some references are made in passing: the Third Poor Man who petitions Gaveston in the opening scene tells him that he is 'A soldier that hath served against the Scot' (1.1.33), and in the second act Lancaster upbraids Edward for his neglect of the territories that have suffered at the hands of all three nations (2.2.161–6). However, Marlowe reduces the length, frequency and complexity of these conflicts, picking up on only Bannockburn and Boroughbridge. The first of these, significantly, is seen in terms of a battle centred around Gaveston and the nobles' dissatisfaction with his place in Edward's favour – in fact, Gaveston had been beheaded by the time Bannockburn was fought in 1314. Boroughbridge (1322) is seen as an attempt by the barons to get rid of the Spencers, but is also seen in terms of revenge on the part of Edward. Again, what we understand to be the facts of these battles are distorted, manipulated and adapted to suit Marlowe's own purposes. What Marlowe wrote when he composed *Edward II* can be seen from a number of different perspectives, and, over the centuries of performance and critical commentary, it has been interpreted as a story about the conflict between the personal and the political; as a story of the legitimacy of revolt against an inadequate and ineffectual monarch; as a homosexual love story; and as a story of an 'overreacher' – Mortimer. Since one of the defining features of drama is its capacity to be reinvented time and again, it is not surprising that a range of different and often contradictory readings have emerged both in critical study and in performance. The rest of this chapter approaches Marlowe's play from a variety of angles: the king's story, Edward's story, Isabella's story, and the usurper's story.

The king's story: class war

Edward II depicts the beginning of the erosion of a rigid, stratified social hierarchy, with clear-cut divisions between the classes, from peasant and labourer, all the way through the ranks to the monarch balanced at the hierarchy's apex. Apparently, what irks the barons is not the nature of the sexual relationship between Edward and Gaveston, but the fact that Gaveston is of a low social class and of obscure birth. At least, this is the story that Marlowe tells. According to Holinshed, Gaveston is a gentleman, the son of a Gascon knight, but in the play Marlowe goes out of his way to identify him as a commoner. In act 1 scene 2 Mortimer Senior refers to him as a 'slave' (25) and Mortimer Junior talks of 'hang[ing] the peasant up' at the court gate (30). In act 1 scene 4, when the barons try to take hold of Gaveston to arrest him, Edward challenges them: 'Whither will you bear him? Stay, or ye shall die.' The scene continues:

Mortimer Senior.	We are no traitors; therefore threaten not.
Gaveston.	No, threaten not, my lord, but pay them home.
	Were I a king –
Mortimer Junior.	Thou villain, wherefore talks thou of a king,
	That hardly art a gentleman by birth?
Edward.	Were he a peasant, being my minion,
	I'll make the proudest of you stoop to him.

[1.4.24–31]

The term 'villain' here has, besides the connotation we are familiar with, a further meaning rooted in its older form 'villein', a feudal serf. Villeins gave service to their lord and in return were allowed to cultivate a portion of land for their own subsistence. Gaveston is not only slighted as someone outside the ranks of the nobility, but also debased to the level of a peasant.

It is important to note the vehemence of the barons and the extent to which their hatred is fuelled by the issue of social class. Notice also that Edward is very much aware of the issue, and knows exactly what he is doing when he rubs salt into the wounds of the barons' injured pride: 'Were he a peasant, being my minion, / I'll make the proudest of you stoop to him (1.4.30–1). Edward's other favourite, Spencer, is a servant in Marlowe's play, while according to Holinshed he is quite clearly of the nobility, though admittedly not of the first rank. The only hint Holinshed provides that social status is a cause of the barons' hatred of Gaveston comes in the description of his execution, in a short passage added to the 1587 edition of the *Chronicles*. His death is described as

> A just reward for so scornful and contemptuous a
> merchant, as in respect of himself (because he was in the
> prince's favour) esteemed the nobles of the land as men of
> such inferiority, as that in comparison of him they
> deserved no little jot or mite of honour . . .

[cited in Thomas & Tydeman, 1994, p. 355]

Marlowe picks up on Gaveston's proud demeanour and contempt for the barons – Warwick notes how 'He nods, and scorns, and smiles at those that pass' (1.2.24), and Mortimer Junior complains:

> Uncle, his [Edward's] wanton humour grieves not me,
> But this I scorn – that one so basely born
> Should by his sovereign's favour grow so pert
> And riot it with the treasure of the realm
> While soldiers mutiny for want of pay.
> He wears a lord's revenue on his back,
> And, Midas-like, he jets it in the court . . .
> Whiles other walk below, the king and he
> From out a window laugh at such as we,
> And flout our train and jest at our attire.

[1.4.401–7, 415–17]

'That one so basely born / Should by his sovereign's favour grow so pert': the barons return obsessively to Gaveston's (and, later, Spencer's) social class. Gaveston further exacerbates such resentment by his penchant for extravagant clothes. Sumptuary laws which were designed to regulate dress codes (materials, ornamentation and often colour) along class lines and so reinforce social hierarchies were in place between 1337 and 1604, though they were often flouted. If this is a slight anachronism on Marlowe's part, it is one that none (or very few) members of his audience would have noticed, since the laws would have been a familiar part of London life at the time the play was written. Although Gaveston is referred to nine times as 'minion' (from the French for 'darling boy'), where the emphasis is on the sexual relationship with Edward specifically, he is more commonly and variously referred to in terms of the baseness of his birth. Among other things, the barons speak of him as 'slave', 'peasant', 'groom', 'thief', 'villain', 'upstart' and 'creeping ant'. The barons' obsession is born out of anxiety over the stability of the social order, an order threatened by a monarch whose lack of restraint in displaying favouritism ignores hierarchy. Their determination to be rid of Gaveston is a panicky response to the threat that this kind of patronage poses, and Gaveston is a concrete personification of it. If 'one so basely born' can rise to a position of authority second only to the king, then their own status and identity, which are based on hereditary principles, are challenged. Elizabethan society was an order founded on patriarchy – public power is transferred from father to son, from former king to his heir. As one generation fades, another matures to replace it, ensuring, in theory, an unbroken line of institutions and ideologies that ensures continuity and stability: the interests of those in power are to be preserved at all costs. As the play proceeds, the threat posed by Gaveston moves from the abstract and symbolic – his place beside Edward on the throne – to the actual and material: Gaveston's accumulation of wealth and titles (Earl of Cornwall, Lord Chamberlain, Secretary and Lord of Man) represents a potential threat to the barons' military control. It is significant that, on Gaveston's return from exile, prompted into greeting him by the king, the barons acidly shower Gaveston with his many titles (2.2.65–8), provoking furious responses from both him and Edward.

Interestingly, the notion of the absolute power of the monarch is emphasized at certain points during the play, but at other times it is called into doubt, and for this reason the play has been considered by some to have been politically radical or subversive. In our own time, with a royal family maintained almost exclusively for its value as a signifier of Britain's cultural heritage, it can be very difficult to imagine a time when such a vast accumulation of authority resided in the king or queen. Although a mixed constitution (monarch, House of Lords, House of Commons) had been established when King John put his seal to the Magna Carta, a considerable amount of power remained centred at the throne. Parliament discussed policy, but the monarch still made it. Furthermore, the Houses of Parliament represented only the top fraction of English society. Often (although not during Edward II's reign) the interests of those at Parliament could be made to synchronize with royal interests. At a rare moment of détente in the play between the king and the baronial class, Isabella rejoices that 'Now is the King of England rich and strong, / Having the love of his renowned peers' (1.4.365–6). But this accord is fleeting. Edward II's reign is characterized more by a fundamental breakdown of the delicate political balance. One of the chief reasons for the failure of that symbiotic relationship is Edward's insistence on elevating his favourites to positions of authority, and in so doing challenging the established order that rests on lines of feudal loyalty where the nobles and the monarch are bound in a kind of mutual obligation to one another. In the first direct confrontation in the play between monarch and subjects, Warwick responds to Kent's challenge 'is this the duty that you owe your king?' with a snarl: 'We know our duties; let him know his peers' (1.4.22–3). By elevating Gaveston or Spencer, Edward is claiming for himself the right to determine those lines of authority. The humiliation and imprisonment of the Bishop of Coventry, for instance, underline this idea of Edward's total control. We witness him abusing and debasing a representative of the church, another central pillar of a carefully structured, hierarchical medieval society.

It is worth noting in passing how time would have altered the way this scene would have been received by its original audience. While it might be shocking in one sense to witness the staging of the Bishop's humiliation, the Elizabethans would also have recognized that this Bishop – a pre-Reformation cleric – is strongly associated with the Pope and papal authority. As we discovered in Part One, Catholic-bashing was an easy way of appealing to the predominantly Protestant audience, and it is a feature that also looms large in *The Jew of Malta*. It is in this light that we should read Edward's threats to burn down the churches in act 1 scene 4:

> Why should a king be subject to a priest?
> Proud Rome, that hatchest such imperial grooms,
> For these thy superstitious taper-lights,

> Wherewith thy antichristian churches blaze,
> I'll fire thy crazed buildings and enforce
> The papal towers to kiss the lowly ground,
> With slaughtered priests make Tiber's channel swell,
> And banks raise higher with their sepulchres.

[1.4.96–103]

The reference to the churches as 'antichristian' signals the vehemence of anti-papist feeling: the more extreme Protestants regarded the Pope quite literally as the Antichrist.

With the baronial class under threat, we see Edward repeatedly challenged by men like Mortimer. Edward is fully aware of the danger that the barons can pose to his authority. In act 2 scene 2 he remarks: 'How oft have I been baited by these peers / And dare not be revenged, for their power is great?' (2.2.200–1). Under pressure to banish Gaveston, Edward is cowed by the Archbishop of Canterbury – in an aside, he mutters, 'It boots me not to threat; I must speak fair' (1.4.63). The conflict between what Edward perceives to be his right as king and the treatment he actually receives is frequently revisited. Time after time he is backed into a corner by the barons, particularly in respect of the treatment of Gaveston. 'Am I a king and must be overruled?' Edward asks, half in defiance and half in disbelief (1.1.134). The answer supplied by both history and the play is that he must. The deposition of a monarch was a particularly sensitive issue, for obvious reasons. We have already seen how volatile the deposition scene in Shakespeare's *Richard II* had proved. Marlowe seems to be fully aware of the explosive potential in his story of Edward II, and it is fascinating to observe the way in which he negotiates his way through difficult territory. The evidence that is accumulated against Edward seems to suggest that he fails to rule justly: it is this fact that makes the challenge to the king a legitimate one. Nevertheless, the play shuttles between justification for the rebellion and reassertions of the king's absolutism.

Act 1 scene 4 is a relatively early flashpoint in the play. The impact of the stage action here can only be fully appreciated in performance, and it is important to visualize it as one reads it. The stage directions draw attention to the fact that Edward '*seats* GAVESTON *beside him on the throne*' (1.4.7. s.d.). Edward's next speech is deliberately provocative:

> *Edward.*   What, are you moved that Gaveston sits here?
> It is our pleasure; we will have it so.

Lancaster.   Your grace doth well to place him by your side,
               For nowhere else the new earl is so safe.

[1.4.8–11]

Lancaster's veiled threat raises the tension, and Gaveston's coolly insolent gaze exacerbates the provocation:

Mortimer Senior.   What man of noble birth can brook this
                     sight?
                     Quam male conveniunt!
                     See what a scornful look the peasant casts.
Pembroke.   Can kingly lions fawn on creeping ants?
Warwick.   Ignoble vassal, that like Phaethon
                     Aspir'st unto the guidance of the sun.
Mortimer Junior.   Their downfall is at hand, their forces down.
                     We will not thus be faced and over-peered.
Edward.   Lay hands on that traitor Mortimer!
Mortimer Senior.   Lay hands on that traitor Gaveston!
                     [*They draw their swords.*]
Kent.   Is this the duty that you owe your king?
Warwick.   We know our duties; let him know his peers.
                     [*They seize* GAVESTON.]

[1.4.12–23]

The outrage the barons feel and express at Gaveston's position on stage – beside Edward on the throne – has three causes: first, a 'peasant' has been raised above them; secondly, another has been installed in the place reserved for the queen; and thirdly, Edward is implying that Gaveston is politically equal to himself. As early as the first scene, Edward publicly invests his favourite with enormous power: 'Receive my seal', he tells him, effectively giving Gaveston the authority to act as his direct representative. 'Save or condemn, and in our name command' (1.1.167–8). Now, provoked beyond endurance, the barons draw their swords, ostensibly in a display of aggression against Gaveston. What is lost when the play is read rather than staged is the fact that, with Edward and Gaveston placed so closely together, the show of arms is as much against the monarch as it is against his minion.

As the play proceeds, two opposing notions are put into circulation: discourses of the lawful and the unlawful, the natural and the unnatural.

As they plot to banish Gaveston, Lancaster gloomily interjects: 'What we confirm the king will frustrate', and Mortimer, with the bold readiness that sets him apart from his peers, replies: 'Then may we lawfully revolt from him' (1.2.72–3). According to Mortimer, Edward is an 'unnatural king, to slaughter noble men / And cherish flatterers' (4.1.8–9). Isabella is an interesting figure in this debate, since she speaks both discourses, as it were, during the course of the play, and the shift from the one to the other signals her change of allegiance. At the beginning of act 3 she remarks on the 'Unnatural wars, where subjects brave their king' (3.1.86). In act 4, however, she lays the blame for civil war precisely and firmly on Edward and his flatterers, declaring that 'Misgovern'd kings are cause of all this wrack' (4.4.9). There are those who remain loyal to Edward, or who return to his service: the Elder Spencer declares, 'Rebel is he that fights against his prince' (4.6.71), and in the figure of Kent we witness a remarkable volte-face in the middle of a battle:

> This way he fled, but I am come too late.
> Edward, alas, my heart relents for thee.
> Proud traitor Mortimer, why dost thou chase
> Thy lawful king, thy sovereign, with thy sword?
> [*Addressing himself*] Vile wretch, and why hast thou, of all
>   unkind,
> Borne arms against thy brother and thy king?
> Rain showers of vengeance on my cursed head,
> Thou God, to whom in justice it belongs
> To punish this unnatural revolt.

> [4.6.1–9]

Kent switches sides twice; his inner turmoil signifies the gravity of the situation, where a king is pitted against his subjects. The difficulties of politics and personal and public moralities that are being fought out are concentrated in the conflict of loyalties experienced by one figure in the play, and this is one of the means by which Marlowe achieves that compression of the action referred to earlier.

It is impossible to make any definitive judgement about the play's stance on the king's divine right. Kent's oblique reference in the quotation above is the closest Marlowe comes to the orthodox position in this regard. As so often in Marlowe's work, it is this lack of definition, this openness, that gives the play its dynamism, particularly when it is interpreted for performance. Edward is a weak king, with a disposition woefully unsuited to the strict duties and responsibilities with which he is charged. However, Mortimer, the man who dethrones him, though seemingly inspired by patriotism and a sense of honour, becomes tyrannical himself, spurred on by arrogance and a thirst for power. The play ends with Edward III installed on the throne, clearly aligned with his dead father, and it may seem that the status quo has been restored. Edward's frequent assertions of his absolute power have been repeatedly undercut by a hasty retreat or defeat throughout the play, and have culminated in his deposition. It is a familiar idea that only those authorities anxious about their stability feel the need to assert their right to power, and will do so at any available opportunity. In this respect Marlowe's Edward prefigures Elizabeth's successor, James I, who ruled from 1603 to 1625 and issued numerous speeches and publications asserting his divine right to rule. Within a quarter of a century of James's death, the English people would execute their king, Charles I, and establish, albeit briefly, a republic.

Edward's story

Marlowe has been seen historically as a radical in his religious perspective, and the accusations of heresy that were levelled against him have sometimes led critics to associate him closely with the sceptical Faustus who is his creation. He has also garnered a reputation for his supposed homosexuality, and as a consequence *Edward II* has been seen as a play that seeks to portray a positive representation of homoerotic desire. The most famous words supposedly spoken by Marlowe in this respect were actually attributed to him by Richard Baines: 'all they that love not tobacco and boys were fools' (MacLure, 1995, p. 37). The saying has subsequently accrued definitive status in framing Marlowe's own sexuality (and his brazenness in declaring it), despite the fact that Baines had some fairly clear motives for slandering Marlowe in this way (and in Elizabethan England it would certainly have been seen as a slander). But this is only the tip of the iceberg in terms of placing Marlowe's debatable sexuality in its historical context. In a society where it was commonplace for men (or, indeed, an entire family) to share beds, where men greeted one another with a kiss because it was fashionable to do so, and where a word like 'love' had a very different set of connotations, it is unwise to try to import our own modern understandings of homosexuality into this historical investigation. The issue of homosexuality in early modern

England is a complex one, and both opinions and theoretical models vary significantly. There is considerable overlap between what Eve Kosofsky Sedgwick has usefully defined as 'homosocial', and homosexual or homo-erotic behaviour (Sedgwick, 1985, pp. 1–2). Homosocial defines the broad spectrum of relations between men that may or may not be sexualized, and the examples of social customs mentioned above give some indica-tion of the complexities involved.

The most important thing to recognize when discussing this issue is that there were no discrete terms for describing homosexual behaviour in early modern England: no Elizabethan man (the case of lesbianism is even more resistant to investigation) would have been able consciously to identify himself as homosexual, since a homosexual identity simply did not exist in the way we understand it now. It is only with the emer-gence of bourgeois culture, and the prioritization of marriage for love as opposed to marriage for property, wealth, status and so on, that homo-sexuality is separated out as a distinct kind of sexuality – and a deviant one at that. Sodomy, which today is recognized as a specific term, was in these times used to refer to a whole range of illicit practices, and while it would have included, in some contexts, sexual relations between men, it also included heterosexual sex in 'unnatural' positions, and bestiality. Neither was it confined to sexual practices, fusing with other forms of 'debauchery' such as excessive eating and drinking, witchcraft and heresy, even cross-dressing. Alan Sinfield suggests that the nearest modern equi-valent would be the catch-all term 'gross indecency' (Sinfield, 1996, p. 130). As such, then, sodomy – and, consequently, homosexuality – was not simply an issue of personal morality but one that was intricately bound up in politics and religion. We see this in Marlowe's own case. Accusa-tions of political sedition go along with charges of atheism, and alleged homosexual practices. However, confusingly perhaps, there is at the same time considerable evidence to suggest that homoerotic behaviour, par-ticularly between males of unequal status – master and servant, master and apprentice, schoolmen and students, for instance – was not uncom-mon during the period. Within these patriarchal structures, the activity seems to have been tolerated and even expected. Juxtaposed against this, we have to recognize that a law prohibiting sodomy was passed in 1533, and the official punishment for the 'crime' was death. The apparent inconsistency may be explained in part by the fact that the law was an element of Henry VIII's legislation that was targeted specifically at Catholic priests, who were commonly associated with sodomy in Protestant pro-paganda. Once again we are reminded of the way in which personal, state and religious politics were tightly enmeshed. The association of sodomy and the devil is illustrated in *Edward II*; there are references to Edward being 'bewitched' by Gaveston (1.2.55), and Lancaster's incredulous reaction to the king's grief at having been parted from his favourite – '*Diablo*, what passions call you these?' (1.4.318) – is significant: the Spanish word for 'devil', evoking witchcraft, is clearly not accidental.

We can discover one perspective on homosexuality in early modern England if we pay attention to medical, legal and religious texts. But a very different picture emerges from a study of literary texts, where same-sex passion is valued quite distinctively, and this is largely due, as Alan Sinfield points out, to the high regard in which classical – Greek and Roman – writings were held at this time (Sinfield, 1995, p. 13). This might take the form Bruce R. Smith identifies as male bonding, as for example in the relationship between Coriolanus and his enemy Aufidius, between Romeo and Mercutio, or Iago and Othello (Smith, 1994, pp. 33–40). The Roman poet Virgil (70–19 BC) provided another model, with his evocation of a pastoral world populated almost exclusively by males: in his second eclogue, he writes of the shepherd Corydon and his male beloved Alexis – the same Alexis referred to in Marlowe's supposed description of Christ's relationship with St John.

If we look more closely at the way the text represents the relationship between Edward and Piers Gaveston in the light of recent studies of homosexuality in Elizabethan England, a complex picture emerges. The opening lines of *Edward II* establish very clearly the particular relevance of studies of early modern sexuality to our understanding of the play. Gaveston enters, according to the stage directions, '*reading on a letter that was brought him from the king*'. His opening lines quote from the letter. The rest of the speech is Gaveston's reflection on it.

> *Gaveston.* 'My father is deceased; come, Gaveston,
> And share the kingdom with thy dearest friend.'
> Ah, words that make me surfeit with delight!
> What greater bliss can hap to Gaveston
> Than live and be the favourite of a king?
> Sweet prince, I come. These, these thy
>   amorous lines
> Might have enforced me to have swum from
>   France,
> And, like Leander, gasped upon the sand,
> So thou wouldst smile and take me in thy arms.
> The sight of London to my exiled eyes
> Is as Elysium to a new-come soul;

183

> Not that I love the city or the men,
> But that it harbours him I hold so dear –
> The king, upon whose bosom let me die,
> And with the world be still at enmity.
> What need the arctic people love star-light
> To whom the sun shines both by day and night?

[1.1.1–17]

The overtones of these lines are undeniably sexual. Gaveston conjures an image of himself and Edward wrapped in each other's arms ('take me in thy arms', 'him I hold so dear', 'upon whose bosom'), and the phrases 'gasped upon the sand' and 'upon whose bosom let me die' emphasize the eroticism – 'die' was a familiar euphemism for orgasm. Furthermore, Gaveston draws upon the story of Hero and Leander (line 8): according to the legend, Leander would swim the Hellespont each night to visit his beloved Hero (a woman) at Sestos. Marlowe wrote his own version of the story, although his unfinished poem does not relate Leander's watery death and Hero's consequent suicide.

Returning to the play's opening scene, having dismissed a procession of poor men seeking to serve him, Gaveston considers his plans for entertaining the king:

> Music and poetry is his delight;
> Therefore I'll have Italian masques by night,
> Sweet speeches, comedies, and pleasing shows;
> And in the day, when he shall walk abroad,
> Like sylvan nymphs my pages shall be clad,
> My men like satyrs grazing on the lawns,
> Shall with their goat-feet dance an antic hay.
> Sometime a lovely boy in Dian's shape,
> With hair that gilds the water as it glides,
> Crownets of pearl about his naked arms,
> And in his sportful hands an olive tree
> To hide those parts which men delight to see,
> Shall bathe him in a spring; and there, hard by,
> One like Actaeon, peeping through the grove,
> Shall by the angry goddess be transformed,
> And, running in the likeness of an hart,
> By yelping hounds pulled down, and seem to die.

[1.1.53–69]

Again, classical references and unmistakable sexual overtones are very evident, and there is a hint here for a sharp director to take the revels Gaveston is seen planning and to stage them in a later scene: the RSC's 1990 production presented a homoerotic dance at court – a 'royal command pornography show', according to one reviewer. Gaveston's speech is an exotic blend of voyeurism, homoeroticism and violence. Marlowe makes playful use of the fact that young men played female roles on the Elizabethan stage: so, for example, the pages are clad like sylvan nymphs, who are specifically female maidens in Greek mythology. Similarly, we have the 'lovely boy in Dian's shape' (the Greek goddess of hunting and the moon, Diana), 'hiding those parts which men delight to see'. The ambiguity over gender – is it a girl? is it a boy impersonating a girl? – leaves us wondering which parts these might be exactly. In an image that splices sex and violence, we see Actaeon pulled down by 'yelping hounds' and 'seem[ing] to die' – again, with a play on the word 'die' as a euphemism for sexual climax. The references to classical literature in the description of these relationships will become familiar as the play unwinds: Isabella compares herself to 'frantic Juno', with Edward cast as her husband Jove, the king of the gods, and Gaveston as Ganymede, the beautiful boy whom Jove took, according to Greek legend, as his cupbearer and lover (1.4.180–1). Marlowe actually depicts Jove and Ganymede in amorous mood in the opening scene of his *Dido Queen of Carthage* (see pp. 203–4). A Ganymede was a familiar Elizabethan term for the younger man in a sexual relationship between males in Marlowe's time. It is worth noting that Gaveston is also compared with Helen of Troy ('the Greekish strumpet', 2.5.15), with an obvious parallel between two wars rooted in erotic love.

From their first scene together, the nature and extent of Edward's love for Gaveston is clear. In a familiar image of lover and beloved, Edward, greeting him, declares 'Knowest thou not who I am? / Thy friend, thy self, another Gaveston!' (1.1.141–2). The trope reappears when Gaveston is banished in act 1 scene 4, when a distraught Edward announces: 'Thou from this land, I from my self am banished' (1.4.118). They exchange miniature portraits in the same scene, according to the stage directions (1.4.127*s.d.*). One of the most touching expressions of that love comes when Edward is forced to sign the document banishing Gaveston, in act 1 scene 4. Asked by Mortimer 'Why should you love him whom the world hates so?', Edward's reply is particularly poignant: 'Because he loves me more than all the world' (1.4.76–7). As Edward signs, he weeps ('Instead of ink, I'll write it with my tears', 1.4.86), and Mortimer's comment might be played by the actor as an incredulous aside, or, equally effectively, as a merciless mock: 'The king is lovesick for his minion' (1.4.87). Some have remarked on the fact that, as soon as the death of Gaveston is announced, Spencer Junior is adopted to take his place, but we should probably not take this as an index of Edward's love for the former. Edward meanwhile justifies bestowing the titles Earl of Gloucester and Lord Chamberlain on Spencer not by any political consideration but 'merely of our love', meaning that the reasoning is purely personal attachment (3.1.145). Spencer is equally unpopular amongst the barons, and his parasitic behaviour is pinpointed by the metaphors used to describe him ('a putrifying branch / That deads the royal vine', 3.1.161–2). The barons identify him as one of those 'smooth dissembling flatterers' that Edward must 'shake off' (3.1.169).

Although the depth of Edward's love for Gaveston seems beyond question, there may be some doubt over the purity of Gaveston's love for Edward: it has certainly been interpreted in various ways in performance. Sara Munson Deats identifies Machiavellian traits in Gaveston, noting his 'skill in dissimulation and flattery' as well as his taste for Italian masques and Italian clothes (1.1.41–5, 54, 412–14) (Deats, 1997, p. 177). In the opening scene, when Gaveston describes the events he is planning to stage for Edward's amusement, he details his need for 'Musicians that, with touching of a string, / May draw the pliant king which way I please' (1.1.51–2). It is clear that Gaveston has titles and all the trappings of power to gain from the relationship (and he clearly revels in them). Edward has less to gain and a kingdom to lose. Spencer's motives are equally suspect, since Marlowe has taken the trouble to show him discussing his strategy to get close to the king – that is, via Gaveston (2.1.1–55). In conversation with Baldock, Spencer spells out his intentions for the benefit of the audience:

> But he that hath the favour of a king
> May with one word advance us while we live.
> The liberal Earl of Cornwall is the man
> On whose good fortune Spencer's hope depends.

> [2.1.8–11]

The same scene also contains a passage that satirizes court fashion, and also serves to hint at Spencer's shallow and self-serving nature. Marlowe is here going against historical record, which actually portrays the two as enemies, but this is a clever way of tightening up the drama.

Holinshed, unsurprisingly, is rather circumspect in his description of the relationship between Edward and Gaveston. Piers Gaveston is the king's 'best beloved familiar'. There are references to his 'company and society' causing Edward to become 'suddenly so corrupted that he burst out into most heinous vices'; he is 'lewdly led'; Holinshed also mentions 'wantonness . . . voluptuous pleasure, and riotous excess' instigated by Gaveston, and the king spending 'days and nights in jesting, playing, banqueting, and in such other filthy and dishonourable exercises', but this is as straightforward as he ever gets. The barons see Edward as 'enchanted', as one who has 'fix[ed] his heart upon a man of such a corrupt humour' (cited in Thomas & Tydeman, 1994, pp. 352–5). In the play, Mortimer Senior puzzles over Gaveston's hold over the king: 'Is it not strange that he is thus bewitched?' he asks, presumably rhetorically (1.2.55). John Stow, in his *Annals of England* (clearly another of Marlowe's sources), notes in his opening description of Edward II that he was 'disposed to lightness, haunting the company of vile persons, and given wholly to the pleasure of the body' (cited in Thomas & Tydeman, 1994, p. 373). Stow, like Holinshed, hints at what would be seen in that context as deviant sexual behaviour, without ever being explicit. Those surrounding Edward often remark on the relationship, frequently referring to Gaveston as the king's 'minion'. The king is seen as 'brainsick' (1.1.124). Isabella speaks of her husband 'frolic[king] with his minion' (1.2.67) and notes how his 'eyes are fix'd on none but Gaveston' (2.4.63). However, what seems to incense the barons and Edward's other opponents most is not the relationship in itself, but the way in which its all-consuming nature impacts on the business of the state. Edward is prepared to sacrifice all for Gaveston, and it is the abdication of his royal duties and responsibilities, not same-sex passion, that alarms the barons most, and presumably would have been most shocking to an Elizabethan audience. He declares himself ready to give up the kingdom so long as he has a corner left 'to frolic with my dearest Gaveston' (1.4.73). After Gaveston's banishment, Edward enters '*mourning*' according to the stage direction, and laments:

> He's gone, and for his absence thus I mourn.
> Did never sorrow go so near my heart
> As doth the want of my sweet Gaveston;
> And could my crown's revenue bring him back,
> I would freely give it to his enemies
> And think I gained, having bought so dear a friend.

[1.4.304–9]

187

The play has an interesting stage history, and it is fairly clear that the theme of homosexuality, impossible to ignore, has influenced the play's popularity in performance. Revived several times in the early modern period, it seems to have been ignored from about 1617 to 1903, when it was revived in Oxford by William Poel. However, the play did not generate any significant interest this century until the 1960s. Since then, it has been more frequently revived: its frank portrayal of homosexual love made it a popular 'find' amidst the sexual revolution of the 1960s and early 1970s. Significant productions include Ian McKellen playing the title role in 1969 (McKellen became familiar as a leading campaigner for gay rights); Ian McDiarmid directed by Nicholas Hytner at the Manchester Royal Exchange (1986); and Simon Russell Beale directed by Gerard Murphy (RSC, 1990). Perhaps the most famous recent interpretation is Derek Jarman's film version, first shown in October 1991, which turns the play into a drama that speaks (according to Jarman) first and foremost 'against the oppression of homosexuals'. A full discussion of Jarman's film can be found in the conclusion, 'Marlowe in our time' (see pp. 236–40). For now, it is worth noting how the play continues to resonate 400 years later, not on account of any 'universal' truths it might be supposed to contain, but because the act of clashing two radically different cultures, set 400 years apart, can make sparks fly. As we shall see, nowhere is this more evident than in the impact made by Jarman's film at its moment of production.

Edward is undoubtedly one of the most complex of Marlowe's creations, and open to wide interpretation by the actors who play him. Between the extremes of his proud fury ('If I be England's king, in lakes of gore / Your headless trunks, your bodies will I trail . . .', 3.1.135–6) and pitiful misery, a prisoner begging for his life, there are a number of different attitudes and positions that are struck. One way of following these is to chart the use of the lion metaphor, a familiar one for a king to choose in asserting (or assessing) his power and authority. The barons' mocking of Gaveston on his second return precipitates a confrontation, and Edward responds with an impressively threatening speech:

> Yet, shall the crowing of these cockerels
> Affright a lion? Edward, unfold thy paws
> And let their lives' blood slake thy fury's hunger.

[2.2.202–4]

The metaphor is highly concentrated here, expressing as it does pride, anger and the desire for revenge, as well as being appropriate to Edward's royal status. Captured by the barons in act 4 scene 7, seeing Spencer and Baldock led away, he projects the lion metaphor onto his conqueror, challenging Leicester to 'rip up this panting breast of mine, / And take my heart in rescue of my friends' (4.7.66–7). When he is ordered to hand over his crown, he is once again a royal lion, only this time the threat is of self-inflicted violence, provoked by the pain of a wound: 'when the imperial lion's flesh is gored, / He rends and tears it with his wrathful paw' (5.1.11–12).

In defeat, in hiding, Edward takes shelter at Neath Abbey. Touching on a theme that also features in Shakespeare's *Henry VI Part 3*, Edward is depicted contrasting his own life with the contemplative life of the monks. Unsurprisingly, Edward finds that 'this life contemplative is heaven' (4.7.20). In this memorable scene he reaches his lowest point so far, and from this time on there is nothing but imprisonment, torture and death ahead of him. The deposition in act 5 scene 1 is a critical scene both in terms of the king's story and Edward's story. Forced to give up, he pleads 'let me be king till night' (59), and the realization that his reign is dwindling away with each passing moment is reminiscent of Faustus's last night on earth. Putting on the crown one last time, he is defiant: 'See, monsters, see, I'll wear my crown' (74). His next line is a clear stage direction to the other actors on stage: 'What, fear you not the fury of your king?' (75). They are unmoved by the display, perhaps even mocking. The scene has deep implications in political terms: the crown is not what Edward believed it to be; it is not of itself invested with any authority. Edward's weak will, his neglect of the realm, his refusal to accept the responsibility of government and his corresponding impulse to pursue his personal sexual and emotional desires, all work to open a gap between the role of kingship and the man who inhabits that role. Stripped of any of the respect due to a monarch, held in contempt by those lined up against him, Edward is only a man, tormented, weakened, ranting and weeping like a spoilt child. The instigator of the rebellion, Mortimer, if defeated, would have suffered the punishment incurred by treasonous acts: the king would have ordered him to be hanged, drawn and quartered. This Edward, king no longer, can only rip into pieces Mortimer's letter with a vain cry: 'So may his limbs be torn, as is this paper!' (5.1.142).

By act 5 scene 3, Edward's use of the lion metaphor has declined even further. Now, struggling against his persecutors as they set about him, shaving off his beard in the water of the sewer, he cries, 'The

wren may strive against the lion's strength, / But all in vain' (5.3.35–6).
No longer a king, no longer a lion, Edward suffers, as he understands
it, not for his misdeeds as a monarch, but for his behaviour as a lover:

> Gaveston, it is for thee that I am wronged;
> For me, both thou and both the Spencers died,
> And for your sakes a thousand wrongs I'll take.

[5.3.41–3]

It is unsurprising that *Edward II* has been appropriated to address the
issue of homophobia. The shift from a political tragedy to a human
tragedy that seems to take place in the final act does invite the kind of
reading of the play that focuses on Edward's sexuality, and his love for
Gaveston in particular. There has been some debate about the manner
in which Edward is executed, but the historical records are fairly clear.
Holinshed records in meticulous, gruesome detail the process by which
Edward, held down by heavy mattresses, had a hot spit thrust into his
anus, the spit being rolled around, burning his entrails, and then
removed to leave his body unmarked. The execution is a cruel parody,
a form of homosexual rape – or else, for the brutally debased Edward,
reduced from monarch to tortured prisoner, a cathartic path to death,
a climax that is at once orgasm and extinction. The 1990 RSC production staged the death scene as sadomasochistic sex that suddenly turns
violent. It also allows for an interpretation that would perceive it as a
punishment fitting the 'crime'. No doubt a proportion at least of Marlowe's
audience would have found it thrilling and cruelly satisfying, as well as
deeply shocking. Marlowe is not only depicting the death of a king on
stage (though admittedly a deposed one), he is portraying it via a taboo
sexual practice that has been turned into a horrifying act of violence.

The queen's story

Mortimer in general assumes greater significance in Marlowe's play than
he does in Holinshed's historical record, where he does not figure
significantly until 1326, when he joins forces with Isabella, who is by
that time estranged from her husband and located in France. Marlowe,
once again condensing the action to achieve a tighter and more powerful dramatic structure, provides a simpler and clearer chain of cause and

effect: Isabella is rejected by her husband, who favours his male lovers
Gaveston and Spencer, and almost as a direct consequence she becomes
Mortimer's lover. Some critics have looked closely at Isabella's choice
of words as she exits at the end of act 1 scene 2, and concluded that
Marlowe plants them as an early sign of intimacy between the queen
and Mortimer. She does call him 'sweet Mortimer' (1.2.80), and, with
hindsight, it is easy to see them in this light; director and actors would
certainly have some scope to invest the parting with deeper significance. As early as act 1 scene 4, there are clues as to what will develop
between these two: in a sharp exchange with Gaveston, just before he
is forced to go into exile, he implies that she has already been unfaithful to Edward:

Edward.	Fawn not on me, French strumpet; get thee gone.
Isabella.	On whom but on my husband should I fawn?
Gaveston.	On Mortimer; with whom, ungentle queen –
	I say no more; judge you the rest, my lord.

[1.4.145–8]

The exchange not only develops the audience's understanding of
Isabella's relationship with Mortimer, it also provides an illuminating manifestation of the sexual jealousy that is sparked from this triangular set
of relationships. Banished from court until she can persuade the barons
to allow Gaveston to return from exile, she seems to focus her persuas-
ive powers on Mortimer:

Isabella.	Sweet Mortimer, sit down by me a while,
	And I will tell thee reasons of such weight
	As thou wilt soon subscribe to his repeal.
Mortimer Junior.	It is impossible; but speak your mind.
Isabella.	Then thus – but none shall hear it but
	ourselves.

[*Draws* MORTIMER JUNIOR *to a seat apart.*]

[1.4.225–9]

The other barons watch them closely, and their remarks, along with
the stage directions noted above, again allow director and actors plenty
of scope to develop the relationship. Elizabethan stage practice would

have been much more heavily emblematic (or pantomimic) than current fashionable acting technique allows. In a modern staging, however, the barons' commentary would operate as a very useful amplifier for the subtle interplay of the two under observation:

> Pembroke. Fear not; the queen's words cannot alter him.
> Warwick. No? But mark how earnestly she pleads.
> Lancaster. And see how coldly his looks make denial.
> Warwick. She smiles! Now, for my life, his mind is
> changed.

[1.4.234–7]

Holinshed chooses to highlight the political rather than the personal nature of the split between Isabella and Edward. Furthermore, Isabella is also given more of the initiative, both here in act 1 scene 4 and elsewhere, marking her out as a strong, wilful, independent, aggressive force in the play – certainly quite different from the rather ineffectual figure she cuts when she first appears on stage, hurrying 'Unto the forest . . . To live in grief and baleful discontent', in despair at Edward's rejection of her now that Gaveston has returned (1.2.47–8). She conforms to the stereotype of the scorned female lover elsewhere, and the performance style adopted by Elizabethan actors, again, would have served to emphasize the deep contours of that stereotype:

> Witness the tears that Isabella sheds,
> Witness this heart, that sighing for thee breaks,
> How dear my lord is to poor Isabel.

[1.4.164–6]

Left alone, she weeps, and Lancaster espies her sitting 'wringing of her hands and beat[ing] her breast' (1.4.188). This version of Isabella derives in part from the patient Griselda figure familiar from medieval literature – Boccaccio and Chaucer both write about her trials at the hands of a tyrannical husband bent on testing her love. Isabella is equally abject in reconciliation with Edward ('O how a kiss revives poor Isabel!', 1.4.332) as she is in despair, and it is not until act 2 scene 4 that she begins to emerge from her role as victim. It is interesting to note that this scene contains both her most moving expression of love for Edward (2.4.16–21), spoken in soliloquy (and consequently difficult to perceive as anything but genuine), and the seeds of her betrayal: urged by Mortimer to sail with him and the barons in pursuit of Edward, whom they have defeated in battle, she declines, lest her 'honour be called in question' (2.4.55). As they leave, she is left alone for another brief soliloquy:

> So well hast thou deserved, sweet Mortimer,
> As Isabel could live with thee for ever.
> In vain I look for love at Edward's hand,
> Whose eyes are fixed on none but Gaveston.

> [2.4.59–62]

It is an intriguing speech, switching as it does from recognition of Mortimer's kindness to her assessment of her failed relationship with Edward. Whether or not Marlowe was writing with some psychological insight here, the actress trained to work within a naturalistic framework is likely to seize upon this as a turning-point for her persona. Another, perhaps more historically sensitive way of understanding it would be to see Isabella moving from one established feminine role (the patient Griselda) to another (the woman of unstable affections and changeable allegiances).

The development of her relationship with Mortimer is open to wide interpretation both in study of the text and in performance. Certainly there is scope to portray Isabella as a woman who uses her sexuality to her advantage, and it is clear that the weak, abandoned queen of act 1 is a long way from the scheming and play-acting power-broker of act 5. What is open to wide interpretation is her trajectory from the beginning to the end of the play. In the context of Elizabethan performance, character consistency and plausibility would not have been the actor's primary concern. Attempts to explain the transformation in psychological terms are motivated by an understanding both of drama and, even more importantly, of the human psyche that are very different from those that would have informed the composition and first performances of the play, and the fact that the role would have been played by a boy only serves to underline the gap between current acting styles and early modern theatre practice. But, however it may be handled in performance, by the second half of act 4 Isabella has been transformed into a deceitful adulteress, conspiring with Mortimer against the throne. Edward hints at hypocrisy: 'And yet she bears a face of love, forsooth. / Fie on that love that hatcheth death and hate' (4.6.14–15). She is 'unnatural' and 'false', and 'unconstant', 'spot[ting] my nuptial bed with infamy' (5.1.17, 30, 31). A modern audience is unlikely to find itself very sympathetic towards Edward, who has presumably been unfaithful himself in his relationships with Gaveston and Spencer – though it would probably not have been understood in this way by Marlowe's contemporaries. Regardless of Edward's royal status, his gender alone means that fidelity is not required or expected of him in the way that it would have been of Isabella (where, ironically, her royal status made it even more of an imperative). What is worth noting is that the 'she-wolf' of the latter half of the play is another stereotype. Anxieties around female sexuality in early modern culture emerge in all kinds of texts from the period, not only dramatic ones, though they reach something approaching hysterical pitch in the revenge tragedies of the early seventeenth century. The duplicitous and untrustworthy female, in the context of sexual relationships and by extension in all other contexts, was already common cultural currency, and would become a staple of the drama over the succeeding decades – Vittoria in Webster's *The White Devil* (1612) and Beatrice-Joanna in *The Changeling* (1622) are obvious examples.

By the time we reach act 5 scene 2, Mortimer and Isabella are clearly acting as partners in crime, the queen happy to let Mortimer determine Edward's fate: 'Conclude against his father what thou wilt, / And I myself will willingly subscribe' (5.2.19–20). She now sets out to deceive Edward deliberately, sending him a jewel and a message that 'I labour all in vain / To ease his grief and work his liberty' (69–70), and her fate, in the final scene, is to be expected. Accused of conspiracy to murder Edward, she is committed to the Tower to await trial. Her parting shot, however, is, again, double-edged: seized by one of the attendant lords, she protests 'Shall I not mourn for my beloved lord, / And with the rest accompany him to his grave?' (5.6.86–7). It is unclear whether she refers here to Edward or Mortimer, who has been marched off to be beheaded. The uncertainty may or may not be intentional on Marlowe's part; in any case, there is room once again for interpretation in the staging of Isabella's arrest and departure.

The usurper's story

As we have already seen, the play manoeuvres with a good deal of care around the legitimacy of the rebellion against Edward, and provides no definitive answers to the question of whether deposition can ever be sanctioned. At the first rumblings of dissatisfaction, Mortimer Junior, predictably, is the most outspoken, promising the queen that they will force Gaveston back into exile, and that 'we have power, / And courage, too, to be revenged at full' (1.2.59–60). The Archbishop of Canterbury immediately interjects, 'But yet lift not your swords against the king', and Lancaster agrees, reminding the company that it is Gaveston, not the king, that they would wish to rid themselves of (61–2). In Holinshed, it seems clear that Mortimer's rebellion against the king is meant to be viewed as unjustifiable. Although the historian's sympathies do shift, it is fairly clear that he supports, in broad principle, the notion of the absolute power of the monarchy. Marlowe's portrayal of Mortimer is far less clear-cut. The play seems more interested in seeking to show how Mortimer tends to follow the king's own path from fortune to disaster. We are back in the territory of the *Mirror for Magistrates*, and the cycles of rising to and falling from a position of power and prosperity. Mortimer in fact makes this most explicit when he reflects on his own career towards the end of the play, using a classical rather than a strictly Christian frame of reference:

> Base Fortune, now I see that in thy wheel
> There is a point to which, when men aspire,
> They tumble headlong down. That point I touched,
> And, seeing there was no place to mount up higher,
> Why should I grieve at my declining fall?

> [5.6.58–62]

On three separate occasions we see Mortimer seeking to legitimate his challenge to the king's rule. When the decision is taken to demand the expulsion of Gaveston, Lancaster remarks, 'What we confirm the king will frustrate'. Mortimer retorts, 'Then may we lawfully revolt from him' (1.2.72–3). Shortly afterwards, presenting the document of Gaveston's exile, Edward overhears a similar remark, and there is a sharp exchange (it is unclear whether Edward's climb-down is spoken as an aside or not, although Forker, editing the version cited here, chooses to interpret it as an aside):

> Mortimer Junior.   [*To* CANTERBURY] Curse him if he refuse,
>   and then may we
>   Depose him and elect another king.

Edward.	Ay, there it goes; but yet I will not yield.
	Curse me. Depose me. Do the worst you can.
Lancaster.	Then linger not, my lord, but do it straight.
Canterbury.	Remember how the bishop was abused;
	Either banish him that was the cause thereof,
	Or I will presently discharge these lords
	Of duty and allegiance due to thee.
Edward.	[*Aside*] It boots me not to threat; I must speak fair.
	The legate of the Pope will be obeyed.

[1.4.54–64]

Certainly Marlowe allows space for some justification of the revolt. To leave aside the struggle for power between the monarch and his nobles, there is in any case some substantial justification for the judgement that Edward is unfit to reign. When Mortimer tries to focus the king's mind on the threat posed by France, whose army has invaded Normandy, Edward's response is dismissive: 'A trifle! We'll expel him when we please' (2.2.10), and he goes on to question Mortimer about the revels that have been prepared to celebrate Gaveston's return from his second period in exile. But the suffering of those subjects Edward has neglected is real:

Lancaster.	The northern borderers, seeing their houses burnt,
	Their wives and children slain, run up and down
	Cursing the name of thee and Gaveston.

[2.2.178–80]

To a warrior like Mortimer, the spectacle of Edward's army ('thy soldiers marched like players, / With garish robes, not armour', 2.2.182–3) that has provoked the ridicule of the Scots is a cause of profound shame to his nation that he himself feels keenly. By the fourth act, Isabella, now in consort with Mortimer, claims that 'Misgoverned kings are cause of all this wrack' (4.4.9), and Mortimer legitimizes the rebellion by casting himself and his fellow barons as the champions of the young prince

Edward ('armed in this prince's right') and Isabella ('That England's queen in peace may repossess / Her dignities and honours'). Furthermore, he talks in terms that suggest the king is himself in peril, and needs to be rescued: 'and withal / We may remove these flatterers from the king' (4.4.17, 23–4, 25). Mortimer adopts a similar approach in justifying the execution of the prisoner Spencer Senior: 'Your king hath wronged your country and himself, / And we must seek to right it as we may' (4.6.67–8). In a final stroke of what we might call audacity, Spencer is referred to as 'this rebel' (69), firmly establishing Mortimer and his followers as the rightful leaders and protectors of the nation, their stand against the king not a revolt but proof of their loyalty to the welfare of their country and its people.

Mortimer the usurper, the antagonist set against the play's protagonist Edward, stands in stark contrast to the monarch. Edward is a weak king, tyrannical in his petulant rages, but finally ineffectual. Mortimer is a schemer, and one who will quickly resort to violence when necessary. In the same way that the play contains several versions of Isabella, so there is a radical disjunction between Mortimer the patriot in the first half and the power-hungry politician of the second. Again, there are ways of interpreting this naturalistically, working on the familiar thesis that power inevitably corrupts. Although he begins the play as one motivated by his concern for his country and its people, and he argues convincingly for the legitimacy of rebellion in the light of this, his moral stance crumbles as he begins his rise. Some critics have claimed that the forthright warrior of the first half is merely a mask, and that the 'real' Mortimer, manipulative and duplicitous, only emerges as he attains a position of authority. There is indeed something Machiavellian about his single-minded pursuit of power. No matter how supportive an audience may be of Mortimer in his fight against Edward and his misrule, we cannot ignore the way in which Mortimer savours his power, and the resemblance this bears to Gaveston's behaviour:

> The prince I rule, the queen I do command,
> And with a lowly congé [bow] to the ground,
> The proudest lords salute me as I pass;
> I seal, I cancel, I do what I will.

> [5.4.46–9]

His arrogance, signalled by such phrases as the Latin line '*maior sum quam cui possit fortuna nocere*' ('I am too great for Fortune to harm me', 5.4.67), marks him out as one destined for a demise as dramatic as his success. It is perhaps more helpful if we perceive this as shaping Mortimer's apparent transformation. This recalls once again the *Mirror for Magistrates*, and the didactic use of history: the trope of *hubris*, of overweening pride leading to a fall from a position of prosperity, would have been a familiar one for Marlowe's audiences.

Nothing illustrates the contrast between Edward and Mortimer more clearly than the way Marlowe depicts their approaches to death: Edward's fortitude in the face of physical and mental torture comes as something of a surprise to the audience, but his end features a more familiar Edward: his spirit broken by imprisonment and torture, he is, he says, 'too weak and feeble to resist', and prays that God will receive his soul (5.5.107–8). Mortimer refuses to beg for clemency ('I will rather die / Than sue for life unto a paltry boy') and departs the stage, condemned to death, as one 'That scorns the world, and, as a traveller, / Goes to discover countries yet unknown' (5.6.64–5). It seems fitting that we do not see him tortured or executed; we do not see him plead for his life to be spared. His refusal to resort to Christian orthodoxy in his final moments would be shocking to many of Marlowe's contemporaries, but of a piece with his Machiavellian tendencies. It is this that some critics have noted as a parallel with other Marlovian heroes, such as Barabas, Tamburlaine and Faustus. The death of Mortimer leaves the legitimate heir to restore order and good government; the realm, purged of its sickness, returns to its established order with the monarch as supreme authority. Moreover, Edward III clearly aligns himself with Edward II: 'in me my loving father speaks' (5.6.40). His words to Mortimer are stark, brooking no contradiction: 'My father's murdered through thy treachery, / And thou shalt die' (5.6.27–8). He orders Isabella to be confined to the Tower until she can be put on trial for conspiracy in the treason, and he is equally uncompromising in his warning to her: 'Think not to find me slack or pitiful', he warns (81).

The play concludes, then, with the monarchy firmly re-established: Edward III is on the throne doling out retribution to those who have conspired in the deposition and murder of his father. But the play's neat resolution belies the complex cross-currents that mark the preceding five acts. Marlowe has drawn an intricate portrait of the interrelation between the personal and the political, playing out a human drama on the stage of state affairs. Edward is both tyrant and victim, self-centred and self-sacrificial; Isabella charts a course that is diametrically opposed to her husband's; Mortimer is transformed from an embodiment of honour and principle into a cruel Machiavell. Once again, the text proves elusive. Is Marlowe playing fast and loose with received notions of kingship and right governance? Does the text offer a bold and defiant presentation of homoerotic love unprecedented in English drama? It may be that there are no definitive answers. Just as history is inscribed and reinscribed by its storytellers, so the play presents itself as a series of potentialities for interpretation and performance.

CHAPTER 7

THE POETRY AND THE
MINOR PLAYS

The Marlowe canon

This chapter draws together three diverse bodies of work in the
Marlowe canon. The two plays *Dido Queen of Carthage* and *The
Massacre at Paris* bookend Marlowe's career, and have been designated
'minor' for very different reasons. *Dido* is evidently the work of a fledgling
playwright and although it is of some interest (chiefly for the way in
which it explores issues of gender and sexuality), it remains perhaps the
least significant text. *The Massacre at Paris*, probably one of the last things
Marlowe wrote, receives less critical attention than one might expect.
The neglect is chiefly due to its textual status: it survives as a fragment
of the original, and it is generally believed to be a memorial reconstruction. Although it is clearly Marlowe's play, it is a ragged and smudged
descendant, or remnant, of the 'original', and is consequently viewed
with a large degree of circumspection. For a while, the play as a material text held a special kind of significance (despite its deeply compromised nature) because it was thought that a single manuscript leaf of the
play held in the Folger Shakespeare Library in Washington, D.C., might
have been penned by Marlowe's own hand. H.J. Oliver, writing in his
introduction to the Revels edition, accepts it as 'holograph' (Oliver, 1968,
p. lviii), and a number of other editors and scholars have followed suit,
although there is no conclusive proof that the fragment was part of
Marlowe's own manuscripts. Finally, the poetry consists chiefly of some
translations of two classical authors, Ovid and Lucan, the long poem
Hero and Leander, and a few miscellaneous pieces including the famous
short lyric 'The Passionate Shepherd to his Love'. Although worthy of
serious attention, Marlowe's non-dramatic work is inevitably seen as less
important than his works for the stage.

It has been customary in book-length studies of Marlowe to neglect
the poetry and these two 'minor' plays. Roger Sales (1991) makes a
few glancing references to the plays but ignores the poems; Thomas

Healy, in his shorter book (1994), devotes half a dozen pages to *Dido* and considers *Massacre*, briefly, in the context of Protestant drama. References to the poems are confined mostly to biographical context. The Longman Critical Reader edited by Richard Wilson (1999) does include an essay on each of the minor plays (though not the poetry), and, intriguingly, Wilson uses *Massacre* as the basis of his provocative introduction to the collection. A new angle comes from writers like Bruce R. Smith (1994) and Jonathan Goldberg (1992), who offer extensive re-readings of *Dido* and *Hero and Leander* in the light of queer theory. A monograph by Patrick Cheney, *Marlowe's Counterfeit Profession* (1997), is exceptional in that it provides a very detailed examination of the poetry, since it posits that Marlowe has been profoundly misinterpreted due to the concentration on his work as a dramatist. Sarah Munson Deats provides one of the most comprehensive readings yet of *Dido* in her *Sex, Gender and Desire in the Plays of Christopher Marlowe* (1997). Nevertheless, these so-called minor works do tend to get overlooked in critical surveys. This chapter aims to consider the work briefly in its own right, and to explore in more detail its relation to the other drama that is the focus of this present study.

Dido Queen of Carthage

In his *2 Henry IV*, Shakespeare misquotes Marlowe's *Tamburlaine* when he has Pistol speak of 'packhorses, / And hollow pamper'd jades of Asia' (2.4.140–1). A few years later, he paid his former rival playwright another tribute, albeit a backhanded one, in act 2 scene 2 of *Hamlet*. Welcoming the players who have come to perform at Elsinore, Hamlet invites the leader of the troupe to perform a speech – 'Aeneas' tale to Dido', describing the death of Priam. Hamlet notes that:

> it was never acted, or, if it was, not above once; for the
> play, I remember, pleased not the million. 'Twas caviare
> to the general. But it was – as I received it, and others
> whose judgements in such matters cried in the top of
> mine – an excellent play, well digested in the scenes, set
> down with as much modesty as cunning.

[*Hamlet*, 2.2.416–22]

The First Player proceeds to recite a speech that is remarkable chiefly for its over-inflated style (although, ironically, Hamlet is deeply moved by it). Although it is clearly not an attempt to imitate the equivalent speech in Marlowe's play (compare *Hamlet* 2.2.432–98 with *Dido* 2.1.213–64), it seems quite likely that Shakespeare is indulging in some good-natured fun at the expense of a youthful effort by a promising rival whose career had been cut tragically short.

The Tragedy of Dido Queen of Carthage was first printed in 1594, although it is thought to date from 1585 or 1586. There is no firm evidence to confirm the speculation, but Marlowe probably worked on it in collaboration with Thomas Nashe (1567–1601). The extent of Nashe's involvement is difficult to judge, since most estimates are based on so-called internal evidence (comparisons of spelling, grammar and style). The play seems to have been written for the Children of the Chapel Royal in Windsor, and they would have performed it in various private indoor performance spaces (such as the Blackfriars theatre) or at court. A short passage plays on Dido's original name Elissa in order to coin a few lines eulogizing Queen Elizabeth, and this is characteristic of these boys' companies' plays that were often intended for court performances:

> Hear, hear, O hear Iarbas' plaining prayers,
> Whose hideous echoes make the welkin howl,
> And all the woods 'Eliza' to resound!

> [4.2.8–10]

Although the title-page announces that *Dido* was played by the Children of the Chapel Royal, there is no evidence of actual performances. Andrew Gurr notes that the tradition of the boy companies giving professional performances (they started to get paid for their work in the 1570s) had a long pedigree, with the staging of plays having been built into their curricula for some time (Gurr, 1996, p. 218). More than any other Marlowe play, perhaps, *Dido* resists traditional character-based interpretation: certainly in performance there would have been nothing 'realistic' about it, since it would have been performed by boys between the ages of eight and thirteen. What would probably have concerned Marlowe most was the verse, rather than the physical staging, since he would have had a right to expect the speeches to be delivered with a high degree of skill. A play like *Dido* was an opportunity both to continue the children's training, and to exploit their talents for a financial profit. Furthermore, the sections of the *Aeneid* that contain the story that *Dido* dramatizes were standard school texts, and probably very familiar to the performers.

The opening scene, depicting Jupiter with Ganymede upon his knee, is striking in terms of its eroticism, bearing in mind the players who would have acted out the scene:

> *Here the curtains draw. There is discovered* JUPITER
> *dandling* GANYMEDE *upon his knee, and* MERCURY
> *lying asleep.*

Jup.   Come, gentle Ganymede, and play with me:
I love thee well, say Juno what she will.

[1.1.1–2]

As the scene proceeds, Jupiter takes Ganymede on his knee (1.1.28), and hangs about his neck jewels that his wife Juno wore on her wedding day (1.1.42). Ganymede responds by simply asking for more:

> I would fain have a jewel for mine ear,
> And a fine brooch to put in my hat,
> And then I'll hug with you an hundred times.

Jup.   And shalt have, Ganymede, if thou wilt be my love.

[1.1.46–9]

A 'ganymede', as we noted in discussion of *Edward II*, was a slang term for the younger partner in a sexual relationship between males: in *Edward II*, Isabella compares herself to Juno, with Edward as Jove and Gaveston in the Ganymede role (1.4.178–81). Joyce Green MacDonald notes that such a relationship was generally not publicly condemned unless it endangered the established social order – 'If the sexual relationship allowed a servant to control a master, for example, it would place an inferior in improper authority over a superior, and would be condemned' (MacDonald, 1999, p. 100). In both these cases, Gaveston in *Edward II* and the Ganymede of the *Dido* play, there is a clear threat to the status quo.

Jackson I. Cope discusses the wider question of young boys performing a tragedy about uncontrollable passion, and points out that passages that have been criticized for their lack of psychological realism can be understood more fully when their performance context is taken into account: 'Marlowe is titillating us . . . with the boys' interesting limitations: instead of declaiming sentiments, he elects to have them enact a farce of love.' In the Dido–Cupid exchanges, 'the paradox of love's absurdity is mocked by the parody of boys playing it absurdly' (Cope, 1974, pp. 320–1). The summary of the action of the play that follows, then, outlines serious, classical material, a tragic tale of titanic passions. However, it is important to bear in mind the company for whom it was written, since this is inevitably going to throw the play into a different light when we come to explore it in greater depth.

The first scene depicts Ganymede complaining to the king of the gods, Jupiter, that Juno (Jupiter's wife) has beaten him, out of jealousy. Venus, meanwhile, complains bitterly that Jupiter neglects her son Aeneas, refugee from the sacked city of Troy, while he lavishes attention on 'that female wanton boy' Ganymede. Jupiter reassures her that he has everything under control, and dispatches Mercury to calm the storms that have been battering Aeneas's ship. Venus, disguised, encounters Aeneas, his son Ascanius and several more of his party on the shore, and having informed him where he has landed, departs. Only after she has gone does Aeneas realize who she was. Act 1 scene 2 introduces us to Iarbas, a suitor of Dido's, who welcomes Aeneas and leads the way to Carthage.

Act 2 finds the party at the gates of the city. They are joined by others of their party, and together they meet Dido, the Queen of Carthage. Aeneas relates the story of the fall of Troy, the death of King Priam, and his escape, and Dido is deeply distressed by the tale. When they have left the stage, Venus transforms Cupid into Ascanius, Aeneas's son, and takes the boy away and hides him in the forest. Cupid is to charm Dido so that she falls in love with Aeneas. In act 3 scene 1, Dido enters with Iarbas, her hopeful suitor. She takes Cupid in her arms and he charms her, and as a result Dido spurns Iarbas, who leaves in despair. (It emerges that Dido's sister Anna is secretly in love with Iarbas.) Aeneas and his company arrive, and Dido offers to repair his wrecked ships on condition that he stay with her. In the following scene (3.2), Juno finds Aeneas's son Ascanius and resolves to kill him, but is interrupted by Venus. The two decide to set aside their enmity and conspire to bring together Aeneas and Dido, whom we next see preparing to go hunting (3.3). Iarbas, meanwhile, bemoans his fate.

A storm interrupts the hunting party (3.4) and Dido and Aeneas, taking shelter in the same cave, declare their love for one another. In act 4 scene 1 they emerge from the cave, and it is clear to the rest of the group, observing them, that they are now lovers. Iarbas despairs, and in the following scene (4.2) he makes a sacrifice to Jove, and rejects Anna's declaration of love for him. Aeneas, meanwhile, seems to have resolved once more to leave Carthage: 'I may not dure this female drudgery', he declares (4.3.55). Dido, hearing that Aeneas and his men are boarding their ships, sends Anna down to the harbour after him (4.4). She returns with Aeneas and his companions, and Aeneas makes it clear that he would not leave without his son Ascanius. Dido crowns Aeneas, who makes a firm promise to stay. Dido impounds the oars, tackling and sails of his ships to make sure. Act 4 ends with a kind of interlude during which a Nurse is teased by Cupid (disguised as Ascanius) after she declares her love for him (4.5).

In act 5, Aeneas shows his companions the city, 'a statelier Troy', that he plans to build at Carthage (5.1.2). Hermes appears with Ascanius and passes on a command from Jove that Aeneas must set sail. Iarbas willingly offers to provide Aeneas with rigging for his ships, and Aeneas takes his painful leave of Dido, who is distraught. She sends Anna after him who tries and fails to convince him to stay. Dido determines to make a fire and burn all traces of Aeneas that have been left behind, which she does with the help of Iarbas and attendants. Then, as the fire burns, she throws herself into the flames. Iarbas, seeing she has killed herself, follows suit, and Anna, in despair now that her beloved is also dead, kills herself too.

Marlowe remains fairly close to his source in this, probably his first play, although he was not the first to dramatize the story, and he may well have drawn on other plays on the same subject. *Dido* dramatizes events recounted in the first, second and fourth books of *The Aeneid* by Virgil (70–19 BC). *The Aeneid* tells the story of the adventures of Aeneas and his Trojan followers after their escape from the city of Troy, whose siege and destruction is recounted in Homer's *Iliad*. It is most likely that Marlowe used Virgil's original Latin as his source text, although Thomas and Tydeman point out that one familiar English translation, by Thomas Phaer (1558), may have been used as well: a copy in the British Library bears the signature of Marlowe's likely collaborator, Thomas Nashe, on the title page (Thomas & Tydeman, 1994, p. 18). There are some passages and phrases that echo Phaer's work fairly closely. Marlowe's chief innovations include his strategy of heightening the significance of Iarbas and Anna so that their own misbegotten loves operate as an (admittedly very simple) kind of subplot. The ending of the play, with Iarbas and Anna following Dido in quick succession onto the funeral pyre, is rather poorly judged, toppling over Dido's tragedy into something awkwardly comical.

However, as we have already noted, it is quite possible that Marlowe had not conceived the play in performance as a straight-faced tragedy. He certainly does not seem to be attempting to emulate the deeply serious tone of Virgil's account of the doomed love affair. The treatment of the classical gods, including Jupiter, Venus and Juno, is irreverent, from the opening depiction of Jupiter as pederast, to the spat between the two goddesses in act 3 scene 2, where Venus unleashes a series of vicious insults at Juno: 'old witch' and 'hateful hag' are two of the epithets she flings her way, as she threatens to 'tear thy eyes fro' forth thy head, / And feast the birds with their blood-shotten balls' if Juno dares to touch Ascanius (3.2.25, 32, 34–5). Venus is similarly acidic in her chiding of Jupiter for neglecting Aeneas and instead sitting 'toying there / And playing with that female wanton boy' Ganymede (1.1.50–1). Cupid's mischievous behaviour in Marlowe's play has some basis in classical myth, but there seems to be no precedent for the decidedly odd act 4 scene 5, which depicts an elderly Nurse stung with erotic desire by Cupid's presence. 'I'll be no more a widow, I am young;' she declares. 'I'll have a husband, or else a lover.' 'A husband, and no teeth!' Cupid responds, in an aside that could just as easily be played aghast as amused (4.5.22–4).

Aeneas is not the noble hero of the Latin epic, but a rather weak and ineffectual figure. Interpretations of the play tend to consider its anatomy of gender and power relations as a central issue, and most frequently it is read fairly straightforwardly as an account of a man having to reassert his masculinity against a threat of female dominance, or of male reason battling and triumphing over the pernicious influence of female passion. It is true, as Sarah Munson Deats points out, that Dido in one sense at least reverses gender stereotypes by playing the 'courtly lover rather than the coy mistress', initiating and directing the action as the love between her and Aeneas develops (Deats, 1997, p. 92). However, Deats elsewhere is forced to acknowledge that Dido performs the more conventional roles of 'victim of divine manipulation' and 'captive of feminine passion' (p. 96). Although Deats argues a forceful and ingenious case for the text as disruptive of accepted categories of gender and sexuality, it seems more likely that the play's more ambiguous representation of Aeneas, for instance, is intended to show a male hero weighed down by female shackles. It is not until the end of act 4 scene 3 that Aeneas finally begins to shake off Dido's thrall, and when he does so, he strikes a rather bathetic note: 'I may not dure this female drudgery', he declares. 'To sea, Aeneas, find out Italy!' (4.3.55–6). In keeping with Marlowe's ironic perspective on his classical story, however,

Aeneas fails to confront Dido with his decision to leave (as he does in Virgil's account), and instead attempts to steal away undetected.

The verse in *Dido* is immature, with many of its lines end-stopped, although there are still some signs of a greater adventurousness and some willingness to experiment. The speeches are composed in a fairly declamatory style: more often than not, one character will begin a speech to another by addressing him or her by name. Furthermore, characters have a tendency to address themselves in the third person, again calling their own names as they begin a speech. The language is ornate and often overloaded by its own opulence, and one can see how it was an easy target for Shakespeare when he was casting around for a style to mimic, or parody. The passage in *Dido* that parallels the deliberately old-fashioned speech Shakespeare wrote for the First Player in *Hamlet* is actually one of the most striking moments in the play. It anticipates the barbarities of the *Tamburlaine* plays with Aeneas's description of the sack of Troy – 'Virgins half-dead dragg'd by their golden hair / And with main force flung on a ring or pikes' (2.1.195–6). In addition, Marlowe's description of Queen Hecuba's defence of Priam, which does not appear in *The Aeneid*, is a startling piece of invention:

> At which the frantic Queen leap'd on his face,
> And in his eyelids hanging by the nails,
> A little while prolong'd her husband's life.
> At last, the soldiers pull'd her by the heels,
> And swung her howling in the empty air . . .

> [2.1.244–8]

The death of the king himself ('Then from the navel to the throat at once / He ripp'd old Priam', 2.1.255–6) is equally brutal and remarkably vivid. The poetry of this speech is perhaps unmatched in the play, culminating in the portrait of the victorious Pyrrhus:

> Yet he, undaunted, took his father's flag
> And dipp'd it in the old King's chill cold blood,
> And then in triumph ran into the streets,
> Through which he could not pass for slaughter'd men;
> So, leaning on his sword, he stood stone still,
> Viewing the fire wherewith rich Ilion burnt.

> [2.1.259–64]

A number of critics have speculated that the play may have been a topical one. William L. Godshalk suggests that anxiety over the mooted marriage of Queen Elizabeth to Francis, Duke of Alençon, may have been Marlowe's point of reference (Godshalk, 1974, p. 57). The Duke of Alençon was the younger brother of Charles IX of France, and the fact that a proposed alliance with Catholic France was unpopular is not altogether surprising, particularly in the wake of the St Bartholomew's Day Massacre of 1572: the prospect of that alliance hung in the air for about twelve years until Francis died in 1584. Philip Sidney and Edmund Spenser, with varying degrees of subtlety, both attacked it. Sarah Munson Deats, however, believes the play might have been designed to recall the marriage of Mary Tudor to Philip of Spain (1554), which had proved disastrous for both Mary and her country (Deats, 1997, pp. 116–17). Such speculations are intriguing but finally impossible to verify or disprove. The play is also interesting for its faint echoes, or anticipations, of later work that lie scattered across its pages. For example, the queen, having fallen in love with Aeneas, declares that 'in his looks I see eternity, / And he'll make me immortal with a kiss' (4.4.122–3). The phrase anticipates Doctor Faustus's reaction to the appearance of Helen of Troy, when he implores her, 'Sweet Helen, make me immortal with a kiss' (*Faustus*, A.5.1.93; B.5.1.96). Marlowe invokes the Icarus myth for the Prologue to *Doctor Faustus*, and here Dido pledges that she will 'make me wings of wax like Icarus, / And o'er his ships will soar unto the sun' (4.4.243–4). Finally, the play stands as an interesting precursor to the chief works. It shows early signs of Marlowe's gift for utilizing his sources imaginatively and, occasionally, mischievously, although it remains essentially a minor piece.

'Blood and cruelty' : *The Massacre at Paris*

At the other end of the Marlowe canon we find *The Massacre at Paris*. When the play received a rare performance – in the format of a rehearsed reading by the Royal Shakespeare Company (15–16 October 1985) – the programme of events billed it as 'a violent cartoon-strip play . . . An anti-Catholic propaganda play or a typical Marlovian attack on organized religion and conventional morality'. The description bears the mark of critical consensus of the first part of the twentieth century. Paul H. Kocher conducted a detailed study of Marlowe's sources (1947a, 1947b) and asserts that Marlowe used very little critical judgement in his study of contemporary Protestant pamphlets that dealt with the affair. His second essay concludes that the 'crudeness and extreme prejudice of most of these views explain in large measure why the drama is the crass and violently partisan thing it is' (Kocher, 1947b, p. 318). Wilbur Sanders spoke for many when he dismissed the play as the work of 'a brutal, chauvinistic propagandist', 'a nasty piece of journalistic bombast' (Sanders, 1968, pp. 20, 22). In the 1990s, however, a number of scholars focused renewed attention on this neglected corner of the Marlowe canon and, in keeping with the shift towards a realignment of Marlowe as radical and subversive, began to refashion it as something more complex.

The play seems to have been very popular in its own time. It was probably premièred in January of 1593 by Lord Strange's Men at the Rose, some four months before Marlowe's death. It reappeared the following year (after the playhouses were closed by plague for most of 1593), and was revived throughout the summer of 1594. Its popularity is rooted in the centrality of the events it depicts in the psyche of the English people at that time: it was an atrocity that, for Protestant England, defined Catholic duplicity and brutality. Many Protestant refugees fleeing persecution were sheltered in England. Catherine de Medici, King Charles IX's mother, plotted to have Admiral Coligny assassinated, and when the attempt failed, she resolved to have all the Huguenot leaders killed, persuading her son Charles IX it was in the interest of public safety. The St Bartholomew's Day Massacre took place in Paris between 24 August and 17 September 1572. The number of Huguenots (French Protestants) that died at the hands of the Catholics is impossible to determine with any degree of accuracy: 3000 may have died in Paris and another 8000 elsewhere across the country. It is thought that between 12,000 and 24,000 women and girls were raped. At the top end of the scale, some contemporary reports put the number of dead as high as 100,000, and although this is fairly obviously an inflated figure, the importance for our purposes is not the historical fact, but the facts as they were presented to Elizabethan England. The reports teemed with detailed anecdotes of savage barbarity: Catholic children slaughtering Protestant babies, individuals taking up 'instruments of everyday domestic life to bludgeon, stab, and drown their neighbours', Protestants being herded into halls to be cut down by bands of local butchers with meat axes (Poole, 1998, p. 1).

The play deals not only with the massacre itself, but also with the aftermath, tracing the political intrigues around the wars of religion that followed up to the assassination of Henry III in 1589. The play opens with Charles IX of France blessing the political marriage between his

Catholic sister Margaret and the Protestant King Henry of Navarre. As the French party leaves to attend mass, the Queen Mother, Catherine de Medici, makes it clear to the audience that she does not intend to allow the marriage to survive. Henry of Navarre, ironically, seems confident that the marriage will keep him and his own people safe from the threats of the Duke of Guise, whom Navarre knows to be plotting against French Protestants. The next scene (2) opens with the Guise plotting the deaths of both the old queen of Navarre (Henry of Navarre's mother) and the Lord High Admiral Coligni. An apothecary hands the old queen poisoned gloves given him by the Guise for the purpose (scene 3) and she dies. A soldier shoots and wounds Coligni. Meanwhile (scene 4), Catherine de Medici and the Guise try to persuade her son King Charles to slaughter the Protestant nobility. News arrives of the botched assassination attempt on Coligni and, as the Guise leaves determined to find a way of finishing him off, Charles promises the wounded admiral his protection.

The night of the massacre (scene 5): Guise and his followers enter Coligni's room and stab him to death, throwing down his body into the street. The massacre continues (scenes 6, 7, 8, 9). In scene 9, Navarre confronts the Guise, before retreating from him and his soldiers. The Guise commands that the order to slaughter the Huguenots be carried to other French cities. The Duke of Anjou, participant in the massacres and next in line to the French throne, sets conditions for taking the Polish crown (scene 10), while the body of the Admiral is strung up for the satisfaction of Catherine de Medici (scene 11), who encourages Guise to continue with the massacre, which he duly does (scene 12). King Charles dies (scene 13) and Navarre considers his options, planning to return home and muster an army in order to claim the French throne that he considers is now his right. However, in the following scene (scene 14) Anjou is crowned as King Henry III of France. At the celebrations, Mugeroun slices off the ear of an offending cutpurse. Catherine de Medici, consulting with the Cardinal, continues her plotting. The Duchess of Guise, it appears, is in love with Mugeroun, and when her husband finds a love-letter addressed to her lover, the Guise, enraged, vows to kill his rival (scene 15).

Navarre is now marching towards France with an army, and a messenger arrives to tell him that the French forces are armed and ready to confront him. Meanwhile, King Henry mocks the Guise for having been cuckolded (scene 17). King Henry warns Mugeroun that the Guise intends to kill him, and Mugeroun decides to try to make peace with the jealous husband. In the following scene (18), Navarre celebrates an early victory over the Duke Joyeux's forces. In scene 19, a soldier shoots Mugeroun dead and is rewarded by the Guise, and in the same scene King Henry confronts the Guise and accuses him of being a traitor to France, forcing him to disband his army, and then proceeding to plot his death. Navarre hears that the Guise has risen up against the King of France and decides he will try and make peace with the king (scene 20). King Henry, meanwhile (scene 21), hatches his plot against Guise. Ostensibly welcoming him in peace, he abandons him to an ambush. The Guise is assassinated and Henry gives orders for the Guise's two brothers, the Duke of Dumaine and the Cardinal of Lorraine, to be killed also. Catherine de Medici curses Henry for what he has done. In scene 22, Henry's order to murder the Cardinal is carried out, and Dumaine, hearing the news in scene 23, fears for his own life. In the final scene (24), Henry and Navarre make peace, but Henry is stabbed and mortally wounded by a friar, who has plotted the assassination with the Guise's brother Dumaine. He gives orders for France to make peace with England before he dies and announces that Navarre will be his successor. Navarre vows revenge on Catholicism for Henry's death.

The Guise is evidently the central character in the play as it stands. For Elizabethan England, he was usefully definable as the key figure in the horror of the Huguenot massacres, and the text certainly identifies him as the villainous anti-hero of the piece. He bears comparisons with other anti-heroes of Marlovian drama, most obviously *The Jew of Malta's* Barabas, with whom he shares Machiavellian tendencies. Just as the Machiavelli of *The Jew's* prologue had claimed to 'count religion but a childish toy' (line 14), the Guise makes it clear that for him religion is used as a cover for his politicking ('My policy hath framed religion', he says, 2.61). He shuns it as a superstition:

> Fie, I am asham'd, however that I seem,
> To think a word of such a simple sound,
> Of so great matter should be made the ground.

[2.64–6]

He has aspects, too, of Tamburlaine ('Give me a look that, when I bend the brows, / Pale death may walk in furrows of my face', 2.97–8), at least in his aspirations. He does seem to fit rather neatly into a pattern of overreachers that we have found to be one template for Marlovian protagonists. Marlowe makes use once more of the Icarus myth when the Guise muses on his ambitions in these terms:

What glory is there in a common good
That hangs for every peasant to achieve?
That like I best that flies beyond my reach.
Set me to scale the high Pyramides,
And thereon set the diadem of France,
I'll either rend it with my nails to naught
Or mount the top with my aspiring wings
Although my downfall be the deepest hell.

[2.37–44]

However, there is little that is impressive about his politicking or his plots and murders. His assassination of the old Queen of Navarre seems to be simply gratuitous, with no clear motivation, and this detail actually contradicts the Huguenot propaganda, which identified Catherine de Medici as the instigator of her death (Roberts, 1995, p. 433). Ultimately, he is presented as one who aspires to diabolical evil but achieves instead an ignominious kind of villainy, the ridiculing of him as a cuckold in scene 17 being a key moment in the text's strategy to undercut his status.

The Guise is most often the perpetrator (or plotter) of the violence that is depicted in the play, and the staged violence of *Massacre*, surprisingly true to life in its messy brutality, contrasts sharply with the rhetorical violence of Aeneas's account of the death of Priam. The poetry of the *Dido* passage, quoted on p. 207 above, is classical in its tone, depicting the terrible warrior Pyrrhus and his pathetic victims in a familiar, heroic vein. The scenes in the later play that represent the massacre itself are brutal and sardonic, and often serve to underline the savagery of the Guise: in scene 7, the Guise runs down the preacher Loreine and accuses him of heresy.

> *Lor.* I am a preacher of the word of God;
> And thou a traitor to thy soul and Him.
> *Guise.* 'Dearly beloved brother' – thus 'tis written.
> *He stabs him.*
> *Anj.* Stay, my Lord, let me begin the psalm.
> *Guise.* Come, drag him away, and throw him in a ditch.
> *Exeunt.*

[7.3–7]

The murders are scruffy and short, rendered more unpleasant by the jokes that accompany them (the Guise mockingly beginning Loreine's sermon for him) and the dehumanization of the victims. When Loreine is dead, the Guise orders Anjou to 'throw him in a ditch' (7.7). In scene 5 he orders the body of the dead Admiral to be thrown down, trampling his corpse into the ground: 'Thus, in despite of thy religion, / The Duke of Guise stamps on thy lifeless bulk!' he crows (5.40–1). H.S. McMillin, in an unpublished dissertation, 'The Staging of Elizabethan Plays at the Rose Theatre', suggests that the rapid succession of short scenes depicting the massacre itself functions almost like the editing of a film documentary, using 'isolated instances to create the idea of a single complex event' (cited in Tydeman & Thomas, 1989, p. 92). It may be that the play provoked the kind of horrified fascination in Elizabethan audiences that televised atrocities do in us today. A number of critics have suggested that Marlowe's theatrical technique in some senses anticipates Brecht's methodology. Certainly there is something Brechtian about the conversation between the two unnamed characters debating how to dispose of Coligni's body at the beginning of scene 11 (lines 1–12), worrying about infecting the air if they burn him, and infecting the fish that they will eat themselves if they throw his body into a river. The Guise's own death is also undercut, as David Hard Zucker notes, by his exchange with the clown-type figure of the Third Murderer who warns him of the plot to murder him (Zucker, 1972, pp. 111–12). His Tamburlaine-like vaunts that precede the murderer's entrance set him up for his fall, both by their arrogant tone and for the note of hubris that they sound:

> So; now sues the King for favour to the Guise,
> And all his minions stoop when I command.
> Why, this 'tis to have an army in the field.
> Now by the holy sacrament I swear:
> As ancient Romans over their captive lords,
> So will I triumph over this wanton king,
> And he shall follow my proud chariot's wheels.

> [21.48–54]

What follows borders on farce. The Third Murderer cringes his way onto the stage to apologize to the Guise for being one of those about to kill him. Marlowe's would-be anti-hero shrugs him off, like the star actor trying to shoo away a stagehand who has inadvertently wandered on stage at the climax of a performance. He attempts to recover his heroic composure by fashioning himself as a Caesar ('Yet Caesar shall go forth. / Let mean conceits and baser men fear death', 21.67–8), a strategy he repeats with his dying breath ('Thus Caesar did go forth, and thus he died', 21.87), but it fails to convince. Always bearing in mind the fact that we are making judgements about a presumably badly damaged version of Marlowe's original, the Guise seems a curious kind of dramatic failure. He is a protagonist full of Tamburlaine-like aspiration but with none of his actual power and grandeur, one who contains all of Barabas's villainy but lacks his sly facility for complicity with the audience.

A number of studies in the 1980s and 1990s attempted to rehabilitate the play, notably essays by Julia Briggs (1983), Andrew M. Kirk (1995) and Penny Roberts (1995). Whether the play is nothing more than crude propaganda remains an open question. Whilst revivals of plays such as *The Jew of Malta* and *Edward II* allow us to reconsider the potentialities that inhere in the texts for the interrogation, subversion or endorsement of various ideological positions, the neglect of *Massacre* in performance terms means that a question mark continues to hang over this particular text. The logical conclusion may still be that the play endorses dominant values, and operates as an indictment of evil Catholic oppression of heroic Protestant martyrs. However, as we have seen time after time in this investigation of Marlowe's work, potential for challenges to the status quo lies deeply embedded in a number of other plays. It would be unwise to write off this play so easily.

The poetry

The context for the production of poetry in the Elizabethan period was very different from the emergent theatre industry in which Marlowe played an essential formative role. The profession of poet had a much longer pedigree, and was much more firmly established in English culture, although the volatility of Henry VIII's court brought about a kind of rupture in the tradition. However, in a period of relative stability in the royal household, Elizabeth maintained and greatly extended the patronage of her court, and London became firmly established as her base. Poets participated in the life of the court both formally and informally. Sir Philip Sidney (1554–1586), Edmund Spenser (1552?–1599) and George Peele (1558?–1597?), amongst others, composed poems to celebrate the public holiday that marked Elizabeth's accession, and poetry was an important part of other royal celebrations. Spenser's 'Prothalamion', for example, marked a double wedding – of Lady Elizabeth and Lady Catherine Somerset – in 1596. A select few were lucky enough to be nurtured at the heart of the court, although even the most successful often had other roles: Spenser worked as a secretary to Lord Grey de Wilton, for instance. More often a poet would rely on the patronage of a courtier: this is the reason behind the plethora of effusive dedications that appear in publications of the day. Shakespeare had his patron early in his career, the Earl of Southampton Henry Wriothesley (1573–1624), to whom both *Venus and Adonis* and *The Rape of Lucrece* were dedicated. Marlowe's patron was Thomas Walsingham, and the first edition of *Hero and Leander* was dedicated to him by the publisher, Edward Blount. Although Marlowe established himself as a playwright at an early point in his career's short, spectacular trajectory, there were times when patrons provided a valuable safety net for those making their way in a still precarious profession. Even dramatists as successful as Marlowe and Shakespeare were sometimes forced to abandon plays in favour of poetry when the plague closed the London theatres: 1593 was one of the worst years, and it is very likely that Marlowe wrote *Hero and Leander* at that time.

Although Marlowe's key poetic work is the unfinished epic *Hero and Leander*, probably the most familiar is his short lyric 'The Passionate Shepherd to his Love'. This first appeared, without an author's name attached, in a 1599 collection of poems entitled *The Passionate Pilgrim*. A year later, the anthology *England's Helicon* printed it with the text slightly altered and including two additional stanzas. This time, the poem was credited to 'Chr. Marlow'. Roma Gill notes that there is considerable evidence to suggest that it had 'widespread appeal' in its own time, and that its tune was also used for a number of other ballads, making it 'among the most pervasive airs of its period' (Gill, 1997, p. 212). The version printed below is the longer version, taken from the *Helicon* of 1600:

> Come live with me, and be my love,
> And we will all the pleasures prove,
> That valleys, groves, hills and fields,
> Woods, or steepy mountain yields.
>
> And we will sit upon the rocks,
> Seeing the shepherds feed their flocks
> By shallow rivers, to whose falls
> Melodious birds sing madrigals.

And I will make thee beds of roses,
And a thousand fragrant posies,
A cap of flowers, and a kirtle,
Embroidered all with leaves of myrtle.

A gown made of the finest wool
Which from our pretty lambs we pull,
Fair linèd slippers for the cold,
With buckles of the purest gold.

A belt of straw and ivy-buds,
With coral clasps and amber studs,
And if these pleasures may thee move,
Come live with me and be my love.

The shepherd swains shall dance and sing
For thy delight each May morning.
If these delights thy mind may move,
Then live with me and be my love.

[Orgel, 1971, p. 211]

'The Passionate Shepherd' is the most frequently anthologized of Marlowe's poems. It is also most well known today as the straight man in a double act, with Sir Walter Ralegh's 'The Nymph's Reply' providing the punchline. Marlowe's poem is such a straight-faced entry into the world of pastoral love poetry that it is hard to take seriously in its own right, although it is quite possible that this impression is itself an effect of cultural transmission: the way it has been so frequently parodied and answered by other writers inevitably colours our reading of the 'original'. Ralegh's is only the most famous of a series of replies. John Donne wrote another, and Marlowe himself makes a satirical reference to it in his *The Jew of Malta*. As Barabas's slave Ithamore woos the prostitute Bellamira, he brings his passionate speech to its climactic conclusion by declaring:

The meads, the orchards, and the primrose lanes,
Instead of sedge and reed, bear sugar-canes:
Thou in those groves, by Dis above,
Shalt live with me and be my love.

[4.2.101–4]

The poet's persona describes for his beloved the pleasures of the ideal-ized life of a shepherd – the beauties of the landscape, the abundance of nature to provide bed, board and clothing, and the pastimes and enter-tainments provided by the birds and the shepherd's swains. The scen-ario is perpetual Spring: the swains, he tells his beloved, will 'dance and sing / For thy delight each May morning' (21–2); the gown he weaves is made of wool pulled 'from our pretty lambs' (14). 'If these delights thy mind may move', he concludes, 'Come live with me, and be my love' (23–4).

Ralegh's 'The Nymph's Reply' shifts the action into 'wayward win-ter' (10). Marlowe's May setting is symbolic of new birth, the tradi-tional month for love, but behind its freeze-frame idyll lurks the familiar theme of the fleeting nature of beauty. The urgency of the poem draws on the same rationale that drives Robert Herrick's familiar proverbial 'Gather ye rosebuds while ye may', from the aptly titled poem 'To the Virgins, to Make Much of Time'. Marlowe sees rocks to sit on, and 'shallow rivers' (7); Ralegh sees the 'rivers rage and rocks grow cold' (6). Marlowe's costume, made of straw, ivy, coral and amber, in Ralegh's world breaks, withers and rots. Marlowe's state of perpetual bliss is succeeded in Ralegh's poem by the reminder of mortality and mutability (21–4):

> But could youth last and love still breed,
> Had joys no date, nor age no need,
> Then these delights my mind might move.

[Orgel, 1971, p. 212]

Piece by piece, Ralegh picks apart the first poem's pastoral fantasy. It is easy to imagine that the poem's sly irony and acidic cynicism, so remin-iscent of much of Marlowe's own work, would have amused Marlowe himself as much as anyone else who read it.

On the face of it, Marlowe's 'The Passionate Shepherd' stands in a well-established tradition of poems addressed by the male courtly lover to the female beloved. However, Bruce R. Smith has offered an intriguing suggestion that would place the poem in a very different genea-logy, more in keeping, perhaps, with the sexual orientation that dom-inates *Hero and Leander*, as well as *Edward II* and, to an extent, *Dido*. Smith argues that 'The Passionate Shepherd' draws on Virgil's second eclogue, which depicts the passion of the shepherd Corydon for the male youth Alexis, and his desperate and doomed attempts to persuade him to be his lover, in what Smith suggests could be read either as 'an indulgence . . . Or a denial of homosexual desire' (Smith, 1994, p. 91). He goes on to argue that Marlowe's poem can be seen as 'a recital of the country pleasures with which Corydon tries to woo Alexis' (p. 92). Although the thesis must remain tentative, it is one potential re-reading of one of the most familiar lyrics in English poetry, further evidence of the continuing provocative potential of Marlowe's work.

Translations

The fact that, at the time of writing, there is no recent edition of Marlowe's poetry signifies the extent to which it tends to be overshadowed by his dramatic works. An old spelling version, edited by Roma Gill, appeared in 1987, but in a hardback edition, effectively consigning it to the shelves of libraries and specialist scholars. The standard modern spelling edition, edited by Stephen Orgel, frequently reprinted in paper-back format, dates back to 1971. The fact that Orgel's edition finds it necessary to include a twenty-page appendix, in close type, providing a dictionary of classical names, proffers one explanation for its marginal status. Much of Marlowe's poetry remains relatively inaccessible to a modern reader because of the density of classical references. Since the bulk of Marlowe's poetry is made up of his translations from Latin works, this is hardly surprising. However, there are some fascinating oddities and some good poetry in these early works, and to neglect them would be to miss a key component in the Marlowe canon. Furthermore, the translation of ancient Greek and Roman literature into English was at the heart of the humanist movement, and it is enlightening to consider the ways in which Marlowe may have been contributing to that new tradition.

The less interesting work of translation is Marlowe's version of Lucan's *De Bello Civili* ('Civil War'), also known as *Pharsalia* (after the battle depicted in the seventh of the ten books). Lucan (AD 39–65) charts the conflicts between Julius Caesar and the Roman Senate; it is gen-erally agreed that the poem was left unfinished on Lucan's death, and that he had intended to conclude it with the assassination of Caesar in 44 BC. Marlowe's translation deals only with Caesar's advance on Rome, including his crossing of the Alps and the River Rubicon, and his conquering of Ariminium. As a number of commentators have noted, the work is of interest chiefly in its political context, describing as it does the horrors of civil war. Stephen Orgel notes its topicality when he makes a connection with the political play *Gorboduc* (Orgel, 1971, p. 253), which is discussed briefly in my analysis of *Edward II* (see pp. 168–9). Roma Gill quotes a passage describing 'These plagues that arise from wreak of civil power' (Gill, 1997, p. 32), and notes that, for the Elizabethans, 'The words have a grim topicality for the decade which experienced the Babington Conspiracy, the execution of a queen who rivalled their own monarch's claim to the throne, and the threat of the Spanish Armada' (ibid., p. 89). Lucan's work is naturally enough a conservative document, spelling out the dangers of disruption within the state with a barely contained, dread horror. Lucan himself, it seems, was a more subversive figure who, if we are to believe the historian Suetonius (c.AD 70–c.160), so offended Emperor Nero that he was forced to take his own life in order to avoid execution (Steane, 1964, p. 255 n. 2). His epic is also notable for the absence of divine intervention, which had been an essential element in the tradition. It is tempting to trace some affinities between Lucan and Marlowe in these respects; it is true also that the two writers share a similar tendency to wallow in their descriptions of savagery in battle: the final section of Marlowe's work includes a vivid description of the sacrifice of a bull, disembowelled so that the prophets can read the future from the appearance of its entrails (607–28). In Lucan's Caesar, there are signs of the genesis of the Marlovian heroic (or anti-heroic) type, and it is possible to draw tentative parallels between him and Tamburlaine in particular.

We can be fairly confident that the translation of Lucan dates from Marlowe's Cambridge years, although the work was not published until 1600. Marlowe's translations of Ovid's elegies are given a similar place chronologically, although their publication history is fairly complex: the sequence was, in Elizabethan times, both popular and controversial, and went fairly quickly through multiple editions. Ovid (43 BC–AD 18) and Marlowe bear some interesting similarities. Patrick Cheney's *Marlowe's Counterfeit Profession* (1997) is a hefty work of scholarship that is predicated on the notion that Marlowe modelled his literary career on an Ovidian paradigm, moving from amatory poetry, through tragedy, to the epic form. Without engaging in the complexities of Cheney's intriguing thesis, we can still note how Ovid was an immensely popular and controversial figure in first-century BC Rome, just as Marlowe's own star burned fast and bright in Elizabethan London. Ovid's poetry challenged established tradition, and offended dominant codes of morality that had been enshrined in law by Emperor Augustus. In a state where the emperor saw fit to banish his own daughter and granddaughter for the crime of adultery, Ovid eventually suffered the same fate, though his own crime seems to have been primarily literary. His unashamed celebrations of promiscuity and playful eroticism in the *Amores* and his *Ars Amatoria* seem to have been one of the chief charges against him in the scandal that ended with his exile. Marlowe provided the first English translation of the *Amores*. Bearing in mind the kind of romantic aura that so often lingers around the mythical Kit Marlowe, it is fairly easy to construct a narrative that posits the irreverent tone and frank eroticism of Ovid's poetry as their chief attraction for him. In truth, the *Amores* was the only work of Ovid's that had not been translated into English, sufficient impetus in itself for the aspiring young poet. Cheney suggests that this work had generally been excluded from the canon of classical writings, 'acquir[ing] the dubious distinction of a cultural taboo', because it was not susceptible to the kind of 'allegorizing and/or moralizing' interpretation that the rest of Ovid's work had been subjected to during the medieval period (Cheney, 1997, p. 49). The significance of Marlowe's translations lies chiefly in their innovative verse form, and in their position at a turning point in interpretations of Ovid's work, in particular his *Metamorphoses*.

Marlowe's work on the *Amores* is for the most part literal, line by line translation, and inevitably this results in some awkward and clumsy passages. The seventh elegy of Book Two provides a representative example:

> Dost me of new crimes always guilty frame?
> To overcome, so oft to fight I shame.
> If on the marble theatre I look,
> One among many is to grieve thee took.

[2.7.1–4]

However, as a number of scholars have established, Marlowe's *Amores* represent a very significant step forward in the development of the so-called heroic couplet and closed heroic couplet: in the former, ten-syllable lines are rhymed in pairs; in the latter, those lines are paired not only by rhyme but by their sense and their structure, so that in each case, the second line concludes a sentence. The heroic couplet would become a very familiar verse form in English poetry of the seventeenth and eighteenth centuries, notably in the work of John Dryden (1631–1700) and Alexander Pope (1688–1744).

Cheney argues that Marlowe's work transcends the dichotomy between the 'medieval Ovid' and the 'Renaissance Ovid', that Marlowe turns away both from the earlier tradition of sanitizing and Christianizing Ovid and from the tendency merely to revel in the poetry's erotic aesthetic (Cheney, 1997, pp. 50–1). The latter is a tendency that we can also trace in Shakespeare's narrative poems *The Rape of Lucrece* and *Venus and Adonis*, as well as some of his comedies. It may be that Marlowe is attempting to forge a new image of Ovid that rejects this simply binary, but it is also clear that Marlowe's work on the *Amores* was an important step forward in the shift away from the tradition that dominated Elizabethan love poetry at the time. The model up to that point had been the sonnets of the Italian poet Petrarch (1304–1374), and Thomas Wyatt (1503?–1542), Philip Sidney (1554–1586) and Shakespeare, among others, worked very much in Petrarch's shadow. Sidney's sequence of poems *Astrophil and Stella* epitomizes the genre. These poems are graced by the presence (and, just as often, the sorely felt absence) of the idealized beloved. The persona of the courtly lover is the abject servant of the woman, and the mood fluctuates from elation to despair, dependent on the way in which his beloved deigns to behave towards him. The poems themselves, as in Edmund Spenser's 'One day I wrote her name upon the strand', are often acknowledged as gestures at immortalizing their subjects:

> [. . . .]
> My verse your virtues rare shall eternise,
> And in the heavens write your glorious name,
> Where, whenas death shall all the world subdue,
> Our love shall live, and later life renew.

> [Jones, 1992, p. 282]

Although there is an evident danger of misrepresentation in selecting extracts from two poems and attempting to use this as the basis for an argument, it is worth comparing Spenser's sonnet with one of Marlowe's racier Ovidian elegies, such as 3.6, whose Latin title translates as 'He bewails the fact that, in bed with his mistress, he was unable to perform' (Orgel, 1971, p. 249). The opening is grimly down to earth: 'Either she was foul, or her attire was bad, / Or she was not the wench I wished t' have had'. The description of attempts at arousal ('And eagerly she kissed me with her tongue, / And under mine her wanton thigh she flung' . . . 'the wench did not disdain a whit / To take it in her hand and play with it') and failure ('Yet like as if cold hemlock I had drunk, / It mockèd me, hung down the head, and sunk') are equally direct.

The poem concludes with the poet addressing his penis directly and admonishing it for its mischievous behaviour:

> Now, when he should not jet, he bolts upright,
> And craves his task, and seeks to be at fight.
> Lie down with shame, and see thou stir no more,
> Seeing thou wouldst deceive me as before.

Ovid's *Amores* frequently feature this kind of cynical, dirty realism, although there is a wider variation of both tone and subject in the collection. Although Marlowe's poetry is weak in places, there are a number of elegies that repay closer study: the thirteenth elegy in Book One is a regretful meditation on the sun rising, and the inevitability of a lover's departure. Elegy 2.6, a curious little poem, is written on the death of a pet parrot: 'Go, godly birds, striking your breasts bewail, and with rough claws your tender cheeks assail'. It should not surprise us that the poems are shot through with a casual misogyny: it is the inevitable flip-side of the idealized portraiture that defines the Petrarchan sonnets. The poems addressed to the poet's mistress Corinna are sometimes tender, more often acidic; elegy 2.19, directed at Corinna's husband, is realistic both about the poet's own motivation for the affair ('We scorn things lawful, stol'n sweets we affect', 3) and his lover's perceptiveness ('Wily Corinna saw this blemish in me, / And craftily knows by what means to win me', 9–10). Elegy 3.13 is a bitter address to his lover, amidst the torments of uncertain jealousies: 'Seeing thou art fair, I bar not thy false playing, / But let not me, poor soul, know of thy straying' (1–2). Unable to face the truth of her infidelities, he teaches her how to keep her secrets hidden from him: 'I'll not sift much, but hold thee soon excused, / Say but thou wert injuriously accused' (41–2). The objects of the poet's lust are frequently fantasy figures, like the woman in 3.6 quoted above, or Corinna in 1.5. They are sexually available, like Ilia in her encounter with the river god in 3.5 ("Tis said the slippery stream held up her breast, / And kindly gave her what she likèd best', 81–2). Elsewhere, we find them as sexual predators, or else as victims, as in 1.7, whose title Orgel translates as 'That his mistress, whom he has beaten, should make peace with him'. The couplets 'But cruelly her tresses having rent, / My nails to scratch her lovely cheeks I bent' and 'Sighing she stood, her bloodless white looks showèd / Like marble from the Parian mountains hewèd' are characteristic of this deeply unpleasant poem (49–52). In 1599, six years after Marlowe's death, the Archbishop of Canterbury and the Bishop of London imposed a blanket ban on verse satire (a genre whose chief exponent was John Donne). As part of that ban, the most recent edition of Marlowe's translation of the *Amores* was burned. Sixteen hundred years on from Ovid's exile, with most of his work established at the centre of the classical canon, these particular works remained off limits, consigned to the margins of the culture.

Hero and Leander

Hero and Leander was one of the most famous poems in the short-lived but phenomenally popular genre of 'erotic epic' – narrative poems, modelled on Ovid, telling tales of passionate love. The other most familiar example is Shakepeare's *Venus and Adonis*, published in 1593. Marlowe's poem was licensed in the same year by John Wolfe, but it appears that it did not find its way into print until 1598. Roma Gill bookends the genre with Thomas Lodge's *Scillaes Metamorphosis* (1589) and James Shirley's *Narcissus* (1646) (Gill, 1997, p. 177). Marlowe's poem is certainly one of the most accomplished forays into a difficult form, cleverly balancing humour and pathos in the depiction of Leander's swim across the Hellespont to make love to Hero. Marlowe's main source is a version of the story by the fifth-century AD Greek poet Musaeus. Clifford Leach points out that, of the poem's 818 lines, 500 are invented by Marlowe (Leach, 1986, p. 179), and the poem is certainly a significant step forward from the dogged translations of Lucan and Ovid's *Amores*.

A comparison of the first description of Hero with that of Leander is instructive, and keys us into one of the most striking aspects of the poem: its representation of sexuality. Hero's garments are in sharp contrast with those woven for the shepherd's beloved in 'The Passionate Shepherd': 'Her veil was artificial flowers and leaves, / Whose workmanship both man and beast deceives' (1.19–20). In the 45 lines devoted to Hero, there are relatively brief references to her hands and neck, a passing comment on her hair, with the rest describing her clothes in close detail, dwelling on the artifice that has created them. Leander, on the other hand, is depicted naked, and Marlowe lingers in his description of his neck ('Even as delicious meat is to the taste, / So was his neck in touching', 1.63–4), his smooth breast, white belly, his back, eyes, cheeks and lips. The admirers of his beauty are almost invariably men and male gods: 'the vent'rous youth of Greece' (57), Jove (62), Hippolytus (77) and the 'barbarous Thracian soldier' (81). The poet concludes that 'Some swore he was a maid in man's attire, / For in his looks were all that men desire' (1.83–4).

An account of Hero's rival lovers follows, and the havoc wreaked among them by her haughty beauty, before we come to the first meeting between her and Leander, and the inevitable mutual love at first sight. Leander's speech praises her beauty above that of Venus, the goddess of love, as he attempts to persuade her to yield to him. His repertoire includes the standard sentiments that we are familiar with from sonnets of the period: 'Ah simple Hero, learn thyself to cherish; / Lone women like to empty houses perish' (1.241–2). The appeal climaxes with the audacious suggestion that Hero is robbing her goddess Venus, 'love's beauteous empress', of 'her name and honour' by vowing chastity (1.300–5). Though Hero refuses him again, she relents to meet him at her solitary tower. When she thinks better of it, and offers Venus renewed vows of chastity, Cupid 'beats down her prayers with his wings' (1.369).

The poem continues with a tale that does not appear in Marlowe's sources: an account of Mercury's sexual assault of a country maid, her escape, and the consequences of Mercury's pursuit of her, including his banishment to earth after he stole from Jove a cup of nectar to satisfy her demands. Marlowe's own little invented myth, which operates as an ironic reflection on the two lovers, concludes the first sestiad. The second sestiad describes Leander's first visit to Hero. They indulge in 'amorous rites' without a sacrifice of Hero's virginity: at the crucial moment, Leander turns out to be all talk and no trousers, seemingly ignorant of what he needs to do. He returns home where he is rebuked by his father for pursuing Hero, but, as Marlowe writes, 'love resisted once grows passionate' (2.139), and Leander throws himself into the Hellespont to swim back to his beloved. As he strives against the waves, his naked body arouses the attentions of the sea-god Neptune, and the description of Neptune's treatment of Leander is (once again) strikingly erotic – much more so, in fact, than the passage devoted to Hero and Leander's love-making:

> He clapped his plump cheeks, with his tresses played,
> And smiling wantonly, his love bewrayed.
> He watched his arms, and as they opened wide
> At every stroke, betwixt them he would slide
> And steal a kiss, and then run out and dance,
> And as he turned, cast many a lustful glance,
> And threw him gaudy toys to please his eye,
> And dive into the water, and there pry

Upon his breast, his thighs, and every limb,
And up again, and close beside him swim,
And talk of love. Leander made reply,
'You are deceived, I am no woman, I.'

[2.181–92]

Leander reaches Hero's tower at last. A typically humorous touch finds
Hero caught unawares: 'Where seeing a naked man, she screeched for
fear; / Such sights as this to tender maids are rare' (2.237–8). Gradually,
Leander argues his way into her bed, and she finally yields her virginity. The poem ends with the dawn of the next day. The printed text
concludes with the Latin line 'Desunt nonnulla' ('Some sections are missing'), and it is often assumed that Marlowe died while the poem remained
unfinished. George Chapman provided the sequel and followed the story
through to its tragic conclusion, recounting the death of Leander as he
swims the Hellespont against wind-driven waves, and Hero's subsequent
death on the discovery of his body.

The comic touches in the poem are some of its chief highlights. The
passionate Leander, having expended enormous amounts of rhetorical
ammunition and physical energy in winning Hero, seems uncertain what
to do when he finally has her in his arms:

Albeit Leander, rude in love and raw,
Long dallying with Hero, nothing saw
That might delight him more, yet he suspected
Some amorous rites or other were neglected.

[2.61–4]

His long-delayed union with Hero comes at last as he seeks her warmth,
having emerged from the water cold and naked. Their fumbling pursuit of sexual satisfaction contrasts, once more, with the proficiency of
Neptune as he fondles Leander's body. Marlowe's erotic epic does not
concern itself solely with the young lovers' stumbling progress to their
consummation, but casts a much wider perspective which allows him
to shed ironic shadows across the central relationship.

Hero and Leander is a confident work; Marlowe seems at home in its
chosen verse form, skilful in his manipulation of the comic and the serious, mischievous in his allusiveness. Marlowe is typically irreverent in
his descriptions of the behaviour of the gods. He is also, unsurprisingly,

casually misogynistic in his representations of women. As Hero gives way to Leander's sexual advances, the poet notes that 'In such wars women use but half their strength' (2.296); in the tale of Mercury and his maid, the woman 'feed[s] him with delays, as women use', and provokes the poet to remark how 'All women are ambitious naturally' (1.426, 428). Leander's successful seduction is seen, again, in a fashion characteristic of the genre, as a military conquest. However, the poem is in some senses as much about Leander's innocent skirmishes with homoeroticism as it is an account of his heterosexual victory, a victory which is itself slyly undercut by his inexperience. The complex sexual dynamics of the poem, particularly when considered alongside the anatomy of relationships explored in *Edward II*, provide tantalizing food for thought when we consider what Marlowe might have achieved had his life not been cut short on that evening in Deptford in 1593.

CHAPTER 8

CONCLUSION: MARLOWE IN OUR TIME

Hell-hound on my trail

'Early this morning,
    when you knocked upon my door
Early this morning,
    when you knocked upon my door
And I said, 'Hello, Satan,
    I believe it's time to go'

[Robert Johnson, 'Me and the Devil Blues']

In August 1938, a young blues singer and guitarist called Robert Johnson was playing at a dance in a small town in Greenwood, Tennessee, where he had secured a regular slot. One night, as Johnson was drinking whisky provided for him by the organizer of the dance, he fell ill. Getting sicker and sicker, but urged by the crowd to play on, he played until he dropped, and he was finally carried out. He lay mortally ill for several days, and when he died his body was taken out and buried in an unmarked grave.

Robert Johnson, 'King of the Delta Blues Singers', is acknowledged as one of the most significant figures in the history of blues music, an innovator who took his country blues tradition and forged something new from its forms and conventions, fashioning a prototypical rock 'n' roll which would prove immensely influential both in the evolution of the blues tradition and in the establishment of rock music. There are obvious but by no means unique parallels between Marlowe and Johnson – they died at roughly the same age, both leaving to their artistic ancestors hugely significant legacies, both of them exemplifying the romantic myth of the genius struck down in his prime. What makes the connection more fascinating are the Faustian overtones that linger around the story of the singer's life and death. As a young man, Johnson had been a poor guitarist, shooed away by the older bluesmen he tried to learn from. He disappeared for a while, only to re-emerge a year later as a guitar prodigy, and it was in the wake of this that the stories began to circulate of a pact with the devil. According to one account, Johnson learnt his art under the 'tutelage of a musician named Ike Zinnerman, who was from Alabama and claimed to have learned to play while visiting graveyards at midnight' (Marcus, 1997, p. 188). Peter Guralnick, in his book *Searching for Robert Johnson*, reports these fragmentary accounts of his death:

> Son House said in 1965: 'We never did get the straight of it. We first heard that he got stabbed to death. Next, a woman poisoned him, and then we heard something else. We never did get the straight of it.' Johnny Shines heard that Robert had been poisoned and 'crawled on his hands and knees and barked like a dog before he died.' Others heard that he lingered for days and suggested that he had finally been struck down by the black arts, his note finally come due.
>
> [Guralnick, 1998, p. 49]

In the same way that the stories about Marlowe's death proliferated in the years following, each new tale embellished with tantalizing details, so the stories about Johnson multiplied too. Beard writes of Marlowe that he 'even cursed and blasphemed to his last gasp' (MacLure, 1995, pp. 41–2); Shines says of Johnson that he ' "crawled on his hands and knees and barked like a dog before he died" ' (Guralnick, 1998, p. 49). Francis Meres claims that Marlowe was 'stabbed to death by a bawdy serving man, a rival of his in his lewd love' (MacLure, 1995, p. 46); according to one of the versions of Johnson's death, he was poisoned by the husband of a woman with whom he had been having an affair (Guralnick, 1998, p. 52).

In a world where God and the devil are actual presences, where good and bad angels hover not as manifestations of conscience but as beings no less real than one's fellow men and women, Faustus's story is a terrifying one, a reminder of the imminence of salvation and damnation, and the thin line that divides them. It is a world that is familiar from our engagement with Marlowe's 400-year-old texts. Greil Marcus talks of an analogous intensity, 'looking for signs of evil and grace, of salvation and damnation, behind every natural fact' when discussing Robert Johnson's art (Marcus, 1997, p. 31). According to Marcus, the resonance of the myth in America owes much to the failure of the Puritan founding fathers to realize their utopian vision – their failures meant that their work had been the devil's, not God's, and 'as they panicked at their failures, the devil was all they saw' (ibid., p. 30). Even when stripped of its specifically religious connotations, and transmuted into a meta-phor for something thoroughly secular, the notion of selling one's soul to the devil can be a powerful signifier. It may be used as a vivid expres-sion of the price that the burden of genius can demand, or of the irre-vocable loss of innocence that accompanies transgressive discoveries. Its deployment (by people like Thomas Beard, Francis Meres and Robert Greene) may also speak of the awe and jealousy inspired by great art.

An exploration of Marlowe in our time – or, strictly speaking, over the past couple of centuries, which is what this chapter covers – needs to take account of several different ways in which he and his work have persisted in Western culture. Marlowe himself operates as a mythical figure in certain contexts. It is certainly the case that the ambiguity of his sexual orientation has made him (like Oscar Wilde) an important rallying point in so-called queer theory, a movement in literary and cultural studies that has, since the 1980s, been challenging accepted notions of hetero- and homosexuality. Elsewhere, he has taken on the dimensions of a Faustus or an Icarus in his own right, as in Charles Nicholl's metaphor which compares him to a burning torch turned downwards, consuming itself as it illuminates (Nicholl, 1992, p. 8). This kind of perception of Marlowe was widespread in the first half of the twentieth century, and remains a potent popular perception. Elsewhere, Marlowe's work (or his sources) provide a springboard for the creativ-ity of other artists. In other contexts, Marlowe's plays are themselves taken up as things to be reworked by his successors to serve their own agendas. Although this chapter inevitably presents only a relatively curs-ory overview, it will touch on each of these areas in an attempt to give an impression, however sketchy, of the breadth of Marlowe's influence.

The Faustus myth in Western culture

Elizabeth M. Butler's three-volume study of the Faust legends – *The Myth of the Magus, Ritual Magic* and *The Fortunes of Faust* – is the most comprehensive study of the myth's genealogy. The bibliographies alone testify to the number of new forms the story has found through the centuries. It is impossible to begin a survey in the space available here, but a number of key texts are worth mentioning, and the monumental, two-part *Faust* that Johann Wolfgang Goethe (1749–1832) wrote has perhaps even eclipsed Marlowe's version of the story. It is not an over-statement to say that *Faust* constituted Goethe's life's work. He started planning it around 1773, and it occupied him on and off until shortly before his death in 1832. Some scenes were published in 1790, the first part appearing in full in 1808, the second just after his death. It was primarily written as a literary, rather than as a dramatic, text, and it was not performed until 1829 and only then in edited form. Today, it is rarely if ever performed in its entirety.

In Goethe's *Faust*, the religious infrastructure of the original has been largely removed from the story, although it remains as a framework for the aesthetic of the piece. Goethe's *Faust* is firmly situated within its secularized age and in particular within its intellectual climate. Philo-sophers as diverse as Immanuel Kant, David Hume and Jean Jacques Rousseau had cast significant doubt, from various perspectives, on the commonly accepted relationship between the human subject and the object: with knowledge centred in the individual (subjectivity), the old order founded on the idea of objective truth (usually underwritten by the existence of the divine) was thrown into disarray. While Marlowe's *Doctor Faustus* texts engage with controversies over Christian doctrine, Goethe's concerns are thoroughly modern, grappling with the philo-sophical, ethical and societal issues that preoccupied his own age. The play retains its basis of a pact with the devil, and the final stages of Part Two depict a struggle between angels and devils for Faust's soul, but the work (particularly the second half) is also populated by a host of classical figures: Paris and Helen, Leda and the swan, Nereus and Galatea. The fact that Goethe depicts God on stage in the 'Prologue in Heaven', something Marlowe did not dare to do, is indicative of how far we have moved away from early modern mindsets. Furthermore, with Goethe's God appearing as a polite, elderly gentleman harried by a cynical, sharp-witted Mephistopheles, it is clear that the specifically Christian dimension of the story has been left far behind.

Goethe's *Faust* was central to the fashioning of German cultural iden-tity, becoming its keystone in the same way that the works of Shakespeare helped crystallize an emerging sense of English or British identity through a similar timespan. *Faust* also had a tremendous impact on the Romantic movement that spread across Europe, and although a number of famous names such as Coleridge and Charles Lamb had their reservations, there were plenty of influential writers who were on hand to lionize Goethe and his achievement. Thomas Carlyle, one of the chief advocates, usefully

identifies one sense in which the Marlowe play seemed strikingly out-
dated to a mid-nineteenth-century reader: it 'presumes a certain degree
of belief in magic and apparitions'. He continues:

> Goethe's conception, both of Faust and Mephistophiles,
> bears not only far more relation to the habits of a refined
> and intellectual age, but it is also far more ingenious and
> poetical in itself. The introduction of magic . . . is intended
> merely to serve as the means of illustrating certain feelings,
> and unfolding certain propensities, which exist in the mind,
> independently of magic; and the belief we are required to
> give it is of the most loose and transient nature.
>
> [cited in Cole, 1989, pp. 187–8]

For the Romantics, Faustus became less of an Icarus figure (the Marlowe
play's analogy in its Prologues), and was constructed instead as a Prometheus, the titan of classical legend who stole fire from the gods to
save humankind. Prometheus's damnation was to be chained to a rock
and preyed on by an eagle; the eagle would peck out his liver each day,
which would then grow back each night, only for the torture to begin
again. To the Romantics, Prometheus was a revolutionary, a daring iconoclast challenging the gods' authority and sacrificing himself for the sake
of the human race. Clearly we have moved a considerable distance away
from Marlowe's Faustus who, though he dreams of some acts of altru-
ism in his first meditation on the power of necromancy ('I'll have them
wall all Germany with brass / And make swift Rhine circle fair
Wittenberg', A.1.1.90–1; B.97–8), quickly collapses into self-interest and
petty self-gratification. Goethe's Faust, in the final section of the second part, dedicates himself to the good of humankind. By the early
twentieth century, scholars were reading *Faust* as the story of heroic aspiration: 'Faust's pact with the devil was understood not as evil but as good;
his restlessness, his drive to achieve and build at all costs, were the ideal
of Western civilization' (Brown, 1992, p. 15).

Inevitably, Goethe's *Faust* has itself become a received, canonical text
that has been refashioned and responded to in various ways: once again,
the myth reverberates, the echoes increasingly difficult to match with
the early legend or its Marlovian incarnation. Heinrich Heine (1797–
1856) produced a dance poem version around 1847, seemingly inspired
(at least in part) by a deep hostility towards Goethe's *Faust II*, in particular its swerve away from a tragic conclusion. Other works from the
nineteenth century include Berlioz's dramatic cantata *La Damnation de*

Faust (1846) and the Italian composer Busoni's opera *Doktor Faust* (left unfinished when he died in 1924). During the Second World War Goethe's *Faust* was appropriated ideologically by the Nazi party. A group of Jewish artists who found themselves unemployed as a result of their Jewishness formed an organization that aimed to create a separate cultural life for their people, and although they did try and incorporate the work of German authors into their repertoire, they soon found themselves forbidden to perform the work of Goethe, among others (Hortmann, 1998, p. 118). Goethe's work was to be preserved and protected as part of the pure Aryan inheritance. Soldiers going to war in 1939, just as they had in 1914, carried their copies of *Faust* in their knapsacks (Brown, 1992, pp. 15–16). The difference between the two wars was that, in 1914, *Faust* had operated as a spur in the collective aspiration towards a national identity, whereas by 1939, the commitment was to maintenance of racial purity. In the 1960s, with the eruption of the counter-culture across the Western world, an inevitable backlash against the figurehead of German culture and his masterwork ensued, with a new generation of theatre practitioners revisiting, often with a vengeance, the *Faust* plays, and interrogating the extent of the text's imbrication within the ideology of nationalism.

Thomas Mann, in his long novel *Doctor Faustus* (1947), updated the story to the first half of the twentieth century, and in part his novel is also an attempt to reconfigure the story (post-Goethe) in the wake of Nazism and the Holocaust. Mann tells the story of Adrian Leverkühn, a musician who makes a pact with the devil in return for the genius that inspires him to invent a new musical form. Mann follows the original story closely, while managing to turn it into a thoroughly modern psychological drama. Although Leverkühn is convinced of the reality of the pact, the reader is aware that Leverkühn's talk of deals with the devil is simply 'the delusion of a mind diseased' (Butler, 1998, p. 322). Mann's novel, then, certainly addresses from a modern perspective the philosophical and religious framework that the legend inevitably drags with it. At the same time it is also an attempt to deal with the wider question, dreadful and inevitable in a post-Holocaust world, of the identity of evil – whether it exists as an independent force in the universe, or whether it is located deep in the fabric of humankind itself.

One of the most interesting reworkings of the myth is Klaus Mann's novel *Mephisto*, subsequently adapted by Istvan Szabó for his film of the same name (1982). Both are set in 1930s Germany and tell the story of a talented but egocentric actor who betrays his left-wing principles and friends in his pursuit of fame and success under the Third Reich.

Mann's novel was recognized as a *roman à clef* when it first appeared in 1936: it was clearly based on the career of Gustav Gründgens, a famous German actor who became a favourite of the Nazi regime, and the title was derived from one of the roles on which he had built his reputation, Mephistopheles in Goethe's *Faust*. Szabó's film is an interrogation of the responsibility of the artist who finds himself operating within a fascist state. As he begins to bend under the pressure of the changing cultural climate, the actor (called Hendrick Höfgen in the film) defends himself by arguing that 'I'm an actor, no? I go to the theatre, play my parts, then go back home. That is all'; and on another occasion, 'The really valuable things, such as theatre and art, rise above everything'. Höfgen survives by living his life as a series of compromises. As the film progresses, he abandons his socialist principles, deserts his friends, and finally abandons his black lover, stripping away his integrity piece by piece and replacing it with one deceit or self-deceit after another. Faustus sells his soul and is condemned to eternal damnation; Höfgen suffers the secular fate of the modern human gradually replacing the layers of the self with a succession of masks, finally terrified to remove them in case he finds that nothing remains underneath.

Bertolt Brecht's *The Life of King Edward II of England*

Faustus aside, it is Marlowe's *Edward II* that has most frequently been revisited, both in terms of revival and 'revision', over the past couple of centuries. Bertolt Brecht's production of *Edward II* is not one of his most familiar works. It comes relatively early in his career, being staged in March 1924. Although he had been hired by the Munich Kammerspiele to direct *Macbeth*, Brecht chose Marlowe's play instead, and adapted the text with the help of his friend and collaborator Lion Feuchtwanger. The script of Brecht and Feuchtwanger's version is certainly not a straightforward translation of Marlowe's original. There is little or no real correlation between speeches at all, and there are a number of substantial formal changes: the Younger and Older Mortimer are condensed into one, and the various clerics of Marlowe's play are subsumed into one figure, the (unhistorical) Archbishop of Winchester. Isabella is renamed Anna, for no discernible reason, and the dynamics and the shape of the whole play have been significantly altered. For Brecht, the story of Edward II is the story of a clash between absolutism and the will of the people. Edward's homosexuality is not seen as significant, working only in terms of characterization as one aspect of a personality that seeks endless gratification. In Brecht's retelling of history, Gaveston's rapid social advancement, 'from butcher's boy to king's whore', is what matters. The play becomes primarily a dissection of class conflict, dramatized as a monumental struggle between two men, Edward and Mortimer.

Brecht's adaptation is concrete evidence of his fondness for plays of the early modern period, and for our purposes, his fascination with these texts is perhaps more significant than his reworking of *Edward II* itself. Brecht's considerable body of work also includes a radical reworking of Shakespeare's *Coriolanus*, and an interesting attempt at an adaptation of John Webster's *The Duchess of Malfi*. The latter was never completed, although a considerable amount of work was done around 1943–5, some in collaboration with the poet W.H. Auden. Although space does not permit a full discussion, Brecht's approach to acting technique is worth some brief consideration. At various points during this study, there has been some discussion of problems associated with interpreting and playing Marlowe's *dramatis personae* as 'characters' in the traditional sense. Drawing on Marxist and other materialist cultural and political theory, Brecht rejected the belief that we possess some given, unalterable essence which makes us human, positing instead a notion of the self primarily determined by socio-economic context. From this perspective, it follows that the self will be understood as specific to that particular culture and set of social circumstances. Brecht allows, then, for an awareness of historical and cultural difference that we have already discovered is crucial to a fuller understanding of Marlowe's work. In 'A Short Organum for the Theatre' he writes that:

> The field has to be defined in historically relative terms.
> In other words we must drop our habit of taking the
> different social structures of past periods, then stripping
> them of everything that makes them different; so that they
> all look more or less like our own, which then acquires
> from this process a certain air of having been there all
> along, in other words of permanence pure and simple.
> Instead we must leave them their distinguishing marks and
> keep their impermanence always before our eyes, so that
> our own period can be seen to be impermanent too.

> [Brecht, 1994a, p. 190]

This methodology, recognizing difference rather than always seeking to establish a commonality based on the principle of 'human nature', can have a tremendous impact on the way we interpret a play like *Edward II* or *The Jew of Malta*, as we have already seen in earlier chapters.

Brecht's work with his actors, influenced on the one hand by the expressionist practitioner Vsevolod Meyerhold (1874–1940) and on the other by his observation of Chinese actors during a visit to Russia in the mid-1930s, encouraged them to get 'outside' their characters, and to emphasize discontinuity rather than consistency. As early as 1926, he was arguing that

> Even when a character behaves by contradictions that's only because nobody can be identically the same at two unidentical moments . . . The continuity of the ego is a myth. A man is an atom that perpetually breaks up and forms anew.

> [Brecht, 1994a, p. 15]

Discontinuity and contradiction are fundamental to a Marxist conception of society: the term *dialectic* is used to describe the notion of dynamic tension or contradiction understood to exist at the heart of social relations. Brecht's approach, rejecting the strictly personal and embracing instead the primacy of the political, liberates us from the strictures of psychological consistency and interiority that dog many attempts, both by actors and by literary critics, to make sense of a play like *Doctor Faustus*. Furthermore, an interpretation (or, more usefully, a staging) of Marlowe's play that is informed by a Brechtian approach might shed new light on the controversies and tensions that lie beneath the surface of the text, both in terms of its ideology (political and religious), and in terms of the form of the play itself. Certainly Brecht's model of performance can be more helpful in approaching *Faustus* than the dominant Stanislavsky-based model that insists on attempting to interpret stage persona as three-dimensional character.

A rare revival of Brecht's *Edward II* was staged by Cherub Theatre Company in London in 1999. The production was devised and rehearsed using Brechtian strategies, with the actors playing their roles as highly defined, hard-edged types within a witty, inventive circus ring setting. There was no attempt to separate the world of the performance from the world of the performers. Stripped of any naturalistic pretensions, the story was presented as a stark demonstration of how history is constructed, while the performance style signalled an awareness of the extent to which it can constantly be *re*constructed in different configurations. There is a political point here, too, and it is in keeping with Brecht's commitment not simply to interpret the world, but to change it. The kind of universalism that Brecht is arguing against is seen as a recipe for political stagnation: if the human is essentially always the same, the implication is that the social order is not susceptible to change. It is fairly evident why someone like Brecht would be sceptical about this kind of understanding of what it is to be human. It is equally clear why those who might seek to reinforce this particular ideology are likely to be those who have a vested interest in the status quo. Brecht's insistence on historical and social specificity energizes a performance of his version of *Edward II*, appropriately devised, with a powerful political charge.

Queer Edward II

Brecht appropriated Marlowe's play to interrogate issues of class and political struggle. The British filmmaker Derek Jarman produced a version of *Edward II* with a starker agenda. This section's subtitle is the title of Jarman's book based on his film, and it provides a concise and uncompromising expression of his intentions. The preface is equally forthright:

> How to make a film of a gay love affair and get it commissioned. Find a dusty old play and violate it.
>
> It is difficult enough to be queer, but to be a queer in the cinema is almost impossible. Heterosexuals have fucked up the screen so completely that there's hardly room for us to kiss there. Marlowe outs the past — why don't we out the present? That's really the only message this play has. Fuck poetry. The best lines in Marlowe sound like pop songs and the worst, well, we've tried to spare you them . . .

> [Jarman, 1992, unpaginated preface]

Jarman's *Edward II* premièred in October 1991 (having been commissioned by the BBC), and was televised in January 1993. The book *Queer Edward II* is dedicated to 'the repeal of all anti-gay laws, particularly Section 28', and the film, though it did have a resonance that extends beyond its immediate context, is best understood within its particular social and political moment. Section 28 of the Local Government Act 1988 in Britain was formulated and passed under the regime of Margaret Thatcher, the Prime Minister of the Conservative government from 1979 to 1990. The law prohibited local authorities from using any financial resources to promote homosexuality, whether by publishing material, or by promoting the teaching in state schools of the acceptability of homosexuality as a 'pretended family relationship'. The deep sense of injustice that such blatant discrimination stirred broods over the film. The letter detailing the terms of Gaveston's exile bears the House of Commons logo. The script notes that the chorus of earls 'resemble the benches of the House of Commons' (Jarman, 1992, p. 32). The men are kitted out in MP-style suits and the women are dressed in parodies of the kind of outfits favoured by Margaret Thatcher. On their first appearance, they are preceded onto the set by a huntsman and his hounds. When they gather to sign the document demanding the banishment of Gaveston, they are arranged around one long table, seated like ministers at a cabinet meeting.

Jarman turns the play into a drama that speaks first and foremost 'against the oppression of homosexuals', as he says himself. The text is, inevitably, heavily cut and reordered (the header that runs across every page of the script reads, with characteristic chutzpah, 'Edward II improved by Derek Jarman'). The style is for the most part naturalistic, the costumes an eclectic palette of twentieth-century 'uniforms' of various kinds – the barons appear in business suits, and we see clashes between policemen in riot gear and gay activists with their own recognizable code of dress; others (notably Mortimer) wear military uniforms. The settings are minimalist and faintly surreal, composed and arranged by Jarman's painterly eye.

The published script is unashamed about its propaganda, with tag lines splashed across the pages: 'HOMO means SAME means EQUAL' (p. 26), 'save queer children from straight parents' (p. 24) and 'gender is apartheid' (p. 36) are representative samples. The climactic fight between Edward and his enemies is staged as a pitched battle between gay 'Outrage' protesters and policemen in riot gear. For Jarman, Edward's only crime is his sexuality, and, in terms of state politics, there is little in his film which engages with state politics beyond the immediate, 1980s/1990s issues of Clause 28 and gay rights, and all that it represents. Consequently, the play's preoccupation with power play in the anatomy of the struggle between the monarch and his barons is ignored. The remarkable actress Tilda Swinton is given little room for manoeuvre in her portrayal of

Isabella; a number of critics have attacked Jarman's depiction of her as casually misogynistic. A diary note in the script is of interest in this respect, describing 'an unsatisfactory bedroom scene with Tilda and Steven [Waddington, playing Edward]'; Jarman records that 'she thought it might be misogynist, I thought the audience would have some sympathy for her, even if she plays it hard' (p. 20). The evidence of some dissent on Swinton's part is significant. Isabella is seen in bed not only with Edward (failing to satisfy him), but also with Mortimer. More surprisingly, we also find her responding to a teasing sexual invitation from Gaveston (who humiliates her by laughing in her face as soon as she begins to respond), and seducing Lightborn as she gives him the order to kill Edward. An odd scene between Mortimer and Isabella is set at a firing range, and we witness her cool brutality as she fires bolts from a crossbow into the hanging carcass of a deer. As the film progresses, her behaviour becomes icier and more perverse. Jarman describes in his journal how 'Tilda looks evil in sick green' (p. 108). In the film's final phase, Isabella becomes increasingly monstrous (and her son, observing all, indulges in increasingly violent play-acting). Kent is tortured and interrogated by Mortimer and Isabella, and Isabella finally kills him herself, sinking her teeth, vampire-like, into his neck, while Mortimer watches, appalled.

Although Jarman's chief concern is with legislation that discriminates against homosexuals, the government is not the only political establishment that comes under attack. The position of the church in relation to the government's repressive policies is another preoccupation. The first time we see the bishop, he is depicted standing at the altar flanked by soldiers. In the chorus of politicians that functions as Jarman's equivalent of Marlowe's barons, a bishop features prominently, and it is he who forces Edward to sign the warrant to banish Gaveston. The banishment itself is represented by a dishevelled Gaveston running a gauntlet of priests, all with their hands clasped in prayer. As he staggers down the lines, the priests spit on him. It should be noted that the hostility is mutual, however, and it is Gaveston who initiates it. In an early scene, the Bishop of Winchester, beaten bloody, is stripped naked by Gaveston and a gang of leather-clad thugs and sexually humiliated. Gaveston then removes his false teeth and makes the sign of the cross over him with them.

The significance of the churchmen in the film lies primarily in the extent to which they are complicit in the actions of Mortimer and his associates. Mortimer himself is almost always dressed in combat fatigues, but his persona is only part sharp military officer – the other part is represented by his numerous bedroom scenes. On his first appearance, he is found in bed with what the script describes as '2 wild girls' (p. 28).

Andrew Tiernan as Gaveston in Derek Jarman's film version of *Edward II* (1991).
(Reproduced by courtesy of the photographer, Liam Daniel.)

When Mortimer gets out of bed, the two women kiss, and it is clear that this, and a later sequence depicting him indulging in sado-masochism with 'three wild girls' (p. 98), is intended to help construct him as a decadent and debauched figure. At the same time, Jarman does not provide his audience with the simple equation of evil hetero-sexuals and saintly homosexuals. The representation of the gay characters is more complex, and at one point in his script/journal, Jarman reflects that 'Andrew [Tiernan] is not playing Gaveston in a way that will endear me to "Gay Times"' (p. 20). Elsewhere he remarks, 'Not all gay men are attractive. I am not going to make this an easy ride. Marlowe didn't' (p. 46). But if the audience is presented with an ambivalent figure in Tiernan's Gaveston, the scene in which he dances with Edward to the accompaniment of Cole Porter's 'Ev'ry Time We Say Goodbye' on the eve of his banishment is crucial in recuperating him and the relationship. Jarman notes that 'Andrew played this scene with subtlety, I hope you can feel a little pity for him' (p. 62). As Kate Chedgzoy points out, 'In the context of AIDS, the song's elegiac quality is intensely poignant' (Chedgzoy, 1995, p. 205). Jarman had himself been diagnosed as HIV+ before the shooting of the film.

Jarman is attempting to reclaim history in making this film in a number of different ways. Part of his project is within the tradition that has sought to construct Marlowe as an iconic figure in English literature who can be claimed by homosexuals as 'one of us' – Oscar Wilde has gone through a similar process (a slogan across a page of Jarman's script reads, 'Queer as Oscar' (p. 54)). At the time of writing, three film projects based on Marlowe's life were being planned, two of them placing a heavy emphasis on a supposed love affair between Marlowe and Thomas Walsingham (Halliburton, 1998, p. 12). For Jarman, it is not only Marlowe whose sexuality needs to be reclaimed, but Edward, too. His script notes that 'by many historians [Edward] isn't even allowed his sexuality' (p. 2). Jarman's film demands another reassessment of the 'facts' in order to tell yet another story of history, both Edward's and Marlowe's. Jarman is also proposing a revision of a tendency in the entertainment industry to depict the past in a nostalgic, cosily conventional fashion (an affliction that has affected television in the UK and the US as much as cinema). Jarman notes that 'Edward's gold robe establishes him for a moment as "the King" as in all those camp old costume versions of Elizabethan plays' (p. 18). Later in the book he offers a more detailed consideration of the film's context:

> Filmed history is always a misinterpretation. The past is
> the past, as you try to make material out of it, things slip
> even further away. 'Costume drama' is such a delusion
> based on a collective amnesia, ignorance and furnishing
> fabrics . . . Vulgarity like this started with Olivier's 'Henry
> V' and deteriorated ever after . . . Our 'Edward' as closely
> resembles the past as any 'costume drama' (which is not a
> great claim).

[Jarman, 1992, p. 86]

A very different costume drama proved to be one of the most critically acclaimed films of 1999. *Shakespeare in Love* is a fantasy woven around Shakespeare's composition of *Romeo and Juliet*. The tone is for the most part light and mischievous, with the co-writer Tom Stoppard given free rein to drop in as many amusing anachronisms and intertextual references as he could muster. *Shakespeare in Love* represents our hero struggling to write his new play, *Romeo and Ethel the Pirate's Daughter*. In the meantime, he falls in love with a woman of nobility, who is due to marry an earl. Their doomed romance provides Shakespeare with the inspiration for his play. The film is populated by familiar figures whose names appear in one of the appendices of this book – Philip

Henslowe, Edward Alleyn, Richard Burbage – and even Queen Elizabeth makes several appearances. In one striking, brief scene, Shakespeare finds himself almost alone in a tavern. At the other end of the bar sits a magnetic, self-assured figure observing him with a quiet curiosity: Christopher Marlowe. Will shamefacedly admits to writer's block, and Kit calmly lays out a plot for his rival playwright that provides Will with all he needs to resume work on his (later to be retitled) *Romeo and Ethel the Pirate's Daughter*. A number of references to Marlowe throughout the film have clearly established him as the more successful writer, with Shakespeare grimly, doggedly soldiering on in his shadow. As Kit leaves the tavern, mentioning in passing his own new work *The Massacre at Paris*, Shakespeare is left to mutter under his breath, admiring and envious, 'Good title'. The next Will knows of Marlowe, he is dead.

Marlowe's modest body of work remains dwarfed by the Shakespearean canon, even though the volatility of his key works – *Faustus*, *Edward II*, *The Jew of Malta* and *Tamburlaine* – has made them especially susceptible to provocative new interpretations in the light of more recent critical theory. *Shakespeare in Love* offers a neat little tribute to Marlowe and his legacy, reversing the polarity that has always underpinned studies of the drama of the period. In view of the many myths that have been layered over him, it is surprising that his fleeting appearance in the film is marked by nothing sensational, instead portraying him as mercurial and quietly self-confident, giving nothing away. He is very far from the dangerous radical Richard Wilson depicts in a recent essay: 'The playwright who staged the scandal of a paedophile god, sado-masochistic killer, immigrant Jew, sodomite king, subversive intellectual, and Catholic terrorist'. Wilson predicts that he 'will be canonised not for normalizing [his characters], but for dramatizing their difference from the normality they outraged' (Wilson, 1999, p. 26), but, finally, this is just one more appropriation. Anti-Catholic propaganda or political satire; anti-Semitic xenophobia or a mirror to reflect back Christian hypocrisy to a dazzled audience; a plea for understanding of sexual difference or a condemnation of a king who would sacrifice his kingdom for his lover; flinty religious orthodoxy or sly atheism? The texts lie open on the desk, blank-faced, and the portrait on the wall at Corpus Christi College looks on, denying nothing, endorsing nothing, while new interpreters inscribe their own preoccupations on the pages.

PART THREE

REFERENCE SECTION

BRIEF BIOGRAPHIES

EDWARD ALLEYN (1566–1626)

One of the two great tragedians of his generation, Alleyn forged a successful partnership with Marlowe as writer and himself as star actor. It was unfortunate that it came to such a sudden, untimely end after only three or four projects. Alleyn led the troupe known as the Lord Admiral's Men. His father-in-law was Philip Henslowe, and between them, Henslowe and Alleyn owned a good proportion of the shares in a number of theatres, including the Rose, where most of Marlowe's plays were premièred. He seems to have gone into temporary retirement in 1597–1600, returning to the stage for five years before finally retiring to his theatre management role in 1605.

RICHARD BURBAGE (1567?–1619)

Burbage began his career in the same company as Alleyn, but joined the Lord Chamberlain's Men as leader when they came together in 1594. He went on to become the other great actor of the time, rivalling Alleyn, and playing many of Shakespeare's key roles, including Hamlet, Othello, Lear and probably Macbeth. Burbage founded the Globe (1599) when the Theatre was no longer viable as a commercial operation, probably stealing the timber from the old playhouse to build his new one. Burbage achieved fame as a painter as well as an actor. It seems he did not share Alleyn's preoccupation with commercial enterprise, and he continued to act to the end of his life.

PHILIP HENSLOWE (d. 1616)

Henslowe was a theatre manager, and related to Edward Alleyn (he was the stepfather of Alleyn's wife). He was closely associated with the Lord Admiral's Men, the company that produced most of Marlowe's plays. Henslowe is of interest to us today chiefly on account of his so-called 'diary', a book that has been invaluable to scholars of the early modern theatre. It includes lists of plays, box office receipts, inventories of props and costumes, etc., and is very revealing about Marlowe's plays in particular. The 'diary' also includes very precise details of alterations made to the Rose theatre in 1592, where Marlowe's major works were first performed.

THOMAS KYD (1558–1594)

Kyd is famous for his play *The Spanish Tragedy* (1587), a key work in the establishment of the so-called revenge tragedy genre, and a popular and much-quoted work in its time. Kyd is also generally thought to have been the author of the so-called *Ur-Hamlet*, the play, now lost, that Shakespeare is believed to have used as the basis for his own famous tragedy. Kyd and Marlowe shared writing chambers. Kyd was arrested on 12 May 1593, when heretical papers were found in his possession. Torture extracted from him a confession that the papers belonged to Marlowe. A day or two after Marlowe's death, Kyd wrote to the Lord Keeper, detailing Marlowe's heretical beliefs. It seems likely that Kyd never fully recovered from his period in custody, and he died a year after Marlowe was killed.

RODERIGO LOPEZ (1520?–1594)

Lopez was a Jewish physician of Portuguese extraction, and a Marrano – that is to say, one whose ancestors had been forcibly converted to Christianity. Contemporary accounts disagree on whether he was a practising Christian or one who continued to practise his own faith in secret. He settled in England in 1559, and after a spell at St Bartholomew's Hospital, he was appointed chief physician to Queen Elizabeth in 1586. Lopez seems to have been involved in some espionage, working with the Earl of Essex to put the pretender Antonio Perez on the throne in Portugal. When this failed, Perez came to England. Lopez and Essex subsequently fell out, and Essex managed to implicate the doctor in a Spanish plot to murder Perez and Queen Elizabeth. Essex presided over the tribunal that convicted him of treason. Elizabeth reluctantly signed the death warrant some months after sentence had been passed and Lopez was hanged, drawn and quartered at Tyburn on 7 June 1594.

NICCOLO MACHIAVELLI (1469–1527)

Machiavelli was a Florentine statesman and political philosopher whose work achieved, perhaps unjustly, a degree of notoriety in Elizabethan England. His treatise *The Prince* was written around 1513, although it was not published until the 1530s. It was based on his observations of the contemporary political scene, and framed as a prospective book of instruction for a future prince who would rule a unified Italian state. Its chief theme is the necessity for the ruler to retain absolute authority over his subjects, and argues that, in politics, the end always justifies the means. *The Prince* was first published in English in 1640, but its influence in England goes back much further than that, via readings of Italian and French versions, and the circulation of translations in manuscript form, long before this publication date. The treatise infiltrated English culture in a rather distorted fashion, and this resulted in Machiavelli becoming a kind of bugbear to Elizabethan culture for his supposed atheism, amorality and willingness to sacrifice everything good and honourable on the altar of opportunism. It is this version of Machiavelli and his theories that informs his appearance as the Prologue figure in Marlowe's *The Jew of Malta*.

THOMAS NASHE (1567–1601)

Educated at Cambridge, Nashe became famous for his spirited, satirical attacks on the Puritans in pamphlets and other works, often using the pseudonym Pasquil. *Pierce Penniless: his Supplication to the Devil* (1592) was one of his most popular satires. His *Christ's Tears over Jerusalem* (1593) seemed to be evidence of an abrupt volte-face, being a desperate expression of regret and act of repentance for his past life and career. However, this did not put a stop to the more daring works of his fertile imagination. He is most well known for his lively picaresque tale *The Unfortunate Traveller*, published the following year (1594), which is a keystone in the development of prose fiction. His play *The Isle of Dogs* (1597), on which he collaborated with the up and coming writer Ben Jonson, was considered so potentially subversive that it led to their imprisonment for several months. Nashe died a few years later, at the age of 33. The chief connection between Nashe and Marlowe is via *Dido Queen of Carthage*: the two probably collaborated on it when both of them were still at Cambridge, around 1586.

SIR WALTER RALEGH (1552?–1618)

Ralegh is most famous for his expeditions, including journeys of discovery to the American continent in the 1580s, and for a number of victories over Spanish forces at sea in the 1590s. He was for a time a favourite at Elizabeth I's court, and was knighted in 1584. He was superseded in Elizabeth's affections by the Earl of Essex, and fell from grace when the queen discovered his affair with Elizabeth Throckmorton, one of her maids-of-honour. He was imprisoned for a while in the Tower of London, and married Throckmorton on his release. James I imprisoned him again in 1603, but released him in 1616 for a final voyage to South America in search of a gold mine. The expedition was a failure and the death sentence that was originally commuted in 1592 was invoked. He was beheaded on 29 October 1618. He was apparently a prolific writer, although much of his work is now lost. His writings include a *History of the World* (1614, unfinished) and about 30 fragments of poetry. These include 'The Nymph's Reply', his cynical response to the pastoral idyll Marlowe evokes in 'The Passionate Shepherd to his Love'.

WILLIAM SHAKESPEARE (1564–1616)

Shakespeare was born in the same year as Christopher Marlowe. He attended a grammar school in Stratford, but unlike Marlowe did not have a university education. He married Anne Hathaway in 1582, and they had three children. He came to London in 1586, probably just before Marlowe arrived there. His activities were at first fairly low key; while Marlowe exploded onto the stage with *Tamburlaine*, a phenomenal success, Shakespeare worked mostly as an actor with the King's Company at the Rose, the Curtain and the Globe. He began to have his own plays performed around 1590–1, including early comedies and the *Henry VI/Richard III* tetralogy. His long poems *Venus and Adonis* and *The Rape of Lucrece* were published in 1593 and 1594, about the time Marlowe wrote *Hero and Leander*. He hit his stride about the time Marlowe died, writing a number of successful comedies and the *Henry IV* history cycle. His tragedies, probably still his most famous works, date from around the turn of the century and the early 1600s. Popular with Elizabeth I, he continued his success after James I came to the throne, retiring from writing for the stage around 1611, some five years before he died. He retired to Stratford in 1611, while keeping up his contacts with the theatrical community in particular in London. His last play was probably *The Tempest*, although it is likely that the unfinished works *Henry VIII* and *Two Noble Kinsmen* were completed by other writers for production during the last years of his life.

SIR PHILIP SIDNEY (1544–1586)

Sidney, in his own time, was one of the most celebrated figures in Elizabethan culture, a poet and soldier who seemed to represent the ideal courtly figure even though, ironically, he himself seemed uncomfortable in that environment. As far as Elizabethan England was concerned, he died an heroic death in the Netherlands fighting Catholic Spain, although the siege of Zutphen itself achieved very little. Fighting to rescue his beleaguered comrade Lord Willoughby, he was wounded in the thigh by a musket ball. He died a few weeks later. One of the stories that circulated depicted the wounded Sidney offering the precious supply in his water bottle to a dying soldier. Although the story is most likely pure invention, it provides an efficient snapshot of Sidney's status and reputation. News of his death prompted literally hundreds of elegies and songs celebrating his achievements and mourning his untimely end. One of Sidney's most significant literary achievements was his series of love sonnets, *Astrophil and Stella*, apparently inspired by his love for Penelope Devereux, daughter of the first Earl of Essex. The sequence circulated in manuscript from around 1582 and was published in 1591. His monumental *Arcadia*, which he began in 1580, was finally published in 1590. He is also remembered for his *Defence of Poesy* (also known as *The Apology for Poetry*), written around 1580 and published in 1595. Sir Francis Walsingham, head of the secret service (and father of Marlowe's friend and patron Thomas Walsingham), was Sidney's father-in-law.

SIR FRANCIS WALSINGHAM (1532–1590)

Educated at King's College, Cambridge, Walsingham, like so many scholars Cambridge turned out at this time, emerged as an ardent Protestant, and became a powerful figure during Elizabeth's reign. He was first employed at her court in 1568, having spent the time of Mary's reign on the continent, where he had devoted himself to a study of European law and politics. By 1572 he had been made Elizabeth's Secretary of State. Motivated by a hatred of Catholicism, he was deeply committed to the removal of the threat posed by Mary Queen of Scots, and the defeat of Spain. He spent his personal fortune on the maintenance of his secret service, and his spies were planted in courts across the continent. Marlowe was one of his agents, and it may well have been Walsingham who intervened to ensure that Marlowe was awarded his MA degree in June 1587. Marlowe's repeated and prolonged absences from college had put the award in doubt, and a letter from the Privy Council made it clear that his absences were due to 'good service' he had done for his country. Walsingham's son Thomas was Marlowe's friend and patron.

SIR THOMAS WALSINGHAM (1568–1630)

Thomas, son of Secretary of State Sir Francis Walsingham, acted as patron to Marlowe and a number of other writers, including George Chapman and Thomas Watson. Watson and Marlowe were friends, and both of them were imprisoned for a time in September 1589 after a street brawl ended in the death of another man, William Bradley. Thomas Walsingham was knighted in 1597. He inherited Scadbury House in Kent, and it was here that Marlowe spent the last few weeks of his life. It is possible that he wrote *Hero and Leander* at that time. Edward Blount, the printer of the first edition of the poem (1598), dedicates the volume to 'the Right Worshipful, Sir Thomas Walsingham, Knight'. He refers to the 'many kind favours' Walsingham bestowed on Marlowe, and declares that 'I cannot but see so far into the will of him dead, that whatsoever issue of his brain should chance to come abroad, that the first breath it should take might be the gentle air of your liking'. Walsingham died at Scadbury in 1630.

FURTHER READING

Editions

The definitive editions of Marlowe's plays remain the Revels series published by Manchester University Press. At the time of going to press, some had recently been reprinted: *Tamburlaine* in 1999, *The Jew of Malta* in 1997. Unfortunately, they were not updated for the reprints, and this undermines the claim on the jacket of the edition of *Tamburlaine* that it includes 'a full survey of recent criticism' – it is in fact some twenty years out of date. Nevertheless, the scholarly apparatus in all the Revels editions remains unsurpassed. The outstanding edition of *Doctor Faustus* in this series is a much more recent one, dating from 1993. Charles R. Forker's *Edward II* appeared in the following year. *Dido and The Massacre at Paris* are collected in one volume, currently out of print. Manchester have recently published student editions of the Revels series. These are significantly cheaper, and feature much more concise (and updated) introductions. So far, *Tamburlaine* (edited by J.S. Cunningham and Eithne Henson, 1998) and *The Jew of Malta* (edited by David Bevington, 1997) have appeared in this series.

The standard original spelling edition of Marlowe's work is under the editorship of Roma Gill and published by Oxford University Press (1986–98). There are a number of one-volume editions of the plays available. These include the Penguin edition, by J.B. Steane, now woefully out of date (1969); the Oxford edition (1995), which omits the two minor plays, but includes *Faustus* in A- and B-text forms; and Mark Thornton Burnett's Everyman edition (1999), which also includes both *Faustus* plays, as well as the minor works. The latter is the best one-volume edition of the plays now available, although, in its first printing at least, it included a guide to further reading which neglected to include the titles and publication details of most of the books and articles to which it referred.

For one-volume editions of the plays, the best of the cheaper alternatives to the Revels editions are the New Mermaids editions. Most have been revised recently, and include James R. Siemon's *The Jew of Malta* (1994), Martin Wiggins and Robert Lindsey's *Edward II* (1997), Anthony B. Dawson's *Tamburlaine Parts One and Two* (1997) and Roma Gill's *Doctor Faustus* (1989). Otherwise, Nick Hern Books publish very cheap, literally pocket-sized editions in their Drama Classics series of *Faustus* (A and B), *The Jew* and *Edward II* with brief introductions and the minimum of critical apparatus.

There are a number of other individual editions of *Faustus* that deserve a mention. Michael Keefer's edition of the A-text provides a substantial introduction, useful appendices (including extracts from the *Faustbook* and Calvin's *Institutes*) and extensive bibliography (Broadview Press, 1991). The Open University Press have published a version of the A-text (1985) in an edition by David Ormerod and Christopher Wortham. Its introduction pays particular attention to the background of magic and the occult. W.W. Greg's 1950 conflated text, *The Tragical History of the Life and Death of Doctor Faustus: A Conjectural Reconstruction* (Clarendon Press), remains of historical interest, but note that the conflated nature of the text means that references to A- and B-texts in this study do not apply. The poems and translations appear in a Penguin paperback edition (edited by Stephen Orgel, 1979) and as volume I in the Oxford original spelling series (edited by Roma Gill, 1986).

Biographical

The standard life of Marlowe remains J. Bakeless's two-volume *The Tragical History of Christopher Marlowe* (Harvard University Press, 1942). William Urry has done an exhaustive study of Marlowe's early years, uncovering some fascinating new insights, in his *Christopher Marlowe and Canterbury* (Faber and Faber, 1988). Although it would be more accurate to describe it as 'a death of Marlowe' than 'a life of Marlowe', Charles Nicholl's *The Reckoning* remains the most fascinating addition to this section (Jonathan Cape, 1991). Its starting point is Marlowe's death and the various accounts of it, but the book actually casts its net much wider than this, providing some intriguing speculation about the Elizabethan criminal underworld and Marlowe's connections there. A.D. Wraight has more recently been responsible for some bizarre accounts of the so-called 'real' Marlowe (that is to say, the one who she believes wrote

Shakespeare's plays). *Christopher Marlowe and Edward Alleyn* (Adam Hart, 1993), *The Story That the Sonnets Tell* (Adam Hart, 1995) and *Christopher Marlowe and the Armada* (Adam Hart, 1996) are to be treated with a healthy dose of scepticism for this reason. However, her 'Pictorial Biography' of Marlowe, written with Virginia F. Stern, is a valuable resource: *In Search of Christopher Marlowe* (MacDonald & Co., 1965) dates from before the sharp left turn, and, helpfully, was reprinted in 1993 by Adam Hart (Publishers) Ltd. It carries a wealth of illustration, including copies of records from the archives of Corpus Christi College, Cambridge. Also worthy of note is Anthony Burgess's *A Dead Man in Deptford*, which provides a subtitle for a section in the present study (Hutchinson, 1993). Burgess's work bears none of the stiffness of the typical historical novel and, more than any other book mentioned here, brings Marlowe and his society vividly to life.

Critical studies of Marlowe's work

A number of excellent studies of Marlowe have been published in the 1990s. Influenced by Foucault's theories of state power, surveillance and coercion, Roger Sales's study *Christopher Marlowe* in the Macmillan Dramatists series (1991) is idiosyncratic in that it studies Marlowe's life and work in the context of a so-called 'dramatised society'. Rich in citations from contemporary documents, it makes for stimulating reading, even if the determination to frame everything within the thesis of a 'stage-play world' occasionally seems forced. There is full discussion of the four major plays, with passing references to *Dido* and *Massacre*, although it does not consider the poetry at all. A shorter study is Thomas Healy's *Christopher Marlowe* in the Writers and their Work series published by Northcote House (1994). Accessible and critically astute, its only limitation is its length (less than 90 pages).

More specialized monographs also appeared in the 1980s and 1990s. Patrick Cheney's *Marlowe's Counterfeit Profession: Ovid, Spenser, Counter-Nationhood* (University of Toronto Press, 1997) posits a densely argued case for placing Marlowe in an Ovidian tradition, and in so doing helps to shift the critical debate from the customary comparisons with Shakespeare. Sarah Munson Deats's *Sex, Gender and Desire in the Plays of Christopher Marlowe* (University of Delaware Press, 1997) argues that Marlowe's work disrupts established categories of sexuality and gender. Emily C. Bartels provides a fascinating study of Marlowe's 'strangers' in her *Spectacles of Strangeness: Imperialism, Alienation and Marlowe* (University of Pennsylvania Press, 1993). Bartels and Deats both show a strong commitment to the notion of Marlowe as radical subversive, following in the tradition established by Simon Shepherd's *Christopher Marlowe and the Politics of Elizabethan Theatre* (Harvester Wheatsheaf, 1986). These new historicist and cultural materialist readings of Marlowe are all indebted to a greater or lesser extent to Stephen Greenblatt's groundbreaking *Renaissance Self-Fashioning From More to Shakespeare* (University of Chicago Press, 1980), which includes substantial discussion of Marlowe, in particular *The Jew of Malta*.

The work of Bartels, Shepherd, Deats and others runs the risk of romanticizing Marlowe in a fashion analogous to those who, in the first half of the century, had chosen to highlight his supposed atheism in order to portray him as a radical iconoclast, notably Una Ellis-Fermor in her study *Christopher Marlowe* published in 1927 (Methuen). Others who have argued a case for Marlowe the iconoclast include Paul H. Kocher in *Christopher Marlowe: A Study of his Thought, Learning and Character* (University of North Carolina Press, 1946) and Harry Levin in *The Overreacher* (Harvard University Press, 1952).

There are some excellent collections of essays available. The most recent, at the time of writing, was Richard Wilson's *Longman Critical Reader: Christopher Marlowe* (Longman, 1999). Others of note are *Christopher Marlowe and English Renaissance Culture* (Scolar Press, 1996), edited by Darryll Grantley and Peter Roberts, and Kenneth Friedenreich's collection *A Poet and a Filthy Playmaker: New Essays on Christopher Marlowe* (AMS Press, 1988). *Christopher Marlowe and the Renaissance of Tragedy*, a collection of essays by Douglas Cole, Josh Beer, Christopher Innes and Simon Williams, focuses on the significance of Marlowe as a theatrical innovator (Greenwood Press, 1996). There are two Casebook collections devoted to Marlowe: John Russell Brown has edited a selection covering *Tamburlaine the Great*, *Edward the Second* and *The Jew of Malta* (Macmillan, 1982) and John Jump oversees a volume devoted to *Doctor Faustus* (Macmillan, 1969). A long overdue New Casebook, reflecting more recent critical trends, was in preparation at the time this book went to press. Finally, for a short and very accessible study of *Faustus*, Michael Mangan's *Doctor Faustus* in the Penguin Critical Studies series (1989) is to be recommended.

The amount published on Marlowe's work in performance has in fact been fairly limited, and the present study has attempted to begin to redress that imbalance. Other titles that are useful in this regard include Clifford Leech's *Christopher Marlowe: Poet for the Stage* (AMS Press, 1986) and a special issue of the *Tulane Drama Review* devoted to Marlowe (Volume 8, Number 4, Summer 1964). George L. Geckle's 1988 publication *Text and Performance: Tamburlaine and Edward II* (Humanities Press International) is useful, but was published too early to cover two key RSC productions, Anthony Sher as Tamburlaine (1992) and Simon Russell Beale as Edward II (1990). William Tydeman provides a study of *Faustus* in performance for the Macmillan Text and Performance series (1984), and both he and Geckle offer fairly straightforward stage histories. Two works that are more theoretical in their approach are David Hard Zucker's *Stage and Image in the Plays of Christopher Marlowe* (Salzburg Studies in English Literature, 1972) and Thomas Cartelli's *Marlowe, Shakespeare, and the Economy of Theatrical Experience* (University of Pennsylvania Press, 1991); the latter, though not an easy read, is a rewarding one, which attempts to imagine Elizabethan audiences' responses to Marlowe's plays.

Finally, two reference works which have been vital to the present study are Millar MacLure's *Christopher Marlowe: The Critical Heritage* (Routledge, 1979) and Vivien Thomas and William Tydeman's *Christopher Marlowe: The Plays and Their Sources* (Routledge, 1994). The latter provides invaluable introductions to each section. There are generous extracts from relevant sources for each play.

Context: literature and theatre

Somewhat inevitably, most of the useful books connecting Elizabethan social and political conditions with literary and theatrical contexts tend to bear the name 'Shakespeare' in their title. With this caveat, Russ McDonald's *Bedford Companion to Shakespeare* is one of the best, comprising commentary and a selection of contemporary documents organized into carefully considered sections (St Martin's Press, 1996). A similar, older publication is G. Blakemore Evans's *Elizabethan–Jacobean Drama: A New Mermaid Background Book* (A. & C. Black, 1989). A collection of essays entitled *A New History of Early English Drama* (Columbia University Press, 1997), edited by John D. Cox and David Scott Kastan, is to be recommended for its scope and depth. It has a broadly new historicist slant. On a similar track is David Scott Kastan and Peter Stallybrass's *Staging the Renaissance* (Routledge, 1991), which also includes useful extracts from criticism by Greenblatt and Jonathan Dollimore on *The Jew* and *Faustus* respectively. Julia Briggs's *This Stage-Play World* (new edition, Oxford University Press, 1997) is a valuable and accessible survey of early modern culture. The first two sections of Peter Hyland's *An Introduction to Shakespeare* (Macmillan, 1996) are also to be recommended.

On Elizabethan theatre specifically, Andrew Gurr's *The Shakespearean Stage, 1574–1642* remains indispensable (Cambridge University Press, 3rd edition, 1992), and his *Playgoing in Shakespeare's London* (Cambridge University Press, 2nd edition, 1996) is also very useful. The *Cambridge Companion to English Renaissance Drama* (Cambridge University Press, 1990), edited by A.R. Braunmuller and Michael Hattaway, is one of the best single-volume guides available. For more specific areas of study, Peter Thomson's *Shakespeare's Theatre* (Routledge, 2nd edition, 1992) is excellent on early modern stage practice. Jean E. Howard's *The Stage and Social Struggle in Early Modern England* is particularly strong on the issue of anti-theatrical discourse (Routledge, 1994); more specialized on this issue of censorship is Janet Clare's *Art Made Tongue-Tied by Authority* (Manchester University Press, 2nd edition 1999). Two important new historicist studies which remain central to debates about the relation between theatre and society are Stephen Mullaney's *The Place of the Stage* (Chicago University Press, 1988) and Leonard Tennenhouse's *Power on Display* (Methuen, 1986).

Society, culture and politics

A number of books dealing with the Elizabethan social and historical context specifically (and so lacking a literary critical or theatre history angle) have been invaluable to the work for this present study. Mary Abbott's *Life Cycles in England, 1560–1720* (Routledge, 1996) focuses on everyday life in Tudor and Stuart England, and comprises commentary and contemporary documents. A more comprehensive study is David Cressy's *Birth, Marriage and Death: Ritual, Religion and the Life-Cycle in Tudor and Stuart England* (Oxford University Press, 1997). Anne Laurence's *Women in England, 1500–1760: A Social History* (Orion Books, 1996) is a fascinating analysis, redressing the traditionally male-centred readings of social history.

For those interested in following up on the issue of homosexuality in early modern culture, the key works (all tending to focus on literary connections) are Alan Bray's *Homosexuality in Renaissance England* (Gay Men's Press, 1982), Bruce R. Smith's *Homosexual Desire in Shakespeare's England* (University of Chicago Press, 1994) and Jonathan Goldberg's *Sodometries* (Stanford University Press, 1992). Mario Digangi's *The*

Homoerotics of Early Modern Drama (Cambridge University Press, 1997) is also useful. On the issue of anti-Semitism, James Shapiro's excellent study *Shakespeare and the Jews* (University of Columbia Press, 1996) includes fairly extensive discussion of *The Jew of Malta*. In relation to the occult (*Faustus*), Keith Thomas's classic study *Religion and the Decline of Magic* (Penguin, 1971) remains seminal.

For further reading in the field of historiography – the study of historical methodology, touched on at various points in this book – the best starting point is Keith Jenkins's *Re-Thinking History* (Routledge, 1991). Recommended for further study of religious conflict in the period are A.G. Dickens's *The English Reformation* (B.T. Batsford Ltd, 2nd edition, 1993) and Christopher Haigh's *English Reformations* (Oxford University Press, 1993); the plural in Haigh's title indicates a shift in perspective that sees the process of the Reformation as one more complex, fragmented and discontinuous than traditional accounts have implied. For more general, introductory reading on Tudor history, see John Morrill's edited collection *The Oxford Illustrated History of Tudor & Stuart Britain* (Oxford University Press, 1996), which includes an essay on theatre and society by Andrew Gurr. More in-depth studies include Christopher Haigh's *Elizabeth I* (1988) and John Guy's *Tudor England* (Oxford University Press, 1988). Although its scope is European, William Manchester's *A World Lit Only by Fire: The Medieval Mind and the Renaissance* (Macmillan, 1996, first published 1993) is a beautifully written account of the momentous cultural shift that took place over a couple of hundred years.

Critical theory

For those wishing to study in greater depth the kind of critical perspectives that inform this study, the market in textbooks in critical theory has expanded massively since the early 1990s, and there are any number of suitable introductions (note that Marlowe himself is marginal or absent from the majority of the studies mentioned under this heading). Two of the best are Peter Barry's *Beginning Theory* (Manchester University Press, 1995) and *A Reader's Guide to Contemporary Literary Theory* by Raman Selden and Peter Widdowson (Harvester Wheatsheaf, 3rd edition, 1993), although the standard text remains Terry Eagleton's *Literary Theory* (Blackwell, 2nd edition, 1996).

Focusing on the specific schools of thought that underpin this work are John Brannigan's *New Historicism and Cultural Materialism* (Macmillan, 1998) and Claire Colebrook's *New Literary Histories* (Manchester University Press, 1997). The seminal work of cultural materialism in relation to Marlowe's period is Jonathan Dollimore and Alan Sinfield's *Political Shakespeare* (Manchester University Press, 2nd edition, 1994). For greater depth on the issue of post-colonialism touched on in the discussion of *The Jew of Malta*, see John McLeod, *Beginning Postcolonialism* (Manchester University Press, 2000) and Ania Loomba's *Colonialism/Postcolonialism* in Routledge's New Critical Idiom series (1998). Loomba's *Gender, Race, Renaissance Drama* (Manchester University Press, 1989) is useful, applying some of these perspectives to the early modern period.

BIBLIOGRAPHY

Abbott, Mary 1996. *Life Cycles in England, 1560–1720.* Routledge

Adams, Joseph Quincy (ed.) 1924. *Chief Pre-Shakespearean Dramas* [including *The Play of the Sacrament*], Cambridge, Mass.

Alexander, Nigel 1971. 'The Performance of Christopher Marlowe's *Dr. Faustus*', *Proceedings of the British Academy*, 57 (1971), pp. 331–49

Althusser, Louis 1971. *Lenin and Philosophy and Other Essays.* Trans. Ben Brewster. New Left Books

Bakhtin, Mikhail 1984. *Rabelais and His World.* Trans. Hélène Iswolsky. Indiana University Press

Barker, Francis 1993. *The Culture of Violence.* Manchester University Press

Barker, Francis 1995. *The Tremulous Private Body: Essays on Subjection.* University of Michigan Press. First published 1984

Bartels, Emily C. 1993. *Spectacles of Strangeness: Imperialism, Alienation, and Marlowe.* University of Pennsylvania Press

Battenhouse, Roy 1964. *Marlowe's Tamburlaine: A Study in Renaissance Moral Philosophy.* First published 1941. Vanderbilt University Press

Bawcutt, N.W. (ed.) 1997. Christopher Marlowe, *The Jew of Malta.* Revels Plays edition. First published 1978. Manchester University Press

Bennett, Susan 1996. *Performing Nostalgia: Shifting Shakespeare and the Contemporary Past.* Routledge

Bevington, David 1962. *From Mankind to Marlowe: Growth and Structure in the Popular Drama of Tudor England.* Harvard University Press

Bevington, David & Rasmussen, Eric (eds) 1993. *Doctor Faustus.* Revels Plays edition. Manchester University Press

Bhabha, Homi K. 1983. 'The Other Question . . .', *Screen*, 24.6, Nov–Dec 1983, pp. 18–36

Billington, Michael 1992. Review of *Tamburlaine* in *The Guardian*, 3 Nov 1992, clipping from Shakespeare Institute Archives

Boal, Augusto 1979. *Theatre of the Oppressed.* Pluto Press

Boas, Frederick S. 1940. *Christopher Marlowe: A Biographical and Critical Study.* Clarendon

Bradshaw, Graham 1993. *Misrepresentations: Shakespeare and the Materialists.* Cornell University Press

Braunmuller, A.R. & Hattaway, Michael (eds) 1990. *The Cambridge Companion to English Renaissance Drama*. Cambridge University Press

Brecht, Bertolt 1976. *Collected Plays Volume 7, 1942–1946*. Ed. John Willett and Ralph Manheim. Eyre Methuen Ltd

Brecht, Bertolt 1994a. *Brecht on Theatre: The Development of an Aesthetic*. Trans. John Willett. First published 1964, 2nd edn 1974. Methuen

Brecht, Bertolt 1994b. *Collected Plays: One*. Ed. & trans. John Willett and Ralph Manheim. First published 1970. Methuen

Briggs, Julia 1983. 'Marlowe's *Massacre at Paris*: A Reconsideration' in *Review of English Studies*, 34, pp. 257–78

Briggs, Julia 1997. *This Stage-Play World: Texts and Contexts, 1580–1625*. Oxford University Press

Bristol, Michael D. 1985. *Carnival and Theater: Plebeian Culture and the Structure of Authority in Renaissance England*. Methuen

Brown, Jane K. 1992. *Faust: Theater of the World*. Twayne Publishers

Burnett, Mark Thornton (ed.) 1999. *Christopher Marlowe: The Complete Plays*. Everyman

Butler, Elizabeth M. 1998. *The Fortunes of Faust*. First published 1952. Sutton Publishing Limited

Calvin, Jean 1961. *Institutes of the Christian Religion*, Vol. II. Ed. John T. McNeill, trans. Ford Lewis Battles. SCM Press Ltd

Campbell, L.B. (ed.) 1938. *The Mirror for Magistrates*. Barnes & Noble

Chambers, E.K. 1945. *The Elizabethan Stage*, Vols. I, III, IV. First published 1923. Clarendon Press

Chedgzoy, Kate 1995. *Shakespeare's Queer Children: Sexual Politics and Contemporary Culture*. Manchester University Press

Cheney, Patrick 1997. *Marlowe's Counterfeit Profession: Ovid, Spenser, Counter-Nationhood*. University of Toronto Press

Cole, Douglas 1989. 'The Impact of Goethe's *Faust* on Nineteenth- and Twentieth-Century Criticism of Marlowe's *Doctor Faustus*', in Peter Boerner and Sidney Johnson (eds), *Faust through Four Centuries: Retrospect and Analysis*. Max Niemeyer Verlag

Cope, Jackson I. 1974. 'Marlowe's *Dido* and the Titillating Children', in *English Literary Renaissance*, 4/1, Winter 1974

Cuddon, J.A. 1992. *Dictionary of Literary Terms and Literary Theory*. 3rd edn. Penguin

Cunningham, J.E. (ed.) 1999. *Tamburlaine the Great*. Revels Plays edition. First published 1981. Manchester University Press

Cunningham, J.E. & Henson, Eithne (eds) 1998. *Tamburlaine the Great*. Revels Student editions. Manchester University Press

Cunningham, J.E. & Warren, Roger 1978. '"Tamburlaine the Great" Re-Discovered', in *Shakespeare Survey*, 31, pp. 155–62

Dawson, Anthony B. (ed.) 1997. *Tamburlaine Parts One and Two.* New Mermaids edition. A. & C. Black

Deats, Sarah Munson 1997. *Sex, Gender and Desire in the Plays of Christopher Marlowe.* University of Delaware Press

Dickens, A.G. 1993. *The English Reformation.* 2nd edn. First published 1989. B.T. Batsford Ltd

Dollimore, Jonathan 1989. *Radical Tragedy: Religion, Ideology and Power in the Drama of Shakespeare and his Contemporaries.* 2nd edn. Harvester Wheatsheaf

Duthie, G.I. 1948. 'The Dramatic Structure of Marlowe's "Tamburlaine the Great" ', *Essays and Studies* [*English Studies*], n.s. 1, pp. 101–26

Easthope, Anthony 1991. *Literary into Cultural Studies.* Routledge

Elton, G. 1969. *The Practice of History.* Fontana

Evans, G. Blakemore 1989. *Elizabethan–Jacobean Drama: A New Mermaids Background Book.* First published 1988. A. & C. Black

Foakes, R.A. & Rickert, R.T. (eds) 1961. *Henslowe's Diary.* Cambridge University Press

Forker, Charles R. (ed.) 1994. Christopher Marlowe, *Edward II.* Revels Plays edition, Manchester University Press

Gardner, Helen 1942. 'The Second Part of *Tamburlaine the Great*', *Modern Language Review*, 37, pp. 18–24

Geckle, George 1988. *Text and Performance: Tamburlaine and Edward II.* Humanities Press International, Inc.

Gill, Roma (ed.) 1997. *The Complete Works of Christopher Marlowe Volume I: All Ovids Elegies, Lucans First Booke, Dido Queen of Carthage, Hero and Leander.* First published 1987. Oxford University Press

Godshalk, William L. 1974. *The Marlovian World Picture.* Mouton

Goldberg, Jonathan 1992. *Sodometries: Renaissance Texts, Modern Sexualities.* Stanford University Press

Greenblatt, Stephen 1994. *Renaissance Self-Fashioning From More to Shakespeare.* First published 1980. University of Chicago Press

Greenblatt, Stephen (ed.) 1997. *The Norton Shakespeare.* Ed. with Walter Cohen, Jena E. Howard and Katharine Eisaman Maus. W.W. Norton & Company

Greg, W.W. (ed.) 1950. *The Tragical History of the Life and Death of Doctor Faustus: A Conjectural Reconstruction.* Clarendon

Gross, John 1994. *Shylock: Four Hundred Years in the Life of a Legend.* First published 1992. Vintage

Grotowski, Jerzy 1964. '*Doctor Faustus* in Poland', *Tulane Drama Review*, 8/4, Summer 1964, pp. 120–33

Guralnick, Peter 1998. *Searching for Robert Johnson.* First published 1989. Pimlico

Gurr, Andrew 1963. 'Who strutted and bellowed?', *Shakespeare Survey*, 16, pp. 95–102

Gurr, Andrew 1992. *The Shakespearean Stage, 1574–1642.* 3rd edn. Cambridge University Press

Gurr, Andrew 1996. *The Shakespearian Playing Companies.* Clarendon Press

Halliburton, Rachel 1998. 'Working-class hero gone bad', *The Independent*, Review section, 30 July 1998, p. 12

Healy, Thomas 1994. *Christopher Marlowe.* Northcote House

Hortmann, Wilhelm 1998. *Shakespeare on the German Stage: The Twentieth Century.* Cambridge University Press

Jarman, Derek 1992. *Queer Edward II.* First published 1991

Jenkins, Keith 1991. *Re-Thinking History.* Routledge

Jones, Emrys (ed.) 1992. *The New Oxford Book of Sixteenth Century Verse.* First published 1991. Oxford University Press

Jones, Robert C. 1986. *Engagement with Knavery.* Duke University Press

Keefer, Michael (ed.) 1991. *Christopher Marlowe's* Doctor Faustus: *a 1604-version edition.* Broadview Press Ltd

Kirk, Andrew M. 1995. 'Marlowe and the Disordered Face of French History', *Studies in English Literature*, 35/2, Spring 1995, pp. 193–214

Kocher, Paul H. 1946. *Christopher Marlowe: A Study of his Thought, Learning and Character.* University of North Carolina Press

Kocher, Paul H. 1947a. 'Contemporary Pamphlet Backgrounds for Marlowe's *The Massacre at Paris*', *Modern Language Quarterly*, 8, pp. 151–73

Kocher, Paul H. 1947b. 'Contemporary Pamphlet Backgrounds for Marlowe's *The Massacre at Paris* Part Two', *Modern Language Quarterly*, 8, pp. 309–18

Laurence, Anne 1996. *Women in England, 1500–1760: A Social History.* First published 1994. Orion Books

Leech, Clifford 1986. *Christopher Marlowe: Poet for the Stage.* Ed. Anne Lancashire. AMS Press

Levin, Harry 1952. *The Overreacher: A Study of Christopher Marlowe.* Harvard University Press

Levin, Harry 1964. 'Marlowe Today', *Tulane Drama Review*, 8/4, Summer 1964, pp. 22–31

Levin, Richard 1984. 'Contemporary Perception of Marlowe's *Tamburlaine*', *Medieval and Renaissance Drama in England*, vol. 1, pp. 51–70

Litvinoff, Barnet 1989. *The Burning Bush: Antisemitism and World History.* First published 1988. William Collins

MacDonald, Joyce Green 1999. 'Marlowe's Ganymede', in *Enacting Gender on the English Renaissance Stage*, ed. Viviana Comensoli and Anne Russell. University of Illinois Press

MacLure, Millar 1995. *Christopher Marlowe: The Critical Heritage.* First published 1979. Routledge

Manz, Beatrice Forbes 1989. *The Rise and Rule of Tamerlane*. Cambridge University Press

Marcus, Greil 1997. *Mystery Train: Images of America in Rock 'n' Roll Music*. 4th rev. edn. First published 1975. Plume/Penguin

Marcus, Leah S. 1996. *Unediting the Renaissance: Shakespeare, Marlowe, Milton*. Routledge

McDonald, Russ 1996. *The Bedford Companion to Shakespeare*. Macmillan

Moretti, Franco 1992. 'The Great Eclipse: Tragic Form as the Deconsecration of Sovereignty', in John Drakakis (ed.), *Longman Critical Reader: Shakespearean Tragedy*. Longman

Morrill, John (ed.) 1996. *The Oxford Illustrated History of Tudor & Stuart Britain*. Oxford University Press

Neale, J.E. 1934. *Queen Elizabeth*. Jonathan Cape

Nicholl, Charles 1992. *The Reckoning*. Jonathan Cape

Oliver, H.J. (ed.) 1968. *Dido Queen of Carthage* and *The Massacre at Paris*. Revels Plays edition, Methuen

Orgel, Stephen (ed.) 1971. *Christopher Marlowe: The Complete Poems and Translations*. Penguin

Palmer, P.M. & More, R.P. 1936. *The Sources of the Faust Tradition*. Oxford University Press

Papetti, Viola 1977. *Arlecchino a Londra: La Pantomima Inglese, 1700–1728*. Istituto Universitario Orientale

Park, Roy (ed.) 1980. *Lamb as Critic*. Routledge & Kegan Paul

Phillips, Melanie 1988. 'A society that can laugh at the Jew of Malta by pretending anti-semitism is dead', *The Guardian*, 1 April 1988

Poole, Kristen Elizabeth 1998. 'Garbled Martyrdom in Christopher Marlowe's *The Massacre at Paris*', *Comparative Drama*, 32/1, pp. 1–25

Pope, Alexander 1985. *Collected Poems*. ed. Clive T. Probyn. Everyman edition, J.M. Dent & Sons Ltd

Rabkin, Norman 1967. *Shakespeare and the Common Understanding*. Free Press

Rasmussen, Eric 1997. 'The Revision of Scripts', in *A New History of Early English Drama*, ed. John D. Cox and David Scott Kastan. Columbia University Press

Ribner, Irving 1953. 'The Idea of History in Marlowe's *Tamburlaine*', *English Literary History*, 20, pp. 251–66

Roberts, Penny 1995. 'Marlowe's *Massacre at Paris*: A Historical Perspective', *Renaissance Studies*, 9, pp. 430–41

Routh, C.R.N. (ed.) 1990. *Who's Who in Tudor England*. Shepheard: Walwyn

Rutherford, Malcolm 1992. Review of *Tamburlaine* in *Financial Times*, 3 Nov 1992, clipping from Shakespeare Institute Archives

Sales, Roger 1991. *Christopher Marlowe*. Macmillan

Sanders, Wilbur 1968. *The Dramatist and the Received Idea*. Cambridge University Press

Sedgwick, Eve Kosofsky 1985. *Between Men: English Literature and Male Homosocial Desire*. Columbia University Press

Shepherd, Simon 1986. *Marlowe and the Politics of Elizabethan Theatre*. St Martin's Press

Simkin, Stevie 1998. '*The Jew of Malta* in The Warsaw Ghetto', *On-Stage Studies*, 21, pp. 31–51

Simkin, Stevie 1999. '"The Artificial Jew of Malta's Nose": Performed Ethnicity in Marlowe's *The Jew of Malta*', *Studies in Theatre Production*, 19, June 1999, pp. 67–92.

Simkin, Stevie & Williams, Carolyn 1999. Interview in *Cahiers Elizabethains*, 55 (April 1999), pp. 65–73

Sinfield, Alan 1992. *Faultlines: Cultural Materialism and the Politics of Dissident Reading*. Clarendon Press

Sinfield, Alan 1994. *Cultural Politics – Queer Reading*. Routledge

Sinfield, Alan 1996. 'How to read *The Merchant of Venice* without being heterosexist', in Terence Hawkes (ed.), *Alternative Shakespeares 2*. Routledge

Smith, Bruce R. 1994. *Homosexual Desire in Shakespeare's England: A Cultural Poetics*. Paperback edition with new preface. First published 1991. University of Chicago Press

Smith, Robert A.H. 1979. 'A Note on *Doctor Faustus* and *The Taming of a Shrew*', *Notes and Queries*, n.s. 26, p. 116

Spenser, Edmund 1979. *The Faerie Queene Book I*. Ed. P.C. Bayley. Oxford University Press

Steane, J.B. 1964. *Marlowe: A Critical Study*. Cambridge University Press

Stone, Laurence 1985. 'Only women', *New York Review of Books*, 11 April 1985, p. 21

Tennenhouse, Leonard 1986. *Power on Display*. Methuen

Thomas, Vivien & Tydeman, William 1994. *Christopher Marlowe: The Plays and their Sources*. Routledge

Thurn, David H. 1989. 'Sights of Power in *Tamburlaine*', *English Literary Renaissance*, 19/1, Winter 1989, pp. 3–21

Tillyard, E.M.W. 1970. *The Elizabethan World Picture*. First published 1943. Penguin

Tydeman, William 1984. Doctor Faustus: *Text and Performance*. Macmillan

Tydeman, William & Thomas, Vivien 1989. *Christopher Marlowe: A Guide Through the Critical Maze*. Bristol Classical Press

Wardle, Irving 1992. 'Marlowe's Rambo Triumphant', in *Independent on Sunday*, 6 Sept 1992, clipping from Shakespeare Institute Archives

Williams, Carolyn 1999. 'Review, *The Jew of Malta*, King Alfred's College, Winchester, December 1997', *Cahiers Elizabethains*, 55 (April 1999), pp. 75–7

Wilson, Richard (ed.) 1999. Introduction, *Longman Critical Reader: Christopher Marlowe*. Addison Wesley Longman

Wraight, A.D. & Stern, Virginia F. 1993. *In Search of Christopher Marlowe*. Adam Hart (Publishers) Ltd reprint. First published 1965 by Macdonald & Co. (Publishers) Ltd

Zucker, David Hard 1972. *Stage and Image in the Plays of Christopher Marlowe*. Salzburg Studies in English Literature

INDEX

The numbers in **bold** signify in-depth discussion.